EXCELGATE

HOW ZIMBABWE'S 2018 PRESIDENTIAL ELECTION WAS STOLEN

Jonathan N. Moyo

Published by SAPES Books
Zimbabwe
www.sapes.org.zw

ISBN: 978-1-52725-529-6

Typeset by BluStrokes
Cover design by Anonymous

Second Printing
Printed by CPI Group (UK) Ltd, Croydon, CRO 4YY

**Dedicated to my family's eternal memory of Our Angel,
Zanele Ntombizodwa Naledi Moyo**

CONTENTS

ABBREVIATIONS

ANC	African National Congress
AU	African Union
BVR	Biometric Voter Registration
CBD	Central Business District
CD-ROM	Compact Disc Read-Only Memory
CEO	Chief Elections Officer
CIO	Central Intelligence Organisation
ConCourt	Constitutional Court
COPAC	Constitution Parliamentary Committee
CSOs	Civil Society Organisations
DLP	Data Loss Prevention
DRC	Democratic Republic of Congo
ESAP	Economic Structural Adjustment Programme
EU	European Union
EU EOM	European Union Election Observation Mission
EVS	Electronic Voting System
GPA	Global Political Agreement
GNU	Government of National Unity
ID	Identity Document
IT	Information Technology
JOC	Joint Operations Command
MDC	Movement for Democratic Change
MDC-A	Movement for Democratic Change Alliance
MID	Military Intelligence Department
NIBMAR	No Independence Before Majority Rule
NCP	National Convergence Platform
NGOs	Non-Governmental Organisations
NPA	National Prosecuting Authority
NTA	National Transitional Authority
PF	Patriotic Front
PF-ZAPU	Patriotic Front Zimbabwe African People's Union
PISI	Police Internal Security Intelligence
SADC	Southern African Development Community
STEM	Science, Technology, Engineering, Mathematics
V.11	Polling Station Return Form
V.16	Electronic Mail Notifying Result of Poll
V.18	Presidential Elections: Result of Poll
V.19	Declaration of Secrecy
V.23A	Ward Return Form
V.23B	Constituency Return Form
V.23C	Provincial Return Form
V.23D	National Command Centre
VOA	Voice of America
UNDP	United Nations Development Programme
UNIP	United National Independence Party
USBs	Universal Serial Buses
ZANLA	Zimbabwe African National Liberation Army
ZANU PF	Zimbabwe African National Union Patriotic Front
ZCTU	Zimbabwe Congress of Trade Unions
ZDF	Zimbabwe Defence Forces
ZEC	Zimbabwe Electoral Commission
ZIPRA	Zimbabwe People's Revolutionary Army
ZNLWA	Zimbabwe National Liberation War Veterans Association
ZRP	Zimbabwe Republic Police
ZUM	Zimbabwe Unity Movement

DIAGRAMS

KEY SOURCE MATERIALS

CONSTITUTION
Constitution of Zimbabwe Amendment (No.20) Act 2013.
Constitution of Zimbabwe, 1980.

STATUTES
Electoral Act [*Chapter 2:13*].
Public Order and Security Act [*Chapter 11:17*].

REGULATIONS
Statutory Instrument 21 of 2005 (Electoral Regulations, 2005).
Statutory Instrument 87 of 2013 (Electoral (Amendment) Regulations, 2013)

RULES OF COURT
High Court Rules, 1971.

CASE LAW
Liberal Democrats & 4 Others v President of the Republic of Zimbabwe E.D. Mnangagwa N.O & 4 Others (CCZ 7/18).

Nelson Chamisa v Emmerson Dambudzo Mnangagwa and 24 Others (CCZ 21/19).

Joseph Evurath Sibanda & Another v President of the Republic of Zimbabwe, Robert Gabriel Mugabe N.O. and 3 Others HC 10820/17.

Emmerson Dambudzo Mnangagwa v The Acting President of the Republic of Zimbabwe and Attorney General of Zimbabwe HC 940/17.

Laxton Group Limited v Zimbabwe Electoral Commission & 3 Others (AC4/18)

Rupa Ashok Hurra v. Ashok Hurra (2002) 4 SCC 388: AIR 2002 SC 1771.

OTHER SOURCES
Zimbabwe Unity Accord, 22 December 1987.

Zimbabwe Electoral Commission, *2013 Harmonised Elections Report*, 2013.

Zimbabwe Electoral Commission, *Zimbabwe 2018 Harmonised Elections Report*, 27 June 2019.

Zimbabwe Electoral Commission, *Electoral Officers Manual for 2018 Harmonized Elections*, 23 July 2018.

Rhodesia Declaration of Independence (UDI), November 1965.

Rhodesia State of Emergency, May 1965.

FOREWORD

AN INVALID ELECTION CASE STUDY

Excelgate: How Zimbabwe's 2018 Presidential Election was stolen is both a historic account of Zimbabwe's political landscape and an academic case study on the country's electoral process. Herein, Jonathan Moyo writes as a renowned scholar with a commendable record in the study of elections, as is evidenced, for example, in his earlier work, **Voting for Democracy: A Study of Electoral Politics in Zimbabwe** (1992). That was published while Moyo was a full-time academic at the University of Zimbabwe. This book, **Excelgate: How Zimbabwe's 2018 Presidential Election Was Stolen**, has been written after he has spent almost two decades in national politics, variously as cabinet minister, a ZANU PF election campaign manager, or, to quote him, as a "strategist" who wrote the party's 2000 and 2013 election manifestos and who participated in the 2002 presidential campaign as Minister of Information and ZANU PF Deputy Secretary for Information and Publicity.

No doubt, many a reader will, at first sight at least, greet this book as the personal reflections of a former "insider" or as one of the "losers" in a military coup that settled a leadership succession dispute within ZANU PF, for even the best of scholars are not immune to subjectivity, not least in the field of social science.

Yet, ultimately, all such studies have to be judged on their merit, on the extent to which they illuminate reality, exposing and exploding myths, while enhancing knowledge and comprehension of social phenomena.

The history of disputed elections is legion in post-independence Africa, including allegations and reports about rigging. This study is perhaps the first, certainly in the case of Zimbabwe, to provide the bare details of how rigging has been done in a specific election – the 2018 Presidential election in Zimbabwe. Against the background of a political legacy in which the military has been central within the context of a state–party conflation, it is difficult to dispute, in the final analysis, Moyo's assertion that "For this reason, ZANU PF has been able to rig elections since 1985 with considerable success".

WHAT IS EXCELGATE?

What is the essence of this case study, **Excelgate: How Zimbabwe's 2018 Presidential Election Was Stolen**? It was the process whereby a **server** (designed to record the results electronically) was severed illegally and irregularly replaced with an **Excel spreadsheet** (into which data were manually and fraudulently entered), all done at ZEC's (Zimbabwe Electoral Commission) national command centre, which had thereby become **a giant polling station**. To quote Nelson Chamisa's founding affidavit which, as Jonathan Moyo reminds us, "was not opposed by ZEC during Chamisa's ConCourt challenge":

> **On the 1st of August 2018 twenty third respondent [ZEC] started what it called a verification process and which it asked Messrs Komichi and Timba to witness. The process involved a group of people in excess of twenty, punching in what was identified as V11 data into an Excel spreadsheet. For close to two days that process continued.**

Therefore, as Jonathan Moyo highlights, this "mishandling of V11s at ZEC's command centre" was nothing less than "highly irregular and scandalously fraudulent …"

> This is because the Electoral Act [*Chapter 2:13*], requires that the data on V11s must be legally collated, verified and compiled at ward centres and aggregated at constituency centres, and not at the national command centre in Harare.

Accordingly,

> Notwithstanding its endorsement by the ConCourt, and even because of that endorsement, ZEC's declaration and announcement of Mnangagwa on 3 August 2018 as the winner of the 2018 presidential election was a coup against the will of the people of Zimbabwe, whose sovereignty over the State is enshrined in the country's new 2013 Constitution.

So, Excelgate

> amounted to turning ZEC's national command centre into a giant polling station to originate new untraceable and unverifiable voting data to generate a new result through an Excel spreadsheet.

The evidence is compelling and expands on the report of the EU Observation Mission, which found ZEC officers in Makoni North completing V11 forms two days after Election Day, "meaning on 1 August 2018, all by themselves in the absence of polling staff and election agents. The ZEC officials shockingly claimed to be doing this because of earlier lack of V11 forms". So, is it not fair to conclude that the Makoni North incident could have been a generalised pattern across the country during those two days? As Moyo observes,

> Where did these V11s that ZEC officials in Makoni North were found by the EU Election Observation Mission completing alone two days after the election go? How many such V11s did these ZEC officials end up completing in the absence of election agents and well after the election? Is there any rational basis for treating the Makoni North incident as isolated and the only such case?

After reading all this, and taking into account both the provisions of the Electoral Act (all of which are clearly outlined in Chapter 1 of the book) and the inadvertent confirmation by ZEC itself in its Electoral Report published on 15 August 2019 (also cited in Chapter 2 of the book), it is difficult not to conclude that **Excelgate** was a "**massive daylight rigging of the 2018 presidential election**". For an Excel spreadsheet has "**no legal or administrative standing in the collation, compilation and verification of election results. None whatsoever.**"

THE RELATIONSHIP BETWEEN THE NOVEMBER 2017 COUP AND THE "COUP ELECTION" OF JULY 2018

As has already been mentioned in the foregoing and in my own work, *The Political Economy of the State in Zimbabwe: The Rise and Fall of the Securocrat State* (2016), there is a close relationship between the military, which has been central even before independence in 1980, on the one hand, and, on the other, the history of election rigging since 1985 as a means of ensuring that the ZANU PF (the state) remains forever at the helm of power. Therefore, elections have served less as a reflection of the requirements of a modern democratic society than as the means towards legitimizing an essentially illegitimate system. Herein, Moyo has sufficiently illustrated the role of the military in the electoral process in Zimbabwe, especially since the 2000 elections in which the emergent Movement for Democratic Change (MDC) had successfully defeated ZANU PF in the constitutional referendum of February 2000; and might have likewise succeeded in the subsequent general election in June that year, had it not been for the "military takeover" of the electoral process, including virtual control of the Electoral Commission. Therefore, it is not difficult to understand the necessary relationship between the November 2017 coup, one of whose objectives was to save ZANU PF from defeat in the 2018 election, on the one hand, and, on the other, the election coup of July/August 2018 poll itself, in which it would have made no sense at all to have ZANU PF lose.

As a former "insider", Jonathan Moyo makes the startling yet accurate observation about the military–political complex in Zimbabwe, namely the Joint Operations Command (JOC):

> **JOC, not cabinet or the politburo, is the pivotal authority in Zimbabwe. Yet JOC is not a statutory or constitutional entity. It has operated like a secret society since its inception in Rhodesia and particularly since its genocidal notoriety in the Gukurahundi years. JOC is the centre of state power in Zimbabwe. It is the system.**

> **JOC's pivotal role is particularly pronounced during elections. This is because of the obvious reason that elections are strategically important for deciding who gets into power, when and how.**

This is a profound conclusion, resonating with the notion of the "securocrat state" about which some of us have written, and putting paid to those analyses that have sought to highlight so called "divisions" and "factions" in the ZANU PF – the state edifice is more important in understanding the nexus of power in contemporary Zimbabwe. As I have pointed out in *The Political Economy of the State in Zimbabwe: The Rise and Fall of the Securocrat State*, the origins of the modern-day JOC in Zimbabwe are to be found in the nature and the role of the Department of Defence and Security of the ZANLA (Zimbabwe African National Liberation Army) days of the struggle, traditionally and strategically headed by the Defence Chief (Josiah Tongogara, Rex Nhongo *aka* Solomon Mujuru, and subsequently Constantino Chiwenga) and around whom civilian politics were guided by the gun – almost literally, as both the "election coup" of 2008 and the November coup itself testify.

The additional dimension to this **military–security–political complex** in the post-independence period has been the entry by the military security hierarchy into the business venture, with all the associated trappings that have made them part of the **comprador bourgeoisie**, within a toxic conflation of power, wealth and corruption. This last factor, and in particular the imperative of protecting ill-gotten wealth, was no doubt one of the motivations behind the military intervention in the 2008 presidential poll in which Mugabe would have relinquished power were it not for the role of Chiwenga and Mnangagwa in orchestrating a runoff on the back of one of the most vicious campaigns of violence against the population, as well as in the November 2017 coup itself and between that and the election in July 2018. But, as Moyo is at pains to illustrate, the common denominator in all these interventions by the military has been the objective of overturning a defeat, as in 2008 when Mugabe lost to Morgan Tsvangirai, or, as claimed by the military as one of the reasons for staging the November 2017 coup, preparing and putting in place a programme to ensure that ZANU PF would not lose the election in July 2018, thereby guaranteeing that ZANU PF won in a poll in which the military was in virtual control of the entire electoral process, particularly the outcome of the presidential election.

In fact, the "Coup Minutes" (which are reproduced in the Appendix) confirm that the army commanders had told Mugabe "that they had to stage the coup because they had received worrying feedback about ZANU PF's electoral prospects from over 2,000 retired army officers they had embedded across the country", and reminded Mugabe of the "2008 election fiasco and told him that the Army had to intervene to prevent what happened to UNIP (United National Independence Party) in Zambia (when it was voted out of power) from happening to ZANU PF".

In retrospect, it was naïve for anyone to have expected otherwise with respect to the outcome of the presidential election in July 2018:

> **Against this backdrop, and having seized political power by ousting Mugabe only seven months before the next general election was constitutionally due by July 2018, and having imposed Mnangagwa as President of Zimbabwe on 24 November 2017 on the back of the coup, the ZDF commanders were determined to use all means available to ensure a Mnangagwa 'electoral victory' in 2018 without fail in order to entrench and consolidate the political gains of the military coup.**

> **As such, the military's principal and overarching goal in undertaking the November 2017 coup was to take over ZANU PF and to rescue it from what the commanders saw as the party's impending electoral defeat seven months down the line. It was inconceivable that the military would let the political power it had grabbed through the barrel of the gun go to the opposition through the ballot box. That was out of the question.**

> **In the circumstances, the commanders treated Zimbabwe's 2018 harmonised election, especially the presidential election, as a military operation of the utmost strategic importance. It was a do or die mission. Losing the election was not an option.**

WHERE DOES THIS LEAVE ZEC, CHIGUMBA AND THE JUDICIARY, PARTICULARLY CHIEF JUSTICE MALABA?

Excelgate exposes ZEC as largely an instrument of a military machine which caused the electoral body to "invent" a route and process of collating, compiling and transmitting the result of the 2018 presidential election outside, and in violation of, the legal manner presented in the Electoral Act. This was after it had become clear on 31 July 2018 that,

> **based on the results from 10,985 polling stations, which the military got to know soon after midnight on 30 July 2018, with 33%, Mnangagwa had lost the presidential election by a landslide to Chamisa, who had 66%. … Collating, compiling and transmitting the presidential election result in terms of s37C(4) of the Electoral Act would have led to the confirmation of Chamisa's crushing victory.**

Therefore, **Excelgate** exposes ZEC itself as a sham institution, a pathetic case indeed. Unsurprisingly, Priscilla Chigumba cast an uncomfortable and tormented figure during the days and hours heading to the announcement of the controversial elections on 3 August, 2018. Likewise, there are reports that she is desperately trying to resign from ZEC, at great risk to her person.

In the final analysis, ZEC has betrayed and exposed the reality of the military state that is Zimbabwe; it can last only as long as the securocrat state itself survives.

Similarly, **Excelgate** has left the judiciary, and particularly the Chief Justice, Luke Malaba, as a compromised and even captured institution when it should ordinarily be both fiercely independent and the virtual soul of the nation. Particularly in Chapter 2, Jonathan Moyo presents a devastating and compelling account of a judiciary that has become an appendage of the military: for example, the purported constitutional case that was fast-tracked in the High Court by Justice George Chiweshe not only to whitewash the coup but also in violation of the provisions of s167(3) of the constitution, which provides that

> **The Constitutional Court makes the final decision whether an Act of Parliament or conduct of the President is constitutional, and must confirm any order of constitutional invalidity made by another court before that order has any force.**

Therefore, concludes, Jonathan Moyo,

> **… Chiweshe's 24 November 2017 High Court Orders [which were rushed through hours before – and in order to facilitate – Mnangagwa's swearing in that morning], corruptly alleged to have been by consent, when Mugabe did not consent and could not have consented, were not and have not been confirmed by the Constitutional Court. As such they have no force of law, to this day."**

On his part, Chief Justice Malaba compounded the (illegality) problem when he ruled – "sitting alone in his Chambers" – and without hearing Mugabe that the former President had "resigned freely and voluntarily" on 21 November 2017.

Second, and most significantly, was the conduct of Malaba with respect to the disputed election itself. In retrospect, and on the strength of the **EXCELGATE** account, it is difficult not to conclude that the ConCourt in general, and Chief Justice Malaba in particular, might have deliberately overlooked the merits of the case before them, especially with regard to an electoral process in which ZEC was found so wanting, in terms of the Electoral Act and in relation to the dominant role of the military therein. This was particularly so with respect to the subject of V11s.

To quote Jonathan Moyo with respect to this issue:

> **Although ZEC and Malaba gave the impression that the presidential election was about V11s … the untold truth is that … the verification and determination of the result of the presidential election is about V23Bs, and not about V11s. There was absolutely no need for Malaba to make misplaced noise about V11s. When it comes to the verification and determination of the result of the presidential election in terms of s110(3)(d) of the Electoral Act, there can be no meaningful argument over a V11 or V23A without reference to one of the 210 V23Bs to which that original copy of the V11 or V23A in dispute must be attached. Quarrelling or making noise over a random V11 or V23A whose original copy is not attached to any V23B whose result it affects, and which V23B affects the final result of the presidential election, is child's play not worth the attention of a competent and reasonable court.**

On the other hand, could it be that this obsession with the V11s was a reflection of ignorance about the electoral process on the part of not only members of ZEC and the ConCourt but also the general public? For, I have to admit, not until the revelations in this book and the attendant details on which Moyo has elaborated in the context of exposing **Excelgate,** was I so aware of the difference between the V11s and V23s. Even members of Chamisa's legal team appeared genuinely confused about the electoral process, particularly on the subject of V11 and V23. So, assuming for a moment that the ConCourt in general and the Chief Justice in particular had acted more out of ignorance than as a deliberate miscarriage of justice in their consideration of the application before them, where do these profound and detailed revelations that is **Excelgate** leave them now? In a genuine democracy, the judiciary, especially its Chief Justice, would hang its head in shame and do the honourable thing and resign.

More than that, what will be the national response, given that **Excelgate** now confirms and compounds the legitimacy problem? And what about SADC (the Southern African Development Community) and the AU (African Union), both of which have over the years overlooked such blatant breaches of the democratic process, and the international community, especially those represented by election observer missions, some of whom, such as the EU, had highlighted some of the problems now so elaborated upon by **Excelgate**?

CONCLUSION: THE IMPERATIVE OF CURING ILLEGITIMACY AND ILLEGALITY

In short, are we all more educated through this book that one can gather the courage to confess and acknowledge that indeed **Excelgate** provides **"substantial and irrefutable statutory grounds that prove beyond any doubt that the 2018 presidential election was brazenly stolen and thus invalidate the result declared and announced by Chigumba on 3 August 2018"**?

Excelgate: How Zimbabwe's 2018 Presidential Election Was Stolen is an amazing and devastating account of an electoral process that was fundamentally flawed, illegal and fraudulent. It is a revelation and confirmation of the nature and content of the state in Zimbabwe as one which, as a securocracy, defies the basic requirements of developmental democracy in the context of the separation of powers between an accountable executive, a vibrant legislature, and a fiercely independent judiciary (which is supposed to be the soul of the nation).

Accordingly, how do we begin as a nation to confront the twin problems of illegitimacy and illegality – both born out of a coup of November 2017 and the "election coup" of July 2018 – and thereby restore constitutional democracy in Zimbabwe?

One of our leading scholars, Sabelo J. Ndlovu-Gatsheni, has aptly summarised the problem (on his Facebook page on 20 November 2019):

> **A government which came to power through non-constitutional means (guns and violence) and only used elections (post-facto) as a ritual to regularise the irregular will always reveal itself through violence. A progeny of violence is always violent.**

Excelgate: How Zimbabwe's 2018 Presidential Election Was Stolen adds invaluable impetus to the current process towards a National Convergence Platform (NCP), as the basis for a possible National Transitional Authority (NTA) – a Political, Electoral, and Economic Reform Agenda – before the next elections in 2023.

Ibbo Mandaza
Publisher
SAPES Books
Harare, December, 2019.

PREFACE

THE 2018 RIGGING CONSPIRACY

IN the wee hours on 31 July 2018, I got a WhatsApp voice call from a senior securocrat in Zimbabwe's Central Intelligence Organisation (CIO) whom I had worked well with in my days as a cabinet minister from 2013 to 2017. In an uncharacteristically animated and excited voice, he asked me: "Have you heard, 63 is gone?" Sensing my answer would be negative, he went on: "63 has been crushed by a landslide, the computers at our Data Recovery Centre show NC has over 66% and 63 has just under 33%. It's a massacre. He's history."

So "NC" is Nelson Chamisa, opposition leader for the Movement for Democratic Change (MDC) and "63" is what some of us in the so-called ZANU PF G40 circles used to and still call Emmerson Mnangagwa, who came to power through a military coup on 24 November 2017.

We gave Mnangagwa that nickname to dispute his claim that he had joined the armed liberation struggle before Sydney Sekeramayi, who the late former President Robert Mugabe said had arrived in Tanzania in 1962, thus making Sekeramayi senior to Mnangagwa in that sense. Mugabe had said on many occasions that Mnangagwa had joined the armed liberation struggle in 1963, hence the origin of his "63" nickname.

Back to the WhatsApp call: I was not surprised by the reported margin of Chamisa's victory nor did I doubt the veracity of the information. The source was a deep state operative in the engine room of the Joint Operations Command (JOC), which brought together police, military and intelligence security service chiefs and their underlings. My source was as credible as they come. I wish to thank the senior CIO securocrat who called me, whose information became my original reference point for what subsequently grew into the case study for this book.

After the WhatsApp call from the CIO securocrat, more calls from a wide spectrum of well-connected contacts started coming through fast and furious with the same message, while I made my own calls to cross-check what I was hearing. By then all media platforms were abuzz with reports of an overwhelming Chamisa victory.

Later in the morning on 31 July 2018 – around 11:00am – a well-connected ambassador in Harare from a SADC (Southern African Development Community) country, with whom I used to closely interact before the coup, sent me screenshots of forwarded WhatsApp messages that Priscilla Chigumba, the chairperson of the Zimbabwe Electoral Commission (ZEC), had sent to some of her close contacts, challenging the reports that were circulating like a veld fire about Chamisa's reported victory.

Chigumba's messages claimed that, based on the results that ZEC had received from across the country that morning on 31 July 2018, Mnangagwa would win with between 53% and 55% of the vote. A vigorous pushback to challenge earlier reports that Chamisa had won was now in full swing.

Later in the afternoon on 31 July 2018, an overzealous ZEC commissioner, apparently keen to be rewarded for leading the propaganda pushback, started deepthroating the media and diplomats, with an outlandish claim that Mnangagwa was set to win by as much as 60%.

The message from the SADC ambassador who had shared the screenshots of Chigumba's WhatsApp messages proved to be very useful. So were the later claims by ZEC that Mnangagwa was heading for a landslide win by at least 60%.

Their assertions, which contradicted the early morning result I had received from a senior CIO official, raised eyebrows and opened a research challenge for me, as a practitioner and student of electoral politics in Zimbabwe.

Then there was a bombshell on 1 August 2018, the day of the Harare Massacre in which, as later officially confirmed by the Motlanthe Commission report cited in this book, the Zimbabwe Defence Forces (ZDF) and the Zimbabwe Republic Police (ZRP) killed six Zimbabweans in cold blood in the streets of Harare and critically injured 35 others.

The bombshell came in the form of another WhatsApp message that Chigumba had sent the previous day to a confidante of hers about the verification and determination process of the result of the presidential election, which ZEC had earmarked to start on 1 August 2018. She had sent emails to election agents of presidential candidates and election observers, and recorded a video message, inviting them to the ZEC national command centre in Harare for the verification exercise to determine the winner of the 2018 presidential election in terms of s110(3)(d) of the Electoral Act [*Chapter 2:13*].

Chigumba's confidante had asked her what the verification exercise was all about and whether it could affect the forecast she had earlier shared, showing Mnangagwa winning by between 53% and 55% of the vote. This was Chigumba's response:

> **They [MDC] don't have to agree. We will announce based on our own V11. We don't need any party's V11. It's just courtesy for us to ask them to verify. Agree or not, we announce.**

The stunning WhatsApp message from Chigumba let the cat out of the bag. ZEC was going to use its own V11 forms and would ignore those in the possession of any party that had contested the 2018 presidential election. The verification exercise, which is mandated by law, would now just be a courtesy, in other words a charade. This was revealing. Chigumba's informative WhatsApp message confirmed that something fundamentally wrong and illegal was afoot at ZEC. This fuelled my curiosity to audit systematically how ZEC had collated, verified, aggregated and determined the result of the 2018 presidential election.

Chigumba had been propositioned and tasked by the military to deliver the election for Mnangagwa at all costs, and she enthusiastically discharged the task, albeit with a plan to leave ZEC immediately after the election.

In October 2019, her agitation to leave had intensified, particularly after her scary encounter with Mnangagwa earlier that month over electoral reforms at which she was threatened and left the meeting running scared, seeking assurance and refugee from a top ZDF commander.

Ahead of the 2018 election Chigumba was rewarded for her role by being variously incentivised, including with a lucrative farm in Mazowe, with a promise to help her to rope in Olivine Industries Zimbabwe, to assist with the commercialisation of the farm to boost production for exports.

Going by what has previously happened to other cronies beholden to the state who get caught up in conflict of interest issues after being allocated farms or being given other spoils of patronage as an incentive to aid and abet political agendas, and indeed given that Chigumba was appointed judge and ZEC chairperson under a cloud of corruption allegations against her, being allocated a farm on top of all this rendered her vulnerable to manipulation and blackmail.

This was further compounded by news reports that she was in a romantic relationship with Winston Chitando, Minister of Mines and Mining Development and a close Mnangagwa ally.

These and related factors combined to compromise Chigumba in a big way, so she became an instrument for the military to ensure a Mnangagwa victory in the 2018 presidential election. Put differently, she became a pawn in the military's quest to use the elections as a means of consolidating the November 2017 coup.

Since the elections were in fact run by the military, Chigumba's role was effectively to help the military have full control of the electoral machinery to ensure that they directly manipulated ZEC's administrative and technical processes. With retired Lieutenant-General Sibusiso Moyo calling the shots and reporting to retired General Constantino Chiwenga – the two men who had led the November 2017 coup – the manipulation was done through army personnel seconded to and embedded within ZEC.

It was also done through military-run companies such as Africom Zimbabwe, which monitored and managed ZEC computers – including the ZEC server that held the election results and which was mirrored by the CIO at its headquarters in Harare – while the CIO's Chiltern Trust was responsible for the accreditation of ZEC officials, election agents, election observers and the media under the tutelage of the military through JOC.

Although the purpose of Chigumba's capture by the military before the elections was to facilitate this rigging infrastructure, the consequences of the capture of her personally only came to the surface in February 2019, when ZEC finalised its Report on the 2018 elections. In a startling disclosure that is tantamount to an admission of having rigged the 2018 presidential election, ZEC revealed on its website on 6 February 2019 that it had used two different processes – it called them "Route A" and "Route B" – to collate, compile and transmit the results of the presidential and parliamentary elections.

As is systematically shown in this book, ZEC's use of two different routes to transmit the presidential and national assembly election results was not only contrary to the principle of harmonised general elections, but is open and shut evidence of gross violation of the Electoral Act [*Chapter 2:13*] by ZEC regarding the transmission of the result of the presidential election. The unprecedented use of two different and conflicting routes to transmit the presidential and parliamentary poll results is now at the centre of how the 2018 presidential election was stolen by the military through ZEC.

Following the finalisation in February 2019 of their Report on the 2018 presidential election, Chigumba came under pressure from within ZEC to engage their line minister, Ziyambi Ziyambi, Minister of Justice, Legal and Parliamentary Affairs, on the reform recommendations in ZEC's Report.

After initial meetings between Chigumba and Ziyambi, they agreed that ZEC should contract a legal mind to draft the recommendations for consideration by the Ministry of Justice before relaying them to Mnangagwa. Chigumba then engaged retired Justice Moses Chinhengo to draft ZEC's proposed electoral reforms. The draft was submitted to the Attorney-General, where it got a positive nod.

One of the key features of the electoral-reform package submitted by Chigumba was that the ZEC chairperson should not be appointed by the president, but should preferably be appointed through a parliamentary process.

Chigumba then sought Mnangagwa's approval of ZEC's proposed electoral reforms. She was granted an audience. To Chigumba's utter shock, Mnangagwa hit the roof and blew his top, asking her a series of politically blinding questions: "What is your motive?"; "Who has sent you with this?"; "You are a sellout!" After viciously and persistently attacking Chigumba, Mnangagwa angrily told her emphatically that there would be no electoral reforms and that she should "just go away".

A shaken Chigumba hurriedly left Mnangagwa's office speechless and fearing for her life. She shared her horrifying experience only with close family members and friends. After her traumatic episode, a concerned intermediary helped Chigumba to approach the ZDF commander, Philip Valerio Sibanda, to seek advice from him on how to proceed after Mnangagwa had angrily rejected ZEC's proposals for electoral reforms and branded her a sellout. Sibanda empathised with Chigumba and advised her to lie low and to take some time off the process.

Chigumba, now feeling it was time to leave ZEC, then further pushed for Cabinet authority to travel to London. She had earlier sought the authority around September 2019 before the meeting, but Mnangagwa had turned it down, fearing that Chigumba wanted to run away, perhaps to spill the beans about how the 2018 presidential election was stolen and what she was made to do to assist the theft. Feeling cornered, she kept a low profile and begged the Office of the President and Cabinet to be allowed to take some time out in South Africa where she wanted to review her options away from ZEC.

After the visit, Chigumba contemplated leaving ZEC. She wanted out, but she was practically held hostage by Mnangagwa, who did not want her to go anywhere.

Chigumba's post-election troubles and her determined efforts to extricate herself from ZEC to the point of wanting to flee Zimbabwe speak volumes about her discomfort with her role in the manipulation of the process and the delivery of a stolen result of the 2018 presidential election to benefit Mnangagwa. Chigumba became trapped by her conscience on the one hand, and the fear of Mnangagwa on the other.

Chigumba's sea of troubles started on 3 August 2018 when, two days after the Harare Massacre, she wrongly and controversially declared Mnangagwa the winner of the 2018 presidential election. This prompted Chamisa to lodge an application with the Constitutional Court (ConCourt) on 10 August 2018, challenging ZEC's declaration.

Over that weekend, Chief Justice Luke Malaba was in Pretoria, South Africa, to attend the wedding of his son who lives in that country. While there, Malaba received a copy of Chamisa's ConCourt application from a senior legal officer at the Judicial Services Commission (JSC), as he was relaxing by the swimming pool at Pretoria Sheraton hotel.

After reading through the application, Malaba turned to the judicial officer and asked him, "Is that all"? To which the officer replied: "Yes, sir." Malaba then shook his head and remarked: "OK. *Akula lutho la* [There is nothing here]." By those words, Malaba meant that there was no case and he was going to have Chamisa's application dismissed even before the case had been heard on its merits.

The conversation between Malaba and the judicial officer was overheard and relayed to me from the scene by a Pretoria Sheraton hotel employee who is originally from Zimbabwe and who had eavesdropped critical parts of the conversation. The information also became an important factor in consolidating my research interest in the unusual events that were unfolding ahead of the hearing of Chamisa's ConCourt challenge.

Malaba's attitude did not surprise me. When I had worked closely with him and Emmerson Mnangagwa between March 2013 and December 2014 in the run-up to his elevation as Vice-President and Second Secretary of ZANU PF at the expense of Joice Mujuru, Mnangagwa used to refer to the late former Chief Justice Godfrey Chidyausiku as *mutengesi* (sell-out) and to Malaba as *munhu wangu uyo* (my man).

In 2016, Mnangagwa abused his position as Minister of Justice, Legal and Parliamentary Affairs and got Chidyausiku to retire as Chief Justice earlier than scheduled, under spurious claims that Mugabe had issued an executive order for him to retire, to get Malaba to act in that position so as to benefit him by having a foot in, pending the appointment of a new head of the judiciary.[1]

Mugabe was shocked when he learnt that Mnangagwa had illegally retired Chidyausiku and replaced him with Malaba behind his back under false pretences without his knowledge or approval. Mugabe was furious. He immediately scuttled Mnangagwa's treacherous arrangement and reinstated Chidyausiku, whom he asked to begin the constitutional process for the appointment of his successor as Chief Justice in terms of section 180 of the Constitution of Zimbabwe enacted in 2013.

When the process of appointing his successor was in motion, Chidyausiku received a letter from Misheck Sibanda, Chief Secretary to the President and Cabinet and Mnangagwa's cousin, claiming that Mugabe was directing him to halt the process pending an amendment of section 180 of the Constitution. I got to know as a Cabinet Minister that Sibanda's letter had been instigated by Mnangagwa and that it was intended to forestall sections 180(2)(c) and (d) of the Constitution, which, prior to Constitutional Amendment Number 1 of 2017, enjoined the JSC to conduct public interviews of prospective candidates to come up with a shortlist of three qualified persons as nominees for the office of Chief Justice. For reasons best known to himself, the prospect of Malaba going through a public interview process petrified Mnangagwa and he pulled out all the stops to try and prevent it. .

Chidyausiku used the official opening of the 2017 legal year to expose the lie that Mugabe had issued an unconstitutional executive order directing the JSC to stop the interviews for filling the post of Chief Justice when he said:

> I also wish to detail the events leading to the holding of the interviews for the post of Chief Justice on 12 December 2016. When the constitution came into force in 2013, it was quite clear that the method of selecting and appointing judges had radically changed.

---

[1] See "Chidyausiku forced into retiring early", *Zimbabwe Independent*, 20 January 2017. While the media reported on Mnangagwa's machinations to force Chidyausiku to retire behind Mugabe's back, using a fake executive order which Mugabe repudiated, claims that Justice George Chiweshe was the intended successor were false and misleading. The true position is that whereas the ZDF "command element" preferred Justice Chiweshe, Mnangagwa's choice was Malaba.

So had the procedure of appointing the Chief Justice and the Deputy Chief Justice. The Judicial Service Commission successfully utilised the new procedure to fill vacancies that had occurred in both the High and Supreme Courts in 2014 and 2015.

My sixth sense, however, told me that the impact of the new procedure, because of its drastic departure from the past process, might have escaped the attention of the Executive in as far as it relates to the appointment of the Chief Justice.

As a cautionary move, I alerted the executive to this new procedure in the appointment of the Chief Justice as early as March 2016. I did not get a response. I inferred from this conduct that the Executive was comfortable with the new procedure. In October 2016, as is required by the constitution, the Judicial Service Commission Secretariat informed the Executive that the Judicial Service Commission had declared the office of the Chief Justice vacant with effect from 1 March 2017 and was initiating procedures to fill the vacancy in accordance with the provisions of the Constitution.

In light of the above, I was surprised to receive communication a few days before the interviews were due to commence that an executive order had been issued ordering the Judicial Service Commission to stop the interviews for filling the post of Chief Justice. I responded to the communication, advising that the Executive's directive could not be complied with without breaking the constitution and that the interviews would proceed as planned and in terms of the constitution. I have since established that the President never issued the alleged executive order to stop the interviews.[2]

Parenthetically, one of the pretexts used by Mnangagwa and the military to justify their coup was that the so-called G40 faction took advantage of Mugabe's old age and alleged incapacity to usurp his constitutional powers, but did not offer even one example to back up their gratuitous claim. Yet here's one very serious example exposed by Chidyausiku, on 16 January 2017, of Mnangagwa using his relative, Mischeck Sibanda, to fake an executive order whose import was to violate and subvert the Constitution in Mugabe's name for the nefarious purpose of assisting Malaba's elevation to the Office of Chief justice.

It is remarkably instructive that, after failing to stop the public interviews for the position of Chief Justice under the cover of a fake executive order in Mugabe's name, Mnangagwa stepped up his efforts to amend section 180 of the constitution to repeal provisions of section 180(2), which required the JSC to advertise the positions of judges, including those of Chief Justice, Deputy Chief Justice and Judge President, and to shortlist three of the most qualified candidates on the basis of their performance in the public interviews.

---

[2] See "Speech by the Zimbabwe Chief Justice, The Honourable Mr Justice GG Chidyausiku CJ [Opening of the Legal Year, 2017]", https://zimlii.org/content/speech-zimbabwe-chief-justice-honourable-mr-justice-gg-chidyausiku-cj-opening-legal-year, page 8.

Mnangagwa's ZANU PF faction, then called Lacoste, used a proxy – one Romeo Taombera Zibani – a University of Zimbabwe law student with military links, to challenge the JSC over Chidyausiku's insistence on proceeding with public interviews in terms of section 180 of the constitution. Zibani cited as respondents the JSC, President Mugabe, Mnangagwa (as Justice Minister), Chidyausiku (as Chief Justice), and the candidates to succeed Chidyausiku – Malaba, Justice Rita Makarau, Justice Paddington Garwe and Justice George Chiweshe.

Mnangagwa presented the Zibani challenge in Cabinet as meant to enable Mugabe to appoint the leadership of the judiciary without his hand tied by "the politics" of public interviews of candidates, which he claimed was smuggled in by the MDC during the constitution-making process. What I got to know then, but which became common cause only after the coup, is that Mnangagwa pushed for Constitution Amendment (No.1) Act 10, 2017, entirely for himself as part of the planning for the coup that he knew would impose him as the country's president.

Mnangagwa knew that a coup was in the making, and that it would impose him as president and he would be the beneficiary of the first amendment to the 2013 constitution. He wanted Malaba to be Chief Justice by all means necessary.

Aware that Mnangagwa was abusing his position as Justice Minister to plan for the coup in pursuit of his personal interest, while also invoking and abusing Mugabe's name and forging his signature, I entered into discussions with Tendai Biti, now MDC Vice-President, on how best to challenge Mnangagwa's plotting through the legal system. To facilitate the challenge, I set up a legal fund coordinated by a local top-notch journalist, Mduduzi Mathuthu, whom I had appointed editor of *The Chronicle* when I was Information Minister in 2013.

With Mathuthu as the contact-person, quite some significant work was done to challenge Mnangagwa on two fronts: one to expose the illegality and personalisation of the first amendment to the new constitution to benefit him and Malaba, the other to expose and challenge the illegal secondment of military personnel at the National Prosecution Authority (NPA). Mnangagwa was using these two fronts as Justice Minister to target his political opponents as part of the plotting for the military coup. Through Biti, with Mathuthu as the link, I sought the legal services of prominent lawyer, Beatrice Mtetwa, to deal with the secondment of military personnel to the NPA and the use of security personnel as prosecutors.

Considerable progress had been made under this two-pronged legal strategy by 15 November 2017, but not much could be done after the coup. To complement the strategy, with support from Cabinet Ministers Patrick Zhuwao and Saviour Kasukuwere, I used to challenge Mnangagwa in Cabinet on his involvement and interest in the first amendment to the new constitution. Mnangagwa would invariably sweat and stammer incoherencies, protesting that Cabinet was not a court of law and pleading for protection from Mugabe. His cronies – such as Prisca Mupfumira, now ironically being hounded by her then master – would challenge us to take our issues with Mnangagwa to parliament, asking Mugabe not to listen to "law school students".

In the end, Mugabe protected Mnangagwa, whose relentless efforts culminated in the promulgation of Constitution of Zimbabwe Amendment (No.1) Act (No.10 of 2017) under which the appointment of the Chief Justice, Deputy Chief Justice and Judge President became exclusively a presidential prerogative with no public input.

When the amendment was introduced by Mnangagwa shortly before the coup, its intended beneficiaries were Mnangagwa himself and Malaba. It is not surprising that, with the amendment in their pocket, Mnangagwa now wants to raise the retirement age for judges to ensure that Malaba remains at the helm of the judiciary to do in 2023 what he did for him in 2018. Many who used to see Malaba as a jurisprudentially progressive judge have been surprised and disappointed by his support of the coup and the escalated suppression of freedoms and violation of human rights since the putsch to the detriment of the Constitution and constitutionalism.

More disappointing, measured against his dissenting opinion in the Jealousy Mawarire election case in 2013, is Malaba's scandalous mishandling of Chamisa's 2018 ConCourt challenge to ZEC's declaration of Mnangagwa as the winner of the presidential election, when the evidence to the contrary was overwhelming and before the court. The point many have missed is that Malaba was anti-Mugabe and pro-Mnangagwa, not a neutral judge bound by constitutionalism. For Malaba it was personal and thus had nothing to do with justice, constitutionalism or progressive jurisprudence.

In the circumstances, trouble bedevilled preparations for the ConCourt case. The way preliminary issues were handled in the case betrayed the palpable fear of losing the election at the polls or in court that was gripping Chigumba, ZEC, Malaba, security officials, especially those embedded in the electoral process, and Mnangagwa himself.

Desperate efforts were made to torpedo Chamisa's ConCourt case.

A lot of dust was kicked to have the case dismissed on the grounds that Chamisa's application had been served out of time on Mnangagwa, Chigumba and ZEC. In particular, ZEC and Chigumba went to ridiculous lengths to try to have the application dismissed on technicalities. This made me even more curious, given that ZEC is a Chapter 12 constitutional body, created as an institution – not of the state but of society – to support democracy.

One would expect an institution such as ZEC to be interested in resolving electoral disputes on merit in order to achieve substantial justice and democratic stability, without seeking refuge or escape through technicalities, some of which were awfully flimsy and even puerile.

In the ensuing drama, and especially after Malaba had blocked Chamisa's *subpoena* on ZEC to produce the server that had the result of the presidential election – which ZEC had abandoned in favour of an Excel spreadsheet that it claimed to have used as a calculator to add the votes in selected V11s and V23As, totally ignoring the necessary V23Bs (presidential constituency returns) to determine the result of the presidential election – it became clear that ZEC wanted the case to be determined on dubious technicalities at the expense of substantive issues. The massive rigging of the 2018 presidential election that had taken place risked being seriously exposed by the merits of the case.

Looking back, Chigumba, ZEC, Malaba and Mnangagwa helped to lay the ground for this book by their suspicious behaviour and actions after Chamisa's application. They tried too hard to have it dismissed on technicalities so that they ended up inviting inevitable scrutiny of their conduct and an audit of the freeness, fairness and legality of result of the 2018 presidential election. This book is in many ways a product of the apprehension they shared and exhibited about a situation that should have been otherwise straightforward in terms of the law.

The writing was on the wall that Chamisa's chances of getting a fair hearing were between slim and none when, at the eleventh hour, Ziyambi – a Mnangagwa ally and loyalist – denied South African Advocates Dali Mpofu and Tembeka Ngcukaiboti licences to represent Chamisa in the ConCourt, and when Malaba barred losing presidential candidates from associating themselves with Chamisa's application as respondents and struck them off the case.

The public interventions in the ConCourt case made by Advocates Mpofu and Ngcukaiboti were helpful. Advocate Mpofu's bid to have the case taken to the African Commission for Human and People's Rights inspired my initial thoughts about using the ConCourt challenge as the focus for the case study in this book.

After struggling for over a year to justify the unjustifiable preliminary judgment that he read on 24 August 2018, drafted by Deputy Chief Justice, Elizabeth Gwaunza, with the assistance of Justice Lavender Makoni, Malaba finally released his "fully dressed judgment" on 7 November 2019. Malaba's much awaited fully dressed judgment has left him naked in the eyes of fair-minded observers.

As is highlighted in this book, Malaba's 137-page judgment is really a self-indulgent and injudicious critique of the applicant, his case and his lawyers, with little regard for the facts of the case and the relevant law. It is a far cry from a legally reasoned and balanced assessment of an important constitutional case with far-reaching implications on the holding of free, fair and credible elections with respect to the rule of law, constitutionalism and democracy in Zimbabwe.

On 26 August 2018, the day Mnangagwa was inaugurated, I wrote a summary of what I had come to understand and frame as "Excelgate" with a view to recording it as a cellphone video to share on my Twitter handle.

This was when I received credible information that, with Military Intelligence Department (MID) officials dictating things, ZEC had deployed a group of twenty or so people at its national command centre to use an Excel spreadsheet to alter the result of the presidential election that had been captured in a server controversially procured from the United States and controlled by the military, which ZEC had abandoned upon failing to manipulate its election-result data.

After failed attempts over a week, I then asked for help from my youngest daughter, then 13 years old, who has a huge interest in video production and film-making.

For her eighth birthday, she asked for a Canon D700 which she put to great and amazing use as a primary school pupil. While my daughter was happy to shoot the "Excelgate" video, she told me upfront that what I was saying was too political and too heavy for her and it needed to be produced professionally and not by an amateur like her. I understood her plea not to be dragged into a political production and accepted that as sign of maturity and good judgement on her part.

I then raised the issue of doing a professional video narrative on "Excelgate" with Edmund Kudzayi, with whom I had done my July 2017 "Blue Ocean Strategy" video for the ZANU PF politburo on Mnangagwa's coup-plotting ahead of the military action that ousted Mugabe and his government from power on 15 November 2017. Kudzayi had been aware of my earlier unsuccessful efforts to video record "Excelgate" on my cell phone, as he had recorded his videos on Chigumba's romantic relationship with Minister Chitando.

Kudzayi considered the possibility of arranging for one of his cameramen to come where I was but the logistics were too complicated and prohibitive.

Meanwhile, I continued to explore other options to get a professional documentary done with the possibility of involving images and voices of some of the key protagonists in the story of how ZEC rigged the 2018 presidential election.

I shared the idea with a colleague in the donor community and asked them if they would consider supporting the production of a documentary on "Excelgate" should Kudzayi submit an application through an NGO called "Voter Education and Development Trust" (VEDT), which Kudzayi had set up to produce video and voice infomercials on the 2018 general election, such as my "Handei Kwekwe" video.

Diligence issues were raised about VEDT's lack of a track record as a new NGO. To save the situation, I approached Ibbo Mandaza and asked him if SAPES Trust could host the project and if he could meet Kudzayi to explore that possibility. In the end, Mandaza proposed a local NGO, which at the time was seized with the tragic situation of the victims of the 1 August 2018 Harare Massacre. Mandaza arranged for Kudzayi to meet with one of the directors after which the NGO agreed to host the documentary project. Unfortunately, only a quarter of the original budget could be availed and only in 2019. This development caused me to rethink the value of a video documentary – more so because I had also come to understand that most of the primary information sources at ZEC were not prepared to speak on camera. I decided to revise the documentary idea in favour of a forensic case study focused on the court papers produced by the parties under oath in the ConCourt challenge.

Based on my familiarity with Zimbabwe's election process, procedures, practice and law, it had become evident to me, from reading the court record, that the ZEC papers were scandalously incoherent and unlawful. I became interested in telling the story of how the 2018 presidential election was massively rigged, based, in the first instance, on compelling evidence contained in the court papers.

Later in April 2019, Kudzayi informed me that the funding had come through, a quarter of the initial budget for a documentary, well after the initial approach, and that he had reconsidered his reservations about doing an underfunded documentary and was now keen to proceed under the banner of his "Kukurigo" outfit. He wanted from me a three-page narrative of "Excelgate" upon which he would develop a script for his documentary. I gave him 37 pages of a narrative that was revised three times in June 2019, after which Kudzyai's documentary and the case study for this book progressed separately.

Subsequently, I continued researching the case study, focusing on the record of the ConCourt, especially the shocking submissions by ZEC and the admission by Mnangagwa that there was indeed a server, whose presidential election result was controversially abandoned by ZEC under a military directive. While ZEC made a bare denial in the ConCourt of the existence of the server, Mnangagwa acknowledged it was there but claimed that it had been hacked.

After sharing my initial manuscript on the case study with SAPES Books, Mandaza felt it was an important work which his publishing house would be keen to publish. He also asked some challenging questions around the "V" forms (election returns) and the server that needed further research and elaboration.

In my preparation of the final manuscript, I received tremendous support from Ibbo Mandaza, Tony Reeler, two anonymous cooperative copy-editors, a senior lawyer who leads one of Zimbabwe's top legal firms for scrutinising my statutory references as well as testing my legal interpretations, and an anonymous graphic designer who designed the cover and did the typesetting.

My special gratitude goes to 11 unnameable ZEC staff members and three ZEC commissioners whose direct and indirect assistance to me was invaluable beyond description. It is unfortunate but understandable that none of them wish to be acknowledged by name.

All told, it is clear from the foregoing that the military had a "rigging conspiracy" or that it had colluded with ZEC through Chigumba and the ConCourt via Malaba. Chigumba's confirmation of that plot was in her WhatsApp messages sent on 31 July 2018, while Malaba's remarks at the Sheraton Hotel in Pretoria just before the election-petition hearing explain why he had scandalously browbeaten the ConCourt to endorse Mnangagwa's stolen result.

Jonathan N. Moyo
December 2019

DISHARMONISING THE 2018 HARMONISED ELECTIONS

SHORTLY after midnight on 3 August 2018, Justice Priscilla Chigumba, the Chairperson of the Zimbabwe Electoral Commission (ZEC), controversially used an Excel spreadsheet, instead of the more secure ZEC server, to calculate the result of the 2018 presidential election, and to declare and announce Emmerson Mnangagwa as the winner with 2,460,463 votes or 50.8%. Chigumba announced that the widely popular opposition candidate, Nelson Chamisa, was the runner-up with 2,147,436 or 44.3%; Mnangagwa's margin of victory was put at 313,027 votes (around 38,000 votes over the 50% threshold).

Just before midnight, ahead of Chigumba's result declaration and announcement, Morgen Komichi, the chairperson of the MDC-Alliance, accompanied by Nelson Chamisa's chief election agent, Jameson Timba, had used the ZEC stage from where election results were being declared to announce that the MDC-Alliance was "totally rejecting the presidential results" and that neither he nor Timba would sign the verification certificate to authenticate the presidential election result.

Four days after declaring Mnangagwa as the winner of the presidential election with 50.8% of the vote, ZEC released a free CD-ROM copy of the presidential results, in what the electoral body claimed was a "protected Excel Format", with a breakdown of the results per polling station, supposedly drawn from original V11s.

Based on the CD-ROM results in the Excel file, ZEC had surprisingly and inexplicably altered the presidential election result that Chigumba had declared for Mnangagwa on 3 August 2018, and this time gave him 50.67% rather than the earlier 50.8%. Eyebrows were raised.

An election scandal of major proportions was brewing, while the nation was still in the middle of coming to terms with the 1 August 2018 Harare Massacre in which lethally armed soldiers had brutally killed, in cold blood, six defenceless and fleeing civilians and critically injured 35 others ahead of the declaration and announcement of the result of the presidential election on 3 August 2018.

The result was bound to trigger a major electoral dispute that was certain to dress Mnangagwa with a cloak of illegitimacy.

Since its independence in 1980, Zimbabwe has not held any general election whose conduct has been deemed by all the contestants, election observers or the media as free and fair, and whose outcome has been accepted as a true and incontestable reflection of the will of the people. The presumption that every election in Zimbabwe is manipulated – or simply rigged – has become prevalent as a widely held belief in society.

Despite this background, persistent claims of manipulated or rigged elections in Zimbabwe have so far not been supported by irrefutable evidence beyond growing allegations of fraud and increasingly common electoral petitions challenging disputed election results in the courts. This has put pressure on the judiciary's handling of election petitions and disputes.

After every general election, particularly since 2000, the courts have found themselves inundated with electoral petitions dealing with alleged violations against prescribed processes and procedures or allegations of fraud that would disgrace even a banana republic. The adjudication of electoral disputes by the courts has not inspired public confidence, especially with respect to petitions challenging the presidential election. The court decision on Morgan Tsvangirai's challenge to the 2002 presidential election "won" by Robert Mugabe is still pending. Both the applicant and respondent are now dead.

This has had a damaging and chilling effect not just on the integrity of the electoral process but also on the confidence of the voters in elections, democracy and political legitimacy.

While a body of literature on electoral politics in Zimbabwe has been developed over the years, virtually all of it has been about the electoral environment. There has been no rigorous empirical case study of how elections have been actually stolen. This void has frustrated not only the possibility of a just resolution of electoral disputes in the courts but also, and more importantly, the formulation and adoption of requisite political and legal measures to reform Zimbabwe's broken electoral system.

EXCELGATE fills that historic void by breaking new ground to show how the 2018 presidential election was actually rigged in the aftermath of the 15 November 2017 military coup that ousted Robert Mugabe and illegally seized power just seven months before the next general election was constitutionally due by July 2018.

After taking over control of the state and its institutions, the military, in a bid to protect and consolidate the gains of the coup, brazenly commandeered the machinery of the Zimbabwe Electoral Commission (ZEC), particularly its server, corrupted its internal system as well as logistics, and illegally changed the route and destination for the collation, compilation and transmission of the result of the presidential election for purposes of rigging the result in favour of Emmerson Mnangagwa, whom it had imposed as president of Zimbabwe on 24 November 2017. This monumental fraud has had a damaging and chilling effect on democracy and development in Zimbabwe at a time when the country was poised to turn a new page on the back of its new democratic Constitution enacted in 2013.

Defining an election as a rule-bound political process which is a legal event, this case study is based on court records, ZEC sources and documents as well as high-level contacts in government and the security sector. Information obtained from these sources and contacts is examined and presented against the backdrop of the Electoral Act (Chapter 2:13), along with Statutory Instrument 21 of 2005 (Electoral Regulations) and the 2018 ZEC Election Officers Manual.

In addition to these sources and contacts, I have also relied on my own direct and intimate knowledge of Zimbabwe's electoral practice, which I gained when I functioned as an election strategist for ZANU PF in the 2000 parliamentary election, the 2002 presidential election and the 2013 harmonised general election, and when I participated as a parliamentary candidate for Tsholotsho in 2005, 2008 and 2013. Prior to this exposure, I studied Zimbabwe's 1985 and 1990 general elections, culminating in my book, *Voting for Democracy: A Study of Electoral Politics in Zimbabwe*, which was published in 1992.

Against this backdrop, **EXCELGATE** painstakingly details the electoral processes and procedures that were generally ignored or misunderstood by ZEC and the military, and exposes how some of these were used while others were subverted as part of a premeditated military plot to audaciously rig the 2018 presidential election, and to produce a scandalously fraudulent result of the presidential election, in gross violation of the Electoral Act and Constitution of Zimbabwe.

Crucially, the core evidence of the rigging of the result of the 2018 presidential election exposed in this book is so glaring that it cannot be rationally or legally refuted or impeached with the usual bare denials that the authorities are accustomed to making. The electoral theft was so blatant and utterly indefensible that it cannot be countenanced by any constitutional democracy without irreparably damaging the fundamental values of constitutionalism, good governance and the political rights enshrined in the Bill of Rights in the Constitution, such as the right to vote, along with the right to free and fair elections.

The setting of the rigging covered in the book is that, on 1 August 2018, as Zimbabweans and international election observers were eagerly awaiting the result of the presidential election held on 30 July 2018, the Zimbabwe Defence Forces (ZDF) and the Zimbabwe Republic Police (ZRP) killed six defenceless and fleeing civilians, and critically injured 35 others in the process, in what has come to be known as the Harare Massacre.

On the same day and riding on this unspeakable atrocity, and having diverted the process of result collation, compilation and transmission from its prescribed route and destination, ZEC started what it called "a verification process" to determine the result of the presidential election held on 30 July 2018. In a telling description by Nelson Chamisa in his founding affidavit in the ConCourt presidential election case, not challenged by any of the respondents, the unprecedented and illegal process invented by ZEC involved "a group of people, in excess of twenty, punching in what was identified as V11 [*sic*] data into an Excel spreadsheet" over two days.

The exercise, which ZEC presented as meant to "verify and determine" the result of the presidential election, was in fact part of a massive rigging of that result, spearheaded by the military from Defence House in Harare and executed by its proxy companies and its operatives embedded deep inside ZEC, using a Microsoft Excel spreadsheet – instead of a Server, to securely store and credibly process election data.

The Excel spreadsheet was used at the 11th hour as a calculator to add up a mixed bag of untraceable and thus unverifiable election returns, called V11s and V23As, to originate new voting data in order to generate a different and fraudulent result of the presidential election.

ZEC's rigged result of the 2018 presidential election was "different" from the lawful result in the V23B forms or constituency returns that are verified and signed by election agents at 210 constituency centres. This is before they are forwarded for collation at the country's 10 provincial command centres, where V23C forms are compiled to enable the collation of the initial result of the presidential election that is recorded in form V23D which is compiled by the Zimbabwe Electoral Commission at its national command centre in Harare.

The lawful result should have been, but was not, collated, compiled and transmitted from 10,985 polling stations, whose V11s are collated and compiled at ward centres into 1,958 V23As.[3] These are then transmitted to constituency centres for collation and compilation into 210 V23Bs, which are transmitted to provincial command centres for collation and compilation into 10 V23Cs, which are transmitted to ZEC's national command centre in Harare for collation and compilation into a V23D, which contains the initial result of the presidential election as defined in s37C(4)(f)(i) of the Electoral Act.

Contrary to ZEC's claim in its Report on the 2018 harmonised elections released only on 15 August 2019, the final result of the presidential election, stipulated in s37C(4)(f)(ii) of the Electoral Act, is not based on form V23D referred to above, but on form V23B, the critical presidential constituency return, which is verified, determined and announced in terms of sections 110(3)(d), (e) and (f) of the Act, respectively.

The lawful result of the presidential election had been captured from around midnight on 30 July 2018 on the V11 returns of 10,985 polling stations and later on the V23A returns from 1,958 ward collation centres and reflected through the ZEC server that the electoral body abandoned after engineers seconded to ZEC by the military and the CIO could not alter the result owing to software challenges they failed to resolve. The delivery of the abandoned server to the Constitutional Court through a subpoena by presidential election petition applicant, the main opposition leader Chamisa, was blocked by Chief Justice Luke Malaba as it would have revealed the lawful result which the military and CIO engineers had failed to alter, in which Chamisa had **66%** and Mnangagwa **33%** of the presidential vote.

Through the subpoena, the server would have exposed the fact that ZEC used an illegal route to collate, compile and transmit the result of the presidential election to enable the illegal use of its national command centre in Harare to be set up as a giant polling station and ward collation centre, rolled into one, to originate fresh V11 and V23A forms.

ZEC confirmed its use of an illegal route and illegal destination for the collation, compilation of the result for the presidential election on page 67 of its Report on the 2018 presidential election, where it says:

> *Results for the presidential and the national assembly elections were transmitted using different routes from the ward collation centre. While the destination for the national assembly election results was the constituency centre, the Presidential results were forwarded to the district centre for onward transmission to the national command centre in Harare.*
>
> **Verification was done at each point by checking the accuracy of every collation return and whether it was properly completed If not, corrections would be effected by use of polling station source documents (V11s).**

It was grossly unlawful for ZEC to use different routes and different destinations from the ward collation centre to transmit the results for the presidential and the national assembly elections.

---

[3] ZEC reported that there were a total of 1,958 elective wards in the country: Zimbabwe Electoral Commission [ZEC] *Zimbabwe 2018 Harmonised Elections Report*, page 70.

On 17 November the *Sunday Mail*, a government-controlled and pro-ZANU PF newspaper, published a curious news item entitled "Government unveils broad electoral reforms", which claimed that

> **A report from the inter-ministerial taskforce seen by the *Sunday Mail* details plans to 'conduct a study in other jurisdictions' to assess the feasibility of adopting a system that allows for the electronic transmission of results to the National Results Centre.**
>
> **'The recommendation for the expeditious transmission of results to the Command Centre (National Results Centre) is already being implemented; for instance, *in the 2018 harmonised elections, the Zimbabwe Electoral Commission used a faster procedure that led to the result forms being transmitted directly from district election centres to the National Results Centre*,' the Report says.**
>
> ***Previously, the results went through the ward, constituency, district and provincial command centres before being transmitted to the National Results Centre*** [emphasis added].[4]

The *Sunday Mail* report was curious because its storyline was cunningly similar to frantic efforts that were underway at the Ministry of Justice, Legal and Parliamentary Affairs to cover up ZEC's admission in its Report on the 2018 harmonised elections that it unlawfully deviated from the prescribed manner and invented a different route with a different destination to collate, compile and transmit the result for the 2018 presidential election.

The government confirmation through the *Sunday Mail* that, "in the 2018 harmonised elections, the Zimbabwe Electoral Commission **used a faster procedure** that led to the result forms being transmitted directly from district election centres to the National Results Centre" is a disclosure of unprecedented electoral corruption by "the system" to brazenly rig the presidential election. What faster procedure did ZEC use? What is the name of the procedure, and what is its legal basis?

What is not disclosed in the *Sunday Mail* is that the alleged faster procedure was applied only to the presidential election, yet this did not lead to a faster release of the results for the election. Furthermore, the *Sunday Mail* article does not mention that the so-called faster procedure meant that the V11s, polling station returns, and the V23As, ward centre returns for the presidential election, which must be collated and verified at constituency centres and at provincial command centres, were illegally taken to ZEC's national command centre in Harare. About this illegality, ZEC says in its Report on the 2018 harmonised elections that:

> **The results were taken to the national command/collation centre physically by the District Elections Officers *where they were captured and collated on a results collation template at the National Collation Centre*** [emphasis added].[5]

---

[4] "Govt unveils broad electoral reforms", *The Sunday Mail*, 17 November 2018: Harare.
[5] ZEC, *Zimbabwe 2018 Harmonised Elections Report*, page 68.

Just consider the staggering implication of the above confession, which no doubt found expression in the ZEC Report by accident or welcome mischief by vigilant staffers: the results of the 2018 presidential election in the form of 10,985 V11s (polling station returns) and 1,958 V23As (ward centre returns) were **"captured and collated on a collation template at the National Collation Centre"** in Harare, when, by law, they should have been collated at 210 constituency centres into V23Bs before being forwarded to ten provincial command centres for further collation into V23Cs.

By inventing a route and destination different from the prescribed process to transmit, capture and collate the V11s and V23As with the result for the presidential election, ZEC disharmonised the 2018 harmonised elections by separating the presidential and national assembly elections in violation of s38 of the Electoral Act. There was no longer a harmonised election after two different routes with two different destinations were used from the ward centres for the collation, compilation and transmission for the results for the two elections. The unlawful implications beggar belief.

Furthermore, and even more fundamentally, the unlawful separation of the two elections, from ward centres, by using two different routes with different destinations to collate, compile and transmit the results for the presidential and national assembly elections substantially violated s37C(4) of the Electoral Act regarding the **mandatory** capturing and collation of all results of the harmonised election; it also violated s110(3) with regard to the verification, determination, declaration and announcement of the result of the presidential election.

How this chain of unprecedented events played out, and the brazen violation of the electoral law to corrupt the route and destination for the collation, compilation and transmission of the result of the 2018 presidential election, and the fraudulent declaration and announcement of Mnangagwa as the elected president, controversially endorsed by the Constitutional Court – a scandal of major proportions with far-reaching implications – culminated in **EXCELGATE**, the shocking story about how Zimbabwe's 2018 presidential election was stolen.

Chapter 1

THE COUP ELECTION

IN this book I show how the military used ZEC to steal Zimbabwe's 2018 presidential election from main opposition leader Nelson Chamisa who, according to the computers at the CIO's Data Recovery Centre that were mirrored with ZEC servers, received 66% of the vote, to benefit Mnangagwa whose tally was 33%. The irrefutable evidence is overwhelming and beyond rational disputation. It's an open and shut case.

An election, as used in this book, is a rule-bound political process which is a legal event. The process starts with the preparation for the registration of voters and the delimitation of polling station, ward and constituency boundaries to enable voter registration. That process culminates in a presidential proclamation for the election, after which it goes into the intensified campaign phase that leads to a voting day or days. This is followed by vote-counting and ends with the declaration of the election results and the announcement of the winning candidates, with any part of the process subject to litigation.

ZEC exposes its rigging scheme

On 6 February 2019, someone at ZEC, perhaps inadvertently but maybe intentionally, uploaded two important diagrams on the ZEC website showing how the electoral body illegally collated, compiled and transmitted the results of the 2018 harmonised elections. Diagram 1 details the process of the collation, compilation and transmission of "all harmonised election results" under what ZEC described as "Route A".

The process outlined in Diagram 1 follows the statutory manner provided in s37C(4) of the Electoral Act (2:13). From the details on this diagram, ZEC

DIAGRAM 1:
PRESCRIBED RESULTS TRANSMISSION IGNORED BY ZEC

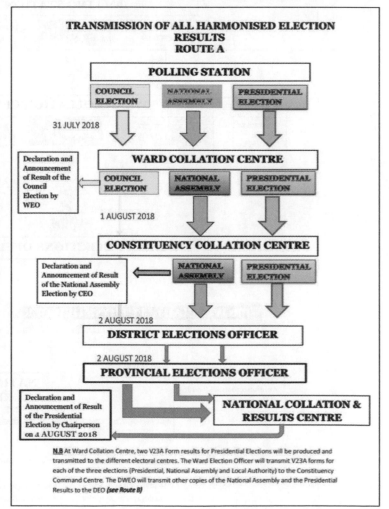

TRANSMISSION OF ALL HARMONISED ELECTION RESULTS ROUTE A

POLLING STATION

COUNCIL ELECTION · NATIONAL ASSEMBLY · PRESIDENTIAL ELECTION

31 JULY 2018

Declaration and Announcement of Result of the Council Election by WEO

WARD COLLATION CENTRE

COUNCIL ELECTION · NATIONAL ASSEMBLY · PRESIDENTIAL ELECTION

1 AUGUST 2018

CONSTITUENCY COLLATION CENTRE

Declaration and Announcement of Result of the National Assembly Election by CEO

NATIONAL ASSEMBLY · PRESIDENTIAL ELECTION

2 AUGUST 2018

DISTRICT ELECTIONS OFFICER

2 AUGUST 2018

PROVINCIAL ELECTIONS OFFICER

Declaration and Announcement of Result of the Presidential Election by Chairperson on 4 AUGUST 2018

NATIONAL COLLATION & RESULTS CENTRE

N.B At Ward Collation Centre, two V23A Form results for Presidential Elections will be produced and transmitted to the different electoral centres. The Ward Election Officer will transmit V23A forms for each of the three elections (Presidential, National Assembly and Local Authority) to the Constituency Command Centre. The DWEO will transmit other copies of the National Assembly and the Presidential Results to the DEO *(see Route B)*

intended to have its Chairperson declare and announce the result of the presidential election on 4 August 2018.

Curiously, on the same day, 6 February 2019, another diagram was uploaded to ZEC's official website detailing how the Commission had a shortcut to – or quicker manner – for the collation, compilation and transmission of the result of the 2018 presidential election.

The second diagram, marked "Urgent Transmission of Presidential Results, Route B", is radically different from the first and is substantially in breach of s37(4) of the Electoral Act. Strangely, the result under this "urgent route" was also projected to be declared and announced by the ZEC Chairperson on 4 August 2018. Apparently the "urgency" was not intended to gain time for ZEC to declare and announce the result sooner within the statutory limit of five days, but to give the military and ZEC opportunity to manipulate the result.

DIAGRAM 2:
URGENT PRESIDENTIAL RESULTS TRANSMISSION ROUTE INVENTED BY ZEC

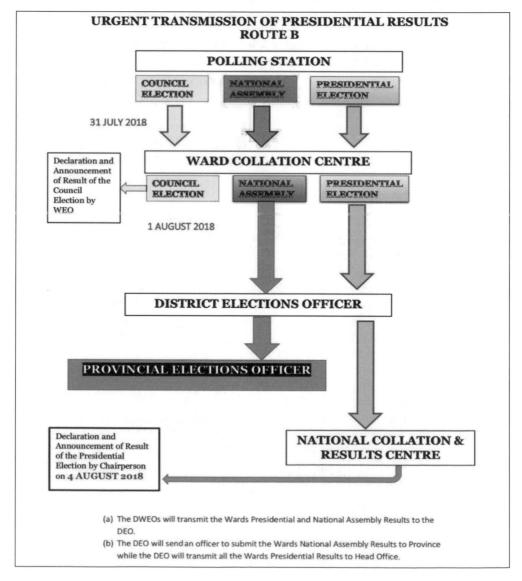

Otherwise, it is common cause that Chigumba declared and announced the presidential election result on 3 August 2018.

What is striking is that the two conflicting diagrams were uploaded by someone on ZEC's website who made them available in a *downloads* folder without any comment and not as part of any documentation. Helpfully, on 8 February 2019, all ZEC commissioners but one affixed their signatures on ZEC's Report on the 2018 harmonised elections, the absent commissioner following suit on 11 February 2019. The Report, which was uploaded to the ZEC website six months later on 15 August 2019, makes this telling disclosure regarding Diagrams 1 and 2:

> **Results for the presidential and the national assembly elections were transmitted using different routes from the ward collation centre. While the destination for the national assembly election results was the constituency centre, the Presidential results were forwarded to the district centre for onward transmission to the national command centre in Harare. Verification was done at each point by checking the accuracy of every collation return and whether it was properly completed. If not, corrections would be effected by use of polling station source documents (V11s).**

ZEC's Report provides an official diagram, displayed below, to make clear and to put beyond disputation that it used two different routes – with the same origin but with two different destinations - to collate, compile and transmit the 2018 presidential and parliamentary result.

DIAGRAM 3:
ZEC'S DISHARMONISED TRANSMISSION OF PRESIDENTIAL AND NATIONAL ASSEMBLY ELECTION RESULTS

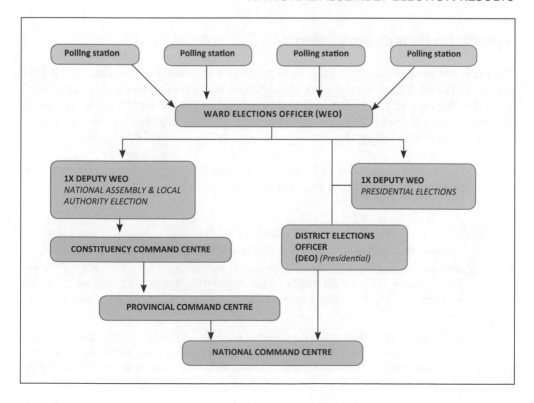

It is abundantly clear from Diagram 3 that what is given in Diagram 2 as "Urgent Transmission of Presidential Results, Route B" was in fact the only route or process that ZEC used to collate, compile and transmit the 2018 presidential election result from the country's 1,958 ward centres direct to the national command centre in Harare. This process, which was different from the one used for the parliamentary election results, was endorsed by all ZEC commissioners who appended their signatures on 8 February 2019 to approve the ZEC Report that contains Diagram 3, thus officially confirming how the result of the presidential election was illegally transmitted on 31 July 2018.

According to ZEC, from the ward centres there were two destinations shown on Diagram 3: the constituency centre (where the original parliamentary V11s and V23As were routed) and the national command centre in Harare (where the original presidential V11s and V23As were routed). This means that the original V11s and V23As with the result of the presidential election could not have been available at the two different destinations through two different routes shown on Diagram 3. The legal implications are staggering. In effect, ZEC disharmonised the 2018 harmonised elections by using two different routes with two different destinations to capture, collate and transmit the results for the presidential and national assembly elections. The disharmonisation was in violation of s38 of the Electoral Act.

Ironically, despite having used an "urgent route", or taken a "shortcut", to collate, compile and transmit the presidential election result, in its public pronouncement ZEC still pretended to be using one route with one destination: the normal, lengthy and arduous route that takes long to process, declare and announce the result. ZEC deliberately lied to the public and to the court, under oath, during the hearing of Chamisa's ConCourt challenge that the declaration and announcement of the result of the presidential election was delayed due to the long and involved process of collating, compiling and transmitting the result.

A grossly invalid presidential election

The route and process used by ZEC to collate, compile and transmit the result of the 2018 presidential election glaringly and scandalously breached the peremptory provisions of s37C (4) of the Electoral Act (2:13) and rendered the whole 2018 presidential election inherently and irretrievably unlawful and thus grossly invalid with the unavoidable consequence of leaving the result declared by Chigumba on 3 August 2018 a legal nullity *ab initio*.

Section 37C(4) of the Electoral Act provides for the collation, compilation and transmission of all the results of the harmonised elections as follows:

(4)   The Commission **shall ensure** that the results of the presidential, national assembly and local authority elections are **collated, compiled** and **transmitted** in the following manner –

   (a) with respect to local authority elections, polling-station returns gathered from every polling station within a ward shall be transmitted to the appropriate ward centre in a return distinctly indicating the results obtained in each polling station relating to those elections;

   (b) with respect to –

       (i) presidential elections, polling-station returns gathered from every polling station within a ward **shall be transmitted to the appropriate ward centre for collation** at that centre, the results of which collation shall be embodied in a return ("presidential election ward return") distinctly indicating the results obtained in each polling station relating to that election; and

(ii) national assembly elections, polling-station returns gathered from every polling station within a ward shall be transmitted to the appropriate ward centre for collation at that centre, the results of which collation shall be embodied in a return ("national assembly election ward return") distinctly indicating the results obtained in each polling station relating to those elections:

Provided that duplicate copies of the polling-station returns gathered from every polling station within a ward for the purposes of subparagraph (i) and (ii) shall also be transmitted through the appropriate ward centre directly to the national command centre;

and

(c) after collation of the results of –

(i) **presidential election at each ward centre, presidential election ward returns gathered from every ward centre within a constituency shall be transmitted to the appropriate presidential constituency centre for collation** at that centre, the results of which collation shall be embodied in a return ("presidential constituency return") distinctly indicating the results obtained in each ward within that constituency relating to that election;

(ii) national assembly elections at each ward centre, national assembly election ward returns gathered from every ward centre within a constituency shall be transmitted to the appropriate national assembly constituency centre for collation at that centre, the results of which collation shall be embodied in a return ("national assembly constituency return") distinctly indicating the results obtained in each ward within that constituency relating to those elections;

and

(d) **after collation of the results of the presidential election at each presidential constituency centre, presidential constituency returns gathered from every presidential constituency centre shall be transmitted to the provincial command centre for collation** at that centre, the results of which collation shall be embodied in a return ("provincial return for the presidential election") distinctly indicating the results obtained in each constituency relating to those elections;

Provided that duplicate copies of the presidential constituency returns gathered from every presidential constituency centre shall also be transmitted directly from the provincial command centre concerned to the national command centre;

and

(e) after collation of the results of the national assembly elections at each national assembly constituency centre, national assembly constituency returns gathered from every national assembly constituency centre shall be transmitted to the provincial command centre, where –

(i) the result of the national assembly election in the province in question will be embodied in a return ("provincial return for the national assembly elections") distinctly indicating the results obtained in each constituency relating to those elections; and

(ii) the results of the election for the party-list candidates for the province in question will be determined in accordance with section 45I on the basis of the provincial return for the national assembly elections, and be embodied in return ("provincial return for elections of party-list candidates") distinctly indicating the results obtained for the Senate, national assembly and provincial council party-list seats;

and

(f) **after the collation of the results of the presidential election at each provincial command centre, provincial returns for the presidential election gathered from every provincial command centre shall be transmitted to the national command centre,** where –

    (i)   the provincial returns shall be collated to obtain the initial results of the presidential election; and

    (ii) the final result of the presidential election shall, after reconciling the provincial returns with the polling station returns and presidential constituency returns referred to in the provisos to paragraphs (b) and (d) respectively, be reflected in a return that distinctly reflects number of votes cast for each presidential candidate at every polling station, ward centre, presidential constituency centre and provincial command centre;

I have emphasised the relevant peremptory provisions of s37C(4) of the Electoral Act to make clear that it is legally mandatory for ZEC to follow and strictly adhere to the statutory process for the collation, compilation and transmission of the results of the harmonised elections, which include the result of the presidential election. As shown on Diagram 4 below, the route used by ZEC breached the Electoral Act by cutting out the presidential constituency centre (which produces the crucially important V23B return necessary for the determination of the final result of the presidential election) and the provincial command centre (which produces the critical V23C return necessary for the determination of the initial result of the presidential election):

DIAGRAM 4:
CONSEQUENCE OF ZEC'S BREACH OF MANDATORY TRANSMISSION ROUTE AND DESTINATION

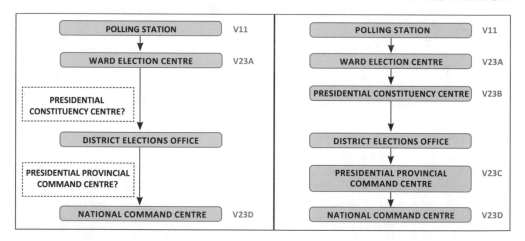

The "different" route that ZEC used to collate, compile and transmit the result of the 2018 presidential election excluded, as destinations, the constituency centres and provincial command centres that collate, compile and transmit V23Bs and V23Cs, respectively. This means that, as shown on Diagram 4, for the purpose of the presidential election, ZEC illegally transmitted the result of the presidential election and, specifically, did not legally collate and compile V23Bs, or constituency returns, to determine the result of the presidential election as required by s110(3)(d), as read with s65A, of the Electoral Act, nor did it legally collate and compile V23Cs, or provincial returns, in terms of s65B as read with s37C(4)(f) of the Act.

ZEC has no discretionary power to invent its own process, as it did in coming up with the transmission manner contained in Diagram 3, whose illegal consequence is highlighted on Diagram 4. On this irrefutable ground alone, the result of the 2018 presidential election declared by ZEC in Mnangagwa's favour cannot legally stand. It is incurably flawed. No reasonable court can condone it.

The question must be asked: why did ZEC invent a different route and process for the collation, compilation and transmission of only the result of the presidential election from the 1,958 wards via District Election Officers, direct to the national command centre in Harare?

There's only one rational answer: to facilitate the rigging of the result of the presidential election.

EXCELGATE unravels the rigging by exposing how the military used ZEC to invent a route and process of collating, compiling and transmitting the result of the 2018 presidential election outside and in violation of the legal manner prescribed in the Electoral Act.

This was after it had become clear on 31 July 2018 that, based on the results from 10,985 polling stations, which the military got to know soon after midnight on 30 July 2018, with 33%, Mnangagwa had lost the presidential election by a landslide to Chamisa, who had 66%. The invention of a different collation, compilation and transmission of only the presidential election result, in a harmonised election where the three elections must be subjected to the same process, was done to enable the alteration of the result. Collating, compiling and transmitting the presidential election result in terms of s37C(4) of the Electoral Act would have led to the confirmation of Chamisa's crushing victory.

Reasons for the November 2017 coup

Various reasons for and triggers of the 15 November 2017 military coup in Zimbabwe have been advanced.[6] There has been quite some debate on what triggered the coup. The propaganda of the coup-makers was that their intervention targeted "criminals around the President". An extension of the same propaganda was that the military had seized power to stop Grace Mugabe, the former First Lady, from succeeding her husband. The putschists, including Mnangagwa and Chiwenga, who pushed the Grace Mugabe fiction knew only too well that Mugabe had vowed on several occasions in politburo meetings that he would not allow his wife to succeed him. He was deadly opposed to the idea. His choice of successor was Sydney Sekeramayi. But, of course, it was convenient propaganda to claim that Grace was on the verge of taking over. On the other hand, the proposition that stopping Grace from succeeding her husband required a military coup was a ludicrous excuse.

---

[6] See, for example, Blessing-Miles Tendi, "The Motivations and Dynamics of Zimbabwe's 2017 Military Coup", *African Affairs*, https://doi. org/10.1093/afraf/adz024.

Equally ludicrous were claims that the coup was necessitated by an urgent need to stop "the G40 cabal" that "had coalesced around Grace Mugabe" and "had usurped President Mugabe's constitutional power and authority". I found this amusing. It remains news to me that I was part of a cabal that had usurped presidential power and authority which could only be regained through a military coup.

For all the political association I'm supposed to have had with Grace Mugabe as an alleged "G40 Kingpin", the fact is that I had very little interaction with her in my days as Cabinet minister. Throughout my tenure as Information Minister between 2000 and 2005, and later between 2013 and 2015, I never had any meeting with her. Not even one. My first ever one-on-one meeting with Grace Mugabe was in August 2017 at her Mazowe Orphanage, some three months before the military coup. And that meeting was about the Robert Mugabe University that it had been proposed be built in Mazowe.

Another popular but utterly false claim is that the military coup was triggered by a foiled attempt by former Commissioner General of Police, Augustine Chihuri, to arrest Chiwenga on his arrival from China at Robert Gabriel Mugabe International Airport on 12 November 2017. The fiction that Chihuri had attempted to arrest Chiwenga at the airport in Harare first came to light when Sydney Sekeramayi, as Defence Minister, raised it with Chihuri on Sunday, 12 November 2017, the day that the incident allegedly happened. Chihuri, who was in Marondera, expressed surprise and told Sekeramayi that he had no knowledge of the alleged incident, and that, in any event, no one had lodged any criminal complaint against Chiwenga, nor had anyone given an instruction for his arrest.

On the next day, Monday, 13 November 2017, at a briefing with President Mugabe, attended by Chief Secretary to the President and Cabinet Misheck Sibanda and other senior officials, Chihuri complained to Mugabe that some people were spreading a malicious rumour that he had attempted to arrest Chiwenga at the airport but was foiled by ZDF commandos. Everyone else in the meeting professed ignorance about the rumour, and the matter ended there.

Following the 15 November 2017 military coup, after the *Zimbabwe Independent* had sensationally reported on 17 November 2017 about the allegedly foiled Chiwenga airport arrest, Chihuri again raised the matter at a briefing meeting for Mnangagwa, as the incoming president, at Munhumutapa Building in the presence of Chiwenga, Misheck Sibanda, the Army's Philip Valerio Sibanda and the Prison's Paradzayi Zimondi. Not even Chiwenga himself confirmed the alleged incident. It became clear that the Hollywood-like fiction about the purported arrest had been fabricated to create legendary myths as part of the propaganda to popularise the military coup.

Some have claimed that the coup was triggered by the dismissal of Mnangagwa from the position of Vice-President on 6 November 2017. Again, this is far-fetched, notwithstanding Mnangagwa's "I'll be back" press statement released on 8 November 2017. Others have suggested that Mugabe's alleged refusal to meet Chiwenga on 13 November 2017 was the trigger of the coup. There was no refusal. The issue was about finding a mutually convenient time, and the expectation was that the meeting would be on Wednesday, 15 November 2017, which turned out to be the day of the military coup.

To insiders who were aware that a military coup in Zimbabwe had been loading for quite some time, and that all hell was set to break loose with blood on the floor ahead of an elective ZANU PF congress that had been slated for December 2017, the 15 November 2017 coup was triggered by a statement released on 14 November 2017 by Simon Khaya-Moyo, then Information Minister and ZANU PF spokesperson, that described as "treasonous", Chiwenga's press statement of 13 November 2017 literally threatening a military coup. In the statement, issued through ZANU PF, SK Moyo charged that

> **Consistent with the guiding principle of the National Liberation Struggle, the ruling Zimbabwe African National Union Patriotic Front (ZANU PF) reaffirms the primacy of politics over the gun. It is against an understanding of this abiding principle that the statement issued by General Constantino Chiwenga purporting to speak on behalf of the Zimbabwe Defence Forces (ZDF) was not only surprising, but was an outrageous vitiation of professional soldiership and his war time record as a high-ranking freedom fighter entrusted with Command responsibilities in a free and democratic Zimbabwe.**
>
> **Clearly calculated to disturb national peace and stability, the said statement by General Constantino Chiwenga which was not signed, and which did not represent the rest of the Command Element, suggests treasonable conduct on his part as this was meant to incite insurrection and violent challenge to the Constitutional Order. Indeed, this is what happens when the gun seeks to overreach by dictating to politics and norms of Constitutionality.**

Chiwenga and the commanders revealed in the "Coup Minutes" how they took SK Moyo's statement seriously and that the statement catalysed the coup as follows:[7]

> **The President and Commander-In-Chief [Mugabe] was informed of concerns of the Command Element over dangerous claims of treasonable conduct arising from a public expression of their disavowal of the state-of-affairs in the country and the Party expressed at the Press Briefing of 13th November, 2017, and the subsequent Operation mounted two days later. The Command Element cited a Press Statement by the Minister of Information, Media and Broadcasting Services, Ambassador S. K. Moyo, which was issued in his capacity as the Spokesperson of the ruling party, and an address by Youth League Secretary [Kudzanai] Chipanga, both of which alleged high treason. They also claimed that the new Minister of Justice, Legal and Parliamentary Affairs, was crafting a legal instrument meant to indict the Commanders for both actions. The noble intentions behind the actions had to be acknowledged to quash fears of indictments in the future.**

The fear of facing treason charges sent shivers down the spines of the "command element" and triggered the coup. Chiwenga and the commanders were convinced, not without good reason,

---

[7] See Appendix: "The Coup Minutes" of the *Zimbabwe Defence Forces*, Harare, 15 November 2017. These Minutes were sent by exiled former ministers in Robert Mugabe's Cabinet to the leadership of the Southern African Development Community (SADC) and the African Union (AU) in January 2018.

that, unless they intervened swiftly, they faced a real risk and possibility of being charged with treason, with a further risk of having the charge opportunistically used to purge the ZDF. Infuriated and scared, they responded by pulling the trigger.

Even so, it should be understood that a trigger is not a cause. As already mentioned, the coup had been loading for quite some time, catalysed for historical, structural and political reasons. In this connection, and considering the issues raised by the commanders in their engagement with President Mugabe during the putsch, there are three reasons for the November 2017 military coup:

- First, the so-called ZDF command element had concluded, from reports of more than 2,000 army commissars embedded in all communities across the country, that ZANU PF was heading for electoral defeat in 2018. The ZDF intervened through their "Operation Restore Legacy" to rescue ZANU PF from assured electoral defeat.

- Second, the ZDF "command element" believed ZANU PF had to be saved from the so-called Generation 40 (G40) caucus which was thought to be on the verge of succeeding Mugabe. Because this ZANU PF faction did not have roots in the armed liberation struggle and its Mgagao culture, the commanders feared that the ascendancy of the grouping would result in a purge of war veterans of the armed liberation struggle from the army and ZANU PF.

- Third, the commanders had become nervous about their security of tenure in the armed forces because of a view, which they strongly opposed, that they all were serving their last term under the two-term clause in the 2013 Constitution affecting senior public officers and permanent secretaries.

Against this backdrop, and having seized political power by ousting Mugabe only seven months before the next general election was constitutionally due by July 2018, and having imposed Mnangagwa as President of Zimbabwe on 24 November 2017 on the back of the coup, the ZDF commanders were determined to use all means available to ensure a Mnangagwa "electoral victory" in 2018 without fail in order to entrench and consolidate the political gains of the military coup.

As such, the military's principal and overarching goal in undertaking the November 2017 coup was to take over ZANU PF and to rescue it from what the commanders saw as the party's impending electoral defeat seven months down the line. It was inconceivable that the military would let the political power it had grabbed through the barrel of the gun go to the opposition through the ballot box. That was out of the question.

In the circumstances, the commanders treated Zimbabwe's 2018 harmonised general election, especially the presidential election, as a military operation of the utmost strategic importance. It was a do-or-die mission. Losing the election was not an option.

Turning ZEC's National Command Centre into a giant polling station

"On the 1st of August 2018 twenty third respondent [ZEC] started what it called a verification process and which it asked Messrs Komichi and Timba to witness. The process involved a group of people, in excess of twenty, punching in what was identified as V11 data into an Excel spreadsheet. For close to two days that process continued".[8]

The above unprecedented goings on at ZEC's national command centre in Harare on 1 August 2018 were narrated by Nelson Chamisa in his founding affidavit. The narration was not opposed by ZEC during Chamisa's ConCourt challenge.

The mishandling of V11s at ZEC's national command centre captured in the narration was highly irregular and scandalously fraudulent. This is because the Electoral Act [*Chapter 2:13*], requires that the data on V11s must be legally collated, verified and compiled at ward centres and aggregated at constituency centres, and not at the national command centre in Harare.

Notwithstanding its endorsement by the ConCourt, and even because of that endorsement, ZEC's declaration and announcement of Mnangagwa, on 3 August 2018, as the winner of the 2018 presidential election was a coup against the will of the people of Zimbabwe, whose sovereignty over the State is enshrined in the country's new 2013 Constitution.

Based on the agreed facts, the essence of Chamisa's unrebutted narration in his founding affidavit is that for a period of two days, from 1 to 3 August 2018, a group of people in excess of twenty were punching data from what ZEC alleged were original V11s and V23s into an Excel spreadsheet. This exercise, which was purported by ZEC to be about the verification and determination of the result of the presidential election, was far from that. Rather, it amounted to turning ZEC's national command centre into a giant polling station to originate new untraceable and unverifiable voting data to generate a new result through an Excel spreadsheet. This was a direct consequence of ZEC's corrupted collation, compilation and transmission of the presidential election result, described in Diagram 3.

But where did the V11s that the group of people, in excess of twenty, who were punching numbers into an Excel spreadsheet come from?

There's no need to look too far for the answer. Recall this WhatsApp message sent on 31 July 2018 by Chigumba to her close contacts:

> **They [MDC] don't have to agree. We will announce based on our own V11. We don't need any party's V11. It's just courtesy for us to ask them to verify. Agree or not, we announce.**

By inventing the process on Diagram 3, ZEC created an illegal avenue for generating its "own V11s" which no other party had. By 31 July 2018, the day ZEC invented its own process for collating, compiling and transmitting the result of the presidential election, Chigumba was dead set on rejecting any presidential election V11 produced in terms of s37C(4), and was determined to treat the verification of election returns by election agents as just a "courtesy", as she readied herself to announce ZEC's own result of the presidential election.

---

[8] This is taken from paragraph 5.1 of Nelson Chamisa's affidavit in his Constitutional Court challenge to ZEC's declaration of Emmerson Mnangagwa as the winner of Zimbabwe's 2018 presidential election (CCZ42/18). See also the affidavits by Jameson Timba and Morgen Komichi (pages 178–182 and 183–186, respectively).

It is in this light that the European Union Election Observation Mission (EU EOM) observed that some party agents and CSOs reported that "polling station return forms, the V11, were altered and return figures changed at ward and constituency collation centres". But even more revealing, from the report of the EU EOM, the evidence of the operation to alter the presidential result included an incident in which EU EOM found ZEC officers in Makoni North completing V11 forms two days after election day, meaning on 1 August 2018, all by themselves in the absence of polling staff and election agents. The ZEC officials shockingly claimed to be doing this because of earlier lack of V11 Forms.[9]

Where did these V11s that ZEC officials in Makoni North were found by the EU EOM completing alone two days after the election go? How many such V11s did these ZEC officials end up completing in the absence of election agents and well after the election? Is there any rational basis for treating the Makoni North incident as isolated and the only such case?

Clearly, these kinds of V11s from Makoni North were among the lot that the "group of people in excess of twenty" were punching into an Excel spreadsheet at the ZEC national command centre between 1 and 3 August 2018.

The significance of the Makoni North incident is that it puts the spotlight on how ZEC contaminated the V11s and why these forms, once they were contaminated, became a convenient, albeit illegal, opportunity for altering and rigging the result of the 2018 presidential election.

Once they had become contaminated through incidents such as the one reported by the EU EOM in Makoni North, which incident has not been rebutted by ZEC, the outcome of the two-day process at the ZEC national command centre that "involved a group of people, in excess of twenty, punching in what was identified as V11 data into an Excel spreadsheet" was also contaminated and could not be relied upon to produce a legitimate result of the 2018 presidential election.

In this connection, the EU EOM report noted that the

> **Presidential results announced by ZEC were based on figures from the provincial level. ZEC also provided a CD-ROM with polling station figures set out in excel format. As this was not a presentation of the actual V11 forms from each polling station, the CD-ROM did not provide the level of transparency, traceability and verifiability which was hoped for and which could have been achieved. Further, the figures presented by ZEC in the CD-ROM contained a large number of errors and inaccuracies.[10]**

When ZEC put together "a group of people in excess of twenty" at its national command centre to have them punch data into an Excel spreadsheet from what was alleged to be original copies of all V11s, presumably from all the country's 10,985 polling stations, it acted irrationally and unlawfully.

In effect, and rather astonishingly so, ZEC set up its national command centre as one giant polling station, which is not provided for in the law. Once so illegally set up, ZEC purported

[9] EU EOM, *Zimbabwe Harmonised Elections 2018: Final Report*, October 2018, page 35. https://eeas.europa.eu/sites/eeas/files/eu_eom_zimbabwe_2018_-_final_report.pdf.
[10] Ibid., page 2.

to collate and verify "original" V11s at its national command centre using "**a group of people, in excess of twenty, punching in what was identified as V11 data into an Excel spreadsheet**" over a period of two days. This was **EXCELGATE**: a massive daylight rigging of the 2018 presidential election.

In terms of the law, data from V11s is punched into V23As, not into an Excel spreadsheet, at designated collation centres in the country's 1,958 ward centres, and nowhere else. The V23A form is the only legal election return that contains collated and verified data from V11s. Once V23As have been legally compiled at ward centres, they are transmitted to constituency centres, not to the national command centre, for collation and compilation into V23Bs or presidential constituency returns. The collated and compiled V23Bs are transmitted to provincial command centres for collation and compilation into V23Cs or provincial returns.

Going by its Report on the 2018 harmonised elections, ZEC was confused or mischievous about the application of "V" forms or election returns. For example, on page 70, regarding the national assembly election, the Report confuses V23s (provincial returns) with V23Bs (constituency returns) as follows:

> **Ward returns for the National Assembly elections were sent to respective constituencies where they were collated, verified, and summed up in the presence of candidates, election agents and observers.** *These were recorded on the constituency return Form V23C. A candidate who attained the majority of votes cast was declared the winner and MP-elect for the constituency. A copy of V23C was displayed outside the constituency centre* **and copies were forwarded to the National Command centre through the Provincial Command centre for information. Political party agents were requested to append their signatures to the forms before they were displayed outside the Constituency centres.**[11]

It cannot be right that, more than a year since the 2018 harmonised general election, ZEC still does not know that a V23C is a provincial command return, whereas a V23B is the correct constituency return.

An Excel spreadsheet has no legal or administrative standing in the collation, compilation and verification of election results. None whatsoever. Whereas V23s with polling station data can be collated, verified and traced back to their original sources or election returns, an Excel spreadsheet simply cannot be verified or aggregated, let alone traced back to any legal source or election return.

There are three source documents that define the forms or returns that must be legally collated and verified: these are the Electoral Act [*Chapter 2:13*], Statutory (Electoral Regulations), as amended, and the ZEC 2018 *Electoral Officers Manual*. None of these key source documents refers to an Excel spreadsheet, with V11 data, as an election return.

Although ZEC claimed to have used an Excel spreadsheet only as "an addition tool", given the fact that the electoral body had invented its own collation, compilation and transmission process direct

---

[11] ZEC, *Zimbabwe 2018 Harmonised Elections Report*, page 70.

from the ward centres to the national command centre, ZEC's use of an Excel spreadsheet had the effect of turning the Excel spreadsheet into an illegal election return, thus giving rise to "Excelgate".

This is an important issue to reflect upon. As already pointed out, by inventing the process on Diagram 3, ZEC created an illegal avenue for generating what Chigumba's WhatsApp message of 31 July 2018 referred to as "our own V11s", which no other party or person had.

ZEC'S "different route" with a "different destination" that it used to collate, compile and transmit the result of the 2018 presidential election did not include, as destinations, the constituency centres and provincial command centres that collate, compile and transmit the critical V23Bs and V23Cs that are, respectively, necessary for the compilation of the final (V23Bs) and preliminary (V23Cs) result of the presidential election. The "different destination" is confirmed by ZEC itself in its Report on the 2018 harmonised elections finalised on 8 February 2019:

> **Results for the Presidential and the National Assembly elections were transmitted using different routes from the ward collation centre. While the destination for the National Assembly election results was the constituency centre, the Presidential results were forwarded to the district centre for onward transmission to the National Command Centre in Harare.**[12]

The Excel spreadsheet used by ZEC at its national command centre to add data from purported "original" V11s and V23As, that legally should have not been there in the manner they got there, became a replacement of the true original V11s and V23As attached to original V23Bs and V23Cs from constituency centres and provincial command centres, which ZEC's "urgent route" illegally avoided as destination centres.

Given the provisions of s37C(4) of the Electoral Act regarding the manner in which the collation, compilation and transmission of the result of the presidential election should be done, s65 of the Act, which is about the procedure that must be followed on receipt of the polling station returns (V11s) stipulates in subsection 7, the destination where the ward returns (V23As) **must be** transmitted as follows:

> **Immediately after causing a copy of the ward return to be displayed outside the ward centre,** *the ward elections officer shall cause the return, certified by himself or herself to be correct, to be transmitted to the constituency centre for the constituency* **in which the ward is situated.**

The Electoral Act is peremptorily clear: **the destination of the original and certified ward return (the V23A) and the original and certified polling station return (the V11) is the constituency centre, not the national command centre in Harare.**

If, for some strange reason, the Ward Elections Officers do not use the original V11s to collate the result of the presidential election to complete entries on the V23As, and if the transmission of the completed original V23As is rerouted to a different destination other than the constituency centre, then the Ward Elections Officers would be in violation of the law and liable to prosecution.

---

[12] ZEC, *Zimbabwe 2018 Harmonised Elections Report*, page 67.

In the same vein, the Constituency Election Officers are required not to open envelopes that do not have original V23As to which the original V11s are attached. If they open and process envelopes without the original V11s and V23As, they are liable to prosecution. ZEC itself makes this position patently clear in its 2018 *Electoral Officers Manual* in these terms:

> The Ward Elections officer will collate Ward results for the Presidential, National Assembly and Local Authority elections. The Ward Elections Officer will make use of one of the original V.11 Forms for each Polling Station to complete entries on the V23A Forms for the three Elections. For each Polling Station in that Ward there must be one corresponding original V.11 Form attached to the back of the V23A Form. *Under no circumstances is the Ward Elections Officer permitted to complete an entry for any Polling Station on the V23A Form without having on hand its original V.11 Form!*
>
> The Constituency Elections Officer will only open the envelope *with the original V23A Forms to which the original V.11 Forms have been attached.* These original V23A Forms will be required by the Constituency Elections Officer to complete Form V23B – also called, the Constituency Collation Form. The Constituency Elections Officer must ensure that the required number of original V23A Forms has been handed over by the Ward Elections Officer for each and every concurrent Election – Photocopies, Facsimiles or anything other than the original V23A Forms will not be accepted!!! [13]

The ZEC *Manual* is emphatic that:

> The Constituency Elections Officer must verify that each and every original V23A Form has its required original V.11 Forms attached. If any such forms are missing or are deemed to be copies then these must under no circumstances be accepted! [14]

Regarding the completion of the presidential constituency returns, the V23Bs, that are required for the collation, verification and determination of the final result of the presidential election in terms of s110(3)(d) of the Electoral Act, the ZEC *Manual* acknowledges in very strong terms the fact that the V23Bs are incomplete unless the original V11s and V23As are attached to them, and directs Constituency Election Officers as follows:

> The Constituency Elections Officer may only complete the V23B Form after receiving the original V23A Forms along with all their relevant original V.11 Forms attached. *Under no circumstances is the Constituency Elections Officer allowed to complete an entry for a Ward's Collated Return on the V23B Constituency Collation Form if he/she does not have the original V23A Form (along with ALL the relevant original V.11 Forms) in his/her possession! The key thing to note here is that original Forms are required at every step in the process!!!*
> ...

---

[13] https://www.zec.org.zw/final/files/ZEC%20Election%20Officers%20Full%20Manual.pdf, page 48.
[14] Ibid., page 49.

The V23B Form is complete when it contains all the collated results for all the Wards in that Constituency. The relevant stakeholders (if present) must be requested to sign the completed V23B Form. *Remember that at the back of every V23B Form, all the original V23A Forms with each and every one of their original V.11 Forms must be attached.*[15]

The ZEC *Manual* goes on to warn against collating the V23Bs without original V11s and V23As because

It is a serious violation of the prescribed results aggregation procedures if any original V23A or its V.11 Forms are found to be missing for any of the captured Ward entries on the V23B Form!

The foregoing means that, as shown on Diagram 4, for the purpose of the presidential election, ZEC did not legally collate and compile V23Bs, or constituency returns, to determine the result of the presidential election as required by s110(3)(d) of the Electoral Act.

Under the First Schedule (Section 2) of Statutory Instrument 21 of 2005 as amended [The Electoral Regulations], there are 25 "V" forms, out of which 14 have since been repealed, leaving 11 that were operational in the 2018 presidential election, out of which only four are election returns (V11, V23A, V23B and V23C).

The four "V" forms, or election returns, that are used by the five electoral centres that are provided in the Electoral Act for the collation, compilation and transmission of the result of the presidential election are:

- **V11** or polling station return (from **10,985** polling station centres)
- **V23A** or ward return (from **1,958** ward collation centres)
- **V23B** or constituency return (from **210** constituency centres),
- **V23C** or provincial return (from **10** provincial command centres)
- **V23D** (at national command centre in Harare with initial national result).

Notably, the Electoral Regulations provide for form V23D, which is not an election return as such, but an administrative form used at ZEC's national command centre to record the total of 10 provincial returns, namely V23Cs, to get the initial or preliminary result of the presidential election.

Section 110(3)(d) of the Electoral Act, on the verification and determination of the result of the presidential election, provides that:

At the time and place notified for the verification of the constituency returns referred to in paragraph (c) and in the presence of such candidates, their chief election agents and observers as are present, the Chief Elections Officer shall display each constituency return to those present and shall, on request, allow a candidate or chief election agent of a candidate to make notes of the contents of each constituency return.

What this means is that the determination of the result of the presidential election begins with the verification – not the collation but the verification – of the constituency returns by ZEC at its national command centre in Harare.

---

[15] Ibid., page 50.

The process requires ZEC to display the constituency returns, one by one, at a time and place notified in advance to enable the candidates or their election agents to verify the returns to confirm or raise queries about them. During this process, there should be no "group of people, in excess of twenty, punching in what was identified as V11 data into an Excel spreadsheet" going on for close to two days, as happened at the ZEC national command centre from 1 to 3 August 2018.

On the procedure for the addition of the votes, and this is where an Excel spreadsheet could have been used as an addition tool, that are in the constituency returns to get the result of the presidential election, s110(3)(e) of the Electoral Act stipulates that

> **When the Chief Elections Officer has completed the verification of the constituency returns under paragraph (d) the Chief Elections Officer shall, in the presence of such persons referred to in paragraph (d) as are present, add together the number of votes received by each candidate as shown in each constituency return.**

The meaning of this section is that the verification of constituency returns at the national command centre cannot rationally or legally start or run concurrently with punching V11 or V23A data into an Excel spreadsheet, to add totals from V11 Forms that have not been collated or verified at the national command centre. Specifically, the addition of votes to determine the result of the presidential election in terms of s110(3)(d) of the Electoral Act cannot be done before the verification has been completed. The verification and addition of votes in the presidential constituency returns are sequential and not simultaneous or concurrent processes.

It is clear that the "V" form to be verified to determine the result of the presidential election is the presidential constituency return, which is form V23B, and not the V11. Yet, in a futile attempt to cover up its rigging with respect to the verification and determination of the result of the presidential election, ZEC's opposing papers in Chamisa's ConCourt challenge only and throughout refer to "V11s" and "V23s", never to any specific V23 form. ZEC's lack of the necessary legal specificity in its reference to "V23s" was deliberate and intended to mislead, given that there are four distinct V23 forms, or presidential election returns, all which are V23 Forms: V23A, the ward return; V23B, the constituency return; V23C, the provincial command return; and V23D, the national command centre form. So, which of these V23s are included or meant by ZEC's catch-all reference to V23s? All or some of them? The law is clear, s110(3)(d) refers to only one of them: V23B; which is the presidential constituency return.

In addition to the unrebutted evidence about a "group of people, in excess of twenty, punching in what was identified as V11 data into an Excel spreadsheet" going on for close to two days at ZEC's national command centre, from 1 August 2018, ZEC did not dispute the following evidence on paragraphs 13 and 14 of the supporting affidavit filed in the ConCourt case by Jameson Timba, Chamisa's chief election agent:

> **13. On the 1st of August 2018, I was invited by ZEC to verify *constituency returns* for the presidential election. On arrival at National Results Centre where ZEC was collating results for the Presidential Election on the basis of data from all ward returns, that is *Form V23a* accompanied by *polling station returns (i.e. Form V11)*, these forms were laid before me by Mr. Murenje, the ZEC Director of Elections and Training.**

14. Mr. Murenje did not present to me the constituency returns (that is Form V23b).

Timba's submission was not rebutted by ZEC in its opposing papers, nor, crucially, did Mr Murenje, the ZEC Director of Elections, submit an opposing affidavit to dispute Timba's key evidence. What emerges and is detailed in this book is that **ZEC used the V23A Forms when it was required by law to use the V23B Forms.** ZEC could not use the V23B Forms because it used a different route to transmit the result of the presidential election whose destination excluded constituency centres where V23Bs are produced.

As such, it is an undisputed fact that the process that ZEC put in place to verify and determine the result of the presidential election was grossly and fraudulently contrary to s110(3)(d) of the Electoral Act because it involved collating and verifying polling station and ward centre returns, V11s and V23s, whose origin could not be verified or traced. The originals of these returns are available only through Form V23B, which ZEC did not avail during its bogus exercise that involved a "group of people, in excess of twenty, punching in what was identified as V11 data into an Excel spreadsheet" going on for close to two days between 1 and 3 August 2018.

Chamisa's factual narration in his founding affidavit, which ZEC did not dispute on the record, that for close to two days ZEC's staff were busy manually entering data from supposedly **original** V11 forms into an Excel spreadsheet is key, given that ZEC cannot legally have **original** V11s that are not attached to V23B forms, the presidential constituency returns. ZEC did not have the V23Bs, the constituency returns, because it used a legally invalid process of collating, compiling and transmitting the result of the presidential election, which is captured in Diagram 3, which diagram was produced by ZEC itself.

The fact that ZEC was collating and compiling original V11s at its national command centre, using an Excel spreadsheet, is confirmation of rigging and nothing else. It is the evidence of Excelgate. Otherwise, the only V11s that ZEC could have, and which it indeed had, are duplicate copies, not originals from polling stations but duplicate copies – those sent electronically directly by polling stations to the national command centre and the **duplicate copies sent by 1,958 ward centres in terms of the provisos of s37C(4)(b) and (d).**

Given the foregoing it is important to note that, in terms of s37C(4)(f) of the Electoral Act, there are two results of the presidential election that ZEC must determine; **one an initial result, and the other a final result.**

The final result of the presidential election requires the reconciliation of four results:

1. First, there's the result based on duplicate copies of all presidential polling station returns (V11s), and there are 10,985 V11s that are verified in terms of s64 of the Electoral Act, and they are sent directly to the national command centre by each polling station (according to the ZEC 2018 *Electoral Officers Manual*) and by 1,958 ward collation centres, according to s37C(4)(b) of the Electoral Act. It is this result that was captured in the ZEC server procured from an American company, which showed Chamisa with 66% of the vote and Mnangagwa with 33%. ZEC used this result in the server to fraudulently and illegally use a different route to collate, compile and transmit the result of the presidential election and to scandalously adopt an Excel spreadsheet,

which it used to alter and rig the result that was in the server. Chamisa sub-poenaed the server based on this result but his subpoena was inexplicably and controversially blocked by Chief Justice Malaba.

2. Second, there is the result based on copies of 210 V23Bs, collated and verified in terms of s65B of the Electoral Act, that are directly sent to the national command centre by constituency centres (according to the ZEC 2018 *Electoral Officers Manual*) and in terms of s37C(4)(d) of the Electoral Act.

3. Third, there is the initial result based on 10 original copies of V23Cs (the provincial returns), verified in terms of s65B(3) and (5) sent directly to the national command centre and contained in a V23D Form, in terms of Statutory Instrument 21 of 2005, Electoral Regulations, *to give the initial result of the presidential election* in terms of s37C(4)(f) of the Electoral Act.

4. Fourth, there is the final result based on 210 original and certified copies of V23Bs (which have attached to them original copies of V23As and V11s) from 210 constituencies, that are collated and verified in terms of s65A and s65B of the Electoral Act and verified according to s110(3)(d) *to determine the final result of the presidential election.*

The duplicate copies in terms of the proviso to s37(4)(b) and (d) serve no purpose other than the reconciliation of the final result of the presidential election in terms of s37C(4)(f)(ii).

In the ConCourt case, ZEC created confusion around all of this and that confusion was unfortunately assisted by Chamisa's averment on paragraph 127 of his heads of argument in the ConCourt case. Instead of challenging ZEC's illegal failure to verify and determine the result of the presidential election on the basis of V23Bs, Chamisa's lawyers misrepresented V23As as follows:

127 The V11 and V23a forms are meant to provide a transparent and reliable means of checking the final election results published by the ZEC. V11 Forms reflect the results at each individual polling station while *V23a forms reflect the combined tally of results at all polling stations in a particular constituency.* The results reflected in these forms should then tally with the overall results announced by the ZEC.

The correct position is that V23A forms reflect the tally of results at all polling stations in a particular ward, whereas V23B Forms reflect the tally of results at all ward collation centres in a constituency.

ZEC did not verify V23Bs, as required by s110(3)(d) of the Electoral Act. Instead, ZEC announced a tainted – that is, a stolen – presidential election result based on a tainted V23D form, which was not based on legally processed provincial returns (V23Cs), given that the collation, compilation and transmission of the result of the presidential election used by ZEC, and captured in Diagram 3, did not include, as destinations, the constituency centres and provincial command centres that collate and compile V23Bs and V23Cs, respectively.

The inculpatory evidence that ZEC illegally used the wrong election return (the V23D) to verify and determine the final result of the 2018 presidential election is in ZEC's Report on the 2018 presidential election, posted on the ZEC website on 15 August 2019, which confirms that:

> The collation and verification of the Presidential election results were completed on the 3rd of August 2018. The voter turnout for the 30th of July 2018 Presidential elections was 85%. *The Chief Elections Officer who was the Returning Officer for the election completed the V23D Form which is a record of results as collated at national level. The results were subsequently announced by the Chairperson of the Zimbabwe Electoral Commission on that same day in accordance with the provisions of the law. A copy of the V23D Form was signed by political party agents and observers present; they were given a copy each.*[16]

ZEC's use of form V23D to collate and announce the final result of the presidential election contravened s37C(4)(f) of the Electoral Act which provides that:

> after the collation of the results of the presidential election at each provincial command centre, provincial returns for the presidential election gathered from every provincial command centre shall be transmitted to the National Command Centre, where –
>
> (i) the provincial returns shall be collated *to obtain the initial results* of the presidential election; and
>
> (ii) *the final result* of the presidential election shall, after reconciling the provincial returns with the polling station returns and presidential constituency returns referred to in the provisos to paragraphs (b) and (d) respectively, be reflected in a return that distinctly reflects number of votes cast for each presidential candidate at every polling station, ward centre, presidential constituency centre and provincial command centre;

It is quite clear that Priscilla Chigumba announced a purported initial result (purported because it was based on an illegal transmission route and destination) as a final result. The V23D that ZEC used to get two different results for Mnangagwa, initially 50.8% of the vote later reduced to 50.67%, was bogus and thus illegal. This result of Zimbabwe's presidential election was a product of an audacious rigging process from 1 to 3 August 2018 which, according to unrebutted evidence in the Constitutional Court record "involved a group of people, in excess of twenty, punching in what was identified as V11 data into an Excel spreadsheet. For close to two days that process continued".

The fact, supported by Timba's unrebutted evidence in the ConCourt case, that, between 1 and 3 August 2018, ZEC did not display the presidential constituency return, the V23B forms, but displayed only V11s and V23As for the verification and determination of the result of the presidential election in violation of s110(3)(d) of the Electoral Act means that, on this score alone, the result declared and announced by Chigumba on 3 August 2018 was invalid, as it

---

[16] ZEC, *Zimbabwe 2018 Harmonised Elections Report*, page 72.

was obtained from a patently illegal process. This stands to reason because it accords with the illegal collation, compilation and transmission of the result of the presidential election result as reflected on Diagram 3.

Although ZEC and Malaba gave the impression that the presidential election was about V11s, and, although they generated unprecedented hullabaloo that turned "V11" into street-slang for "evidence", the untold truth is that the hullabaloo was much ado about nothing, because the verification and determination of the result of the presidential election is about V23Bs, and not about V11s.

There was absolutely no need for Malaba to make misplaced noise about V11s. When it comes to the verification and determination of the result of the presidential election in terms of s110(3)(d) of the Electoral Act, there can be no meaningful argument over a V11 or V23A without reference to one of the 210 V23Bs to which that original copy of the V11 or V23A in dispute must be attached. Quarrelling or making noise over a random V11 or V23A whose original copy is not attached to any V23B whose result it affects, and which V23B affects the final result of the presidential election, is child's play not worth the attention of a competent and reasonable court.

To recap, there are two glaring, substantial and irrefutable statutory grounds that prove beyond any doubt that the 2018 presidential election was brazenly stolen and thus invalidate the result declared and announced by Chigumba on 3 August 2018. These are:

1. **The result of the 2018 presidential election declared by ZEC in Mnangagwa's favour cannot legally stand and no reasonable court would condone or endorse it because the route and process used by ZEC to collate, compile and transmit that result glaringly and grossly breached the peremptory provisions of s37C(4) of the Electoral Act [*Chapter 2:13*] with the effect of rendering the entire 2018 presidential election fundamentally flawed and inherently unlawful in a corrupt and scandalous manner that invalidates the result declared by Chigumba on 3 August 2018, regardless of the vote tallies.**

2. **The fact, which ZEC did not refute or rebut, that it did not display the presidential constituency return, the V23B Forms, for the verification and determination of the result of the presidential election as required in terms of s110(3)(d) of the Electoral Act, means that the result declared and announced by Chigumba on 3 August 2018 is invalid as it was obtained from a corrupt and scandalous process that was not in substantial compliance with the law and which no competent and reasonable court can condone or endorse.**

These two issues that invalidate the result of the presidential election declared and announced by Chigumba on 3 August 2018 are not about figures, which Malaba said he did not care about when he delivered the preliminary ConCourt judgment on 24 August 2018, but they are about facts and the law.

It is a fact that ZEC used an illegal route, different from the one it used for the parliamentary election results, to collate, compile and transmit the result of the 2018 presidential election. That "different" route was in and of itself an exercise in rigging, not least because the illegal route opened the result of the presidential election to corrupt and scandalous manipulation.

Chapter 2

ROOTS OF RIGGING

MOST Zimbabweans believe that elections in the country are rigged but don't know how the rigging is done, yet they think there is one rigging formula that the ruling authorities apply to every election.

This is what I understand from the endless questions I get as a former Cabinet Minister "who should know", apparently because of my role as a former ZANU PF election campaign manager or "strategist" who wrote the party's 2000 and 2013 election manifestos and who participated in the controversial 2002 presidential campaign as Minister of Information and ZANU PF Deputy Secretary for Information and Publicity.

The widespread assumption that former and current Cabinet Ministers or ZANU PF politburo members *ex officio* know something useful about goings on in the corridors of power is understandable but wrong. The true position is that the vast majority of former and current Cabinet Ministers or politburo members are ignorant of "the system" and what goes on in it. This is because the *modus operandi* of the system is that information is shared among and between its officials strictly on a "need to know" basis. Only a few "connected" Cabinet Ministers or politburo members who attend JOC (Joint Operations Command) meetings, or who are linked to it as former intelligence operatives or securocrats, are in the know.

JOC, not Cabinet or the politburo, is the pivotal authority in Zimbabwe. Yet JOC is not a statutory or constitutional entity. It has operated like a secret society since its inception in Rhodesia and particularly since its genocidal notoriety in the Gukurahundi years. JOC is the centre of state power in Zimbabwe. It is the system.

JOC's pivotal role is particularly pronounced during elections. This is because of the obvious reason that elections are strategically important in deciding who gets into power, or who stays in power, or who gets out of power, when and how. As such, to unpack the roots of election rigging in Zimbabwe is to unpack JOC.

Broadly, two types of election rigging are experienced in Zimbabwe. One is *anticipatory rigging*, whose target is the intimidation of the voter to induce a particular electoral outcome by manipulating the political or electoral environment. The other is *constructive rigging*, whose target is the manipulation of the electoral process as a legal event to affect the election result. The modalities or tools used in either of these two approaches to rigging, including the choice and scale of approach, depend on the situation and circumstances of the election in question.

Anticipatory rigging

The target of anticipatory rigging in Zimbabwe has been the intimidation of the voter within his or her surrounding political or ethnic associations. An example of this is ZANU PF's 1990 television message targeting supporters of Edgar Tekere's ZUM (Zimbabwe Unity Movement) whose campaign against the introduction of a legislated one-party state resonated with the electorate. The ZANU PF video showed a speeding car veering out of its lane with a sound of screeching brakes and crashing into another vehicle, after which a voice-over warns eerily:

> This is one way to die. Another is to vote ZUM. Don't commit suicide. Don't be foolish. Vote ZANU PF and live.

Earlier versions of this typical ZANU PF approach to anticipatory rigging, without reference to ZUM, was witnessed in the 1985 parliamentary election and later in the 2002 presidential election campaigns. The approach is undergirded by the message that voting for the opposition risks death, while voting for ZANU PF is a life assurance.

On 5 March 1983, at the height of the Gukurahundi atrocities, the Bulawayo-based *Chronicle* newspaper reported that Emmerson Mnangagwa made death threats at a rally in Matabeleland by charging that:

> Blessed are they who will follow the path of the government laws, for their days on Earth will be increased. But woe unto those who will choose the path of collaboration with dissidents for we will certainly shorten their stay on Earth.

Mnangagwa made a similar threat in February 2019 against lawyers who represent clients arrested during demonstrations and medical doctors who treat patients injured during demonstrations, warning:

> To those who choose demonstrations and mayhem, we are equal to the task and we are fully prepared for you; but to those who choose peace and harmony, Alleluia to them, they will live long in our black African country; but those who choose demonstrations, their lives will be shortened.

ZANU PF's idea behind its use of this kind of anticipatory rigging through death threats is that voters respond positively to "project fear".

As is shown in this chapter, anticipatory rigging of this kind – and, even worse, rooted in ZANU PF's *"pungwe"* culture – has been the system's chosen approach since Zimbabwe's independence in 1980.

Between 1980 and 1987 the target of this culture was ZAPU, Joshua Nkomo and Matabeleland. In 1990 it was ZUM, Edgar Tekere and Manicaland. In 2000 it was Morgan Tsvangirai, the MDC and white farmers. In 2008 it was Morgan Tsvangirai, the MDC, and Solomon and Joice Mujuru. In 2013 it was Morgan Tsvangirai, the MDC and Joice Mujuru. And in 2018 it was Robert Mugabe, the so-called G40, Nelson Chamisa, the MDC and Mashonaland provinces. All these targets are reviewed in this chapter.

Constructive rigging

Whereas anticipatory rigging focuses on the environment to target the voter, *constructive rigging* targets the election as a political process which is a legal event to technically manipulate the rules, processes or procedures to change the result of the election to a desired outcome. Constructive rigging has the intent of affecting an election result in order to change its outcome one way or another through an illegal act of commission or omission.

An example of constructive rigging, which has become prevalent in the Zimbabwean electoral experience in recent years, is the manipulation of ballot papers by ZEC officers during the counting of votes.

In order to determine the result of an election at the polling station – it could be a council, parliamentary or presidential election – the valid ballot papers in each ballot box are counted in "lots" and "bundles" by a ZEC counting officer. A lot consists of 10 ballots and a bundle consists of 100 ballots or 10 bundles of 10. Where polling agents are absent or functionally illiterate – which is common nowadays, as exemplified by the absence of MDC-Alliance polling agents from 500 polling stations in the 2018 harmonised elections – ZEC counting officers can play games. A common trick is to undercount the votes of a targeted candidate by putting more than 10 votes in that candidate's lots, while overcounting the votes of the favoured candidate by putting fewer than 10 votes in his or her lots.

In 2013 my votes were undercounted through this ploy, leading to my defeat in Tsholotsho North constituency. Upon learning what had happened, I challenged the outcome and demanded a recount. ZEC authorities granted me the recount, only for the system to intervene to get ZEC to cancel the recount to my detriment.

A particularly pertinent example of constructive rigging is ZEC's decision to use two different routes with two different destinations to collate, compile and transmit the result of the 2018 presidential and parliamentary election in violation of s37C(4) of the Electoral Act.

The presumption of rigging

Since an election is a rule-bound process which is a legal event, its result is at law presumed to be valid. The presumption is based on the expectation that an election is organised, run or conducted and its result determined in accordance with existing law.

There are four sources of election rules: the Constitution; the Electoral Act [*Chapter 2:13*], as amended; Statutory Instrument 21 of 2005 (Electoral Regulations), as amended, and the ZEC *Electoral Officers Manual*, as modified.

Whereas political parties, election candidates, agents and observers are expected to understand that an election is a rule-bound political process which is a legal event, the fact is that most do not. This fact is the *zone of opportunity for rigging*. This is because rigging is simply the manipulation and corruption of one rule or another to affect the result towards a desired outcome.

In Zimbabwe, ZANU PF rigs as a matter of course, especially through anticipatory rigging. There are two major reasons why this is so.

The first is that since 1980 ZANU PF has evolved, institutionalised and entrenched itself not as a political party but as an extension or part of the state. ZANU PF meetings – from the cell or village, the branch (a group of cells or villages), the district (a group of branches), the province (a group of districts), the politburo, the central committee to the party's annual people's conference or congress – are attended and even organised by state functionaries, especially from the Army, CIO, Police and key civil servants, whose ranks are higher depending on the level of the structure holding the meeting.

The clearest evidence of the link between the state and ZANU PF is in the "Coup Minutes" on the military ouster of Robert Mugabe on 15 November 2017.[17]

---

[17] See Appendix: "The Coup Minutes", 15 November 2017.

The pervasive rationale for the November 2017 military coup was all about the control of ZANU PF by the Army, through which other organs of the state, notably the judiciary and ZEC, are roped in. It is in this regard that the presumption of validity of the result of elections in Zimbabwe inherently favours ZANU PF. The individual and institutional makers, implementors and interpreters of an election as a rule-bound political process, which is a legal event, are either ZANU PF or are commanded by the party. For this reason, ZANU PF has been able to rig elections since 1985 with considerable success.

The second reason why ZANU PF rigs elections as a matter of course is because its opponents do not, from the start, treat or understand that an election is a rule-bound political process which is a legal event. Typically, ZANU PF opponents wake up to the reality that an election is a legal event after the fact, when the rigging has occurred, when the damage has been done and when the presumption of validity of the result is operational. This tends to trigger last-minute decisions to find lawyers and, once they are found, most of these lawyers would not have been following the election as a rule-bound political process, which is a legal event.

Given the historical circumstances under which ZANU PF has evolved as an extension of the state, circumstances which dramatically came to the fore on 15 November 2017 and which have been openly playing out since then, an alternative, counterintuitive presumption, the presumption of rigging, should inform the participation of opposition political parties, candidates and civil society in any election in Zimbabwe. They should assume that the election will be rigged and hire lawyers to gather the rigging evidence right from the time ZEC starts the preparations for the delimitation of constituencies and registration of voters.

Society should proceed under the presumption that, in the prevailing circumstances in which the state and ZANU PF are organically linked, the presumption of rigging should guide opposition parties and candidates who wish to challenge ZANU PF in any election.

Bullets for votes

Although it appeared to have been an afterthought or an eleventh-hour intervention, the 15 November 2017 military coup was long coming, with its roots in the violent presidential election run-off held on 29 June 2008.

When Mugabe lost the first round of the presidential election to Morgan Tsvangirai, who nevertheless did not garner the required 50% plus one vote on 29 March 2008, and after the MDC formations had won 110 out of 210 parliamentary seats, the writing was on the wall that Mugabe would lose a free-and-fair run-off election by a wide margin. The die had been cast.

The military, headed by Chiwenga, who by then had started working closely with Mnangagwa in opposition to Joice Mujuru and her husband, who at the time was the key kingmaker in ZANU PF, intervened to reverse Tsvangirai's electoral gains, block his momentum ahead of the run-off and guarantee Mugabe's victory before the fact. Widespread anticipatory rigging was in full force.

A few days after the result of the 29 March 2008 presidential election in which Tsvangirai had defeated Mugabe became known, some 200 serving senior officers of the armed forces were deployed countrywide to campaign for Mugabe through intimidation and brute violence. They were assisted by war veterans and other pro-ZANU PF militants. The teams were deployed on 8 April 2008 to campaign for Mugabe in the run-off. Except for two, all the deployed officers were senior serving officers of the armed forces. Lt. Gen. PV Sibanda commanded the operation with the assistance of Maj. Gen. Nick Dube, while General Chiwenga was the overall commander of the operation with Major General Last Mugova and Colonel S. Mudambo providing back-up assistance.

The army deployment for the 2008 presidential election runoff was as follows:[18]

Harare Metropolitan Province	**AVM Karakadzai + CIO**
Bulawayo Province	**Col. C. Sibanda**
Bulawayo central	Maj. J. Ndhlovu
	Maj. J. Ncube
Manicaland	**Brig. Tarumbwa**
Mutare South	Brig. Tarumbwa
Buhera Central	Col. M. Mzilikazi (MID)
Buhera North	Maj. L. M. Svosve
Buhera South	Maj. D. Muchena
Buhera West	Lt. Col. Kamonge
	Major Nhachi
Chimanimani East	Lt. Col. Murecherwa
Chimanimani West	Maj. Mabvuu
Headlands	Col. Mutsvunguma
Makoni North	Maj. V. Chisuko
Makoni South	Wing Commander Mandeya
Mutare Central	Lt. Col. Tsodzai
	Lt. Col. Sedze
	Mandi Chimene
Mutare West	Lt. Col. B. Kashiri
Mutare North	Lt. Col. Chizengwe
	Lt. Col. Mazaiwana
Mashonaland Central	**Brig. Gen. Shungu**
Bindura South	Col. Chipwere
Bindura North	Lt. Col. Parwada
Muzarabani North	Lt. Col. Kazaza
Muzarabani South	Maj. H. Maziri
Rushinga	Col. F. Mhonda
	Lt. Col. Betheuni
Shamva North	Lt. Col. Dzuda
Shamva South	Makumire
Midlands	**AVM Muchena**
	Brig. Gen. S. B. Moyo
	Lt Colonel Kuhuni

---

[18] I first made public this nationwide army deployment list for the 2008 presidential election run-off on @Twitter handle @ProfJNMoyo on 16 January 2018.

Chirumhanzu South	Maj T. Tsvangirai
Mberengwa east	Col. B. Mavire
Mberengwa West	Maj T. Marufu

Matabeleland South — **AVM Abu Basutu**

Beit Bridge East	Group Cpt. Mayera
	Rtd. Maj. Mbedzi
	Lt. Col. B. Moyo
Gwanda South	Maj J. D. Moyo
Gwanda Central	Maj. B. Tshuma
Matopo North	Lt. Col. Maphosa

Matabeleland North — **Brig. Gen. Khumalo**

Binga North	Maj E. S. Matonga
Lupane East	Lt Col. Mkwananzi
Lupane West	Lt Col. Mabhena
Tsholotsho	Lt. Col. Mlalazi
Hwange Central	Lt. Col P. Ndhlovu

Masvingo — **Maj. Gen. E. A. Rugeje**

Rtd. Maj. Gen. Gibson Mashingaidze
Rtd. Brig. General Rangwani

Bikita West — **Maj. B. R. Murwira**

Chiredzi Central	Col G. Mashava
Chiredzi West	Maj. E. Gono
Gutu South	Maj. Chimedza (Medical Doctor)
	AVM Muchena
Masvingo	Lt. Col. Takavingofa
Mwenezi West	Lt. Col. Muchono
Mwenezi East	Lt. Col. Mpabanga
Zaka East	Maj. R. Kwenda

Mashonaland West — **Brig. Gen. Sigauke**

Chinhoyi	Col Gwekwerere
Chegutu East	Lt. Colonel W. Tutisa
Hurungwe East	Lt. Col. B. Mabambe
Mhondoro Mubaira	Col. C. T. Gurira
Zvimba North	Cpt. T. Majongwe

Mashonaland East — **Brig. Gen. D. Nyikayaramba**

Rtd. Brig Gen Rungani

Chikomba Central	Lt. Col. Marara
Goromonzi North	Lt Col. Mudzimba
	Maj F. Mbewe
Marondera Central	Maj. Gen. Chedondo (COSG)
	Lt. Col B. Kashiri
Marondera West	Squadron Leader U. Chitauro
Murehwa South	Maj. Gurure
Murehwa North	Lt. Col. Mukurazhizha
	Lt. Col. Chinete

What ensued was a bloody orgy of violence, not only against MDC supporters but also against ZANU PF members perceived to have been Mujuru supporters accused of voting for Tsvangirai in what was known as "Bhora musango".[19] More than 200 people were killed, many more were tortured, and tens of thousands were displaced both internally and externally.

Before the bloody army-run campaign for Mugabe in the 2008 presidential election run-off, save for some isolated incidents that some political parties complained of, the 29 March 2008 election was the most peaceful, freest and fairest election in Zimbabwe. It is the only election since 1980 in which ZANU PF has lost its majority in Parliament.

It was in response to this, plus the fact that Mugabe failed to get a majority of 50% + 1 votes in the presidential election, that the army, under General Chiwenga working in cahoots with Mnangagwa, became involved and effectively carried out a violent poll coup against the MDC and its supporters and against supporters of Joice Mujuru in ZANU PF, targeting her supporters in the Mashonaland, Masvingo and Manicaland provinces. Chiwenga and Mnangagwa entered into a pact under which the army would campaign for Mugabe in the run-off; in return, Mugabe would commit to serving no more than one additional term, after which he would pass the presidential baton to Mnangagwa.

The poll coup that took place against the MDC after the 29 March 2008 general election was spearheaded by the same military commanders who staged the open and full-blown coup against Robert Mugabe on 15 November 2017. When Mugabe seemed to dither, indicating his readiness to hand over power to Tsvangirai, arrangements were made for a military takeover in 2008, but General Chiwenga later baulked at announcing the coup out of fear of the reaction of SADC, the AU and the international community through the United Nations. In the circumstances, the commanders opted for a silent but bloody poll coup.

Although this silent coup was against the opposition, it had a collateral effect of holding Mugabe beholden to the military commanders, to whom he owed his controversial 2008 electoral tenure. It was as a result of the 2008 silent coup that the military took over the procurement of regalia and the organisation and management of the ZANU PF election campaign in the 2013 general election, with Chiwenga and Mnangagwa calling the shots. Mugabe was a hostage candidate in the 2013 general election.

Consequently, the military commanders believed that Mugabe's 2013 election victory belonged to them. As such, the 2017 military coup was an act of reclaiming a mandate that they saw as theirs – a mandate they believed had been usurped by the so-called Generation 40 (G40) politicians whom they described as "criminals around President Mugabe".[20]

---

[19] "Bhora musango" (literally, "kick the ball off the field of play") was first introduced in ZANU PF as a strategy of throwing away the votes against Robert Mugabe in the 29 March 2008 general election whose first round Mugabe lost to Morgan Tsvangirai; see Lyton Ncube, "Bhora Mugedhi versus Bhora Musango: The interface between football discourse and Zimbabwean politics", *International Review for the Sociology of Sport*, 51(2), March 2016 (first published 20 January 2014).
[20] The statement that the military coup was targeting "criminals surrounding President Mugabe" was made by General Sibusiso Moyo on 15 November 2017; see https://www.enca.com/africa/full-statement-by-zim-army-on-state-broadcaster.

Back to Mgagao

Mugabe's ouster by the military was branded as "Operation Restore Legacy". It is important to contextualise the meaning of this branding and the impact it had on the prospects for a free-and-fair general election that was due in seven months following the coup.

Mugabe was first imposed as ZANU leader by ZANLA guerrilla commanders who had deposed the then leader, Reverend Ndabaningi Sithole, in 1975 at Mgagao guerrilla training camp in Tanzania. By deposing Mugabe and imposing Mnangagwa in November 2017, the military was in effect restoring the 1975 Mgagao legacy, whose ideological essence is that "the gun dictates politics". Put differently, "Operation Restoration Legacy" was meant to bring back or reassert the operational dictum that the leader of ZANU PF is chosen by the barrel of the gun, not by the ballot box. The understanding of the Mgagao legacy is a prerequisite to the understanding of the November 2017 coup, its architects, their ideology, leadership style, political outlook, as well as how and why the military captured the 2018 presidential election by brazenly stealing it.

Fashioned along the lines of how ZANLA commanders deposed Ndabaningi Sithole and imposed Mugabe in 1975, the historical and ideological justification of the November 2017 military coup was the "Mgagao Declaration" made in 1975 by the young combatants in the Zimbabwe National Liberation Army, at Mgagao training camp for guerrillas in Tanzania.[21]

On the one hand, the historical significance of the Mgagao Declaration is that it simultaneously laid the foundation for the removal in 1975 of the President of the Zimbabwe African National Union (ZANU), Sithole, and paved the way for the elevation of Mugabe to the position of President and First Secretary of ZANU, which was later confirmed in Mozambique in 1977 at a controversial party congress. The ideological significance of the Mgagao Declaration is that it turned upside down the deeply held principle in the Zimbabwean nationalist movement for independence that "politics must lead the gun" to declare that "the gun must lead politics".

The Mgagao Declaration is thus the ideological foundation not just of the November 2017 military coup but also of the state violence and the impunity of its perpetrators. The atrocities committed by the army on 1 August 2018, ahead of the announcement of a stolen result of the presidential election, were the ugly manifestation of "Operation Restore Legacy" with the gun dictating politics in the vein of the Mgagao Declaration.

The Gukurahundi backdrop

Given the influences of the Mgagao Declaration and the 1980 to 1990 extension of the Rhodesian State of Emergency on the ZDF, a disturbing dimension of the orientation and experience of the military commanders behind the November 2017 military coup is that they are the architects and enforcers of independent Zimbabwe's darkest time, known as the Gukurahundi. This is the period during which some 20,000 Ndebele were massacred in the country's Matabeleland and Midlands provinces between 1980 and 1987. In this connection,

---

[21] Wilfred Mhanda, *Dzino: Memories of a Freedom Fighter* (Harare: Weaver Press, 2011).

the widespread claims that the coup, by only deposing Mugabe, represented a new dispensation in a new and ostensibly better Zimbabwe were unfounded. The Gukurahundi link of the coup-makers explains the continuing scourge of violence with impunity in Zimbabwe, as witnessed on 1 August 2018 and between 14 and 28 January 2019.

For the better part of its first decade of independence, Zimbabwe was governed under the Rhodesian State of Emergency, enacted in 1965 when the country did not have a justiciable Bill of Rights, and whose import was to suspend the respect for and the implementation of fundamental rights that had been enshrined in the Lancaster House Constitution. The continuation of the Rhodesian State of Emergency, mixed with the Mgagao ideological mantra that the gun must lead politics, entrenched the entitlement view among Zimbabwe's former ZANLA guerrilla combatants and the new military commanders that their guns indeed dictated politics. It is this view, based on their experience of leading the implementation of the State of Emergency, that led Zimbabwe's military commanders to unleash Gukurahundi and develop a coup mentality as their default orientation.

It is in this context that the military commanders, such as Chiwenga, who imposed Mugabe at Mgagao in 1975 and deposed him in November 2017, are the same who reposed him in power as ZANU PF's and Zimbabwe's leader from April 1980 to November 2017. The agenda for this started with the Gukurahundi genocide that targeted for elimination Joshua Nkomo, PF-ZAPU, which he led, and the Ndebele in Matabeleland and the Midlands province who were presumed to be Nkomo's political base.

Some 20,000 Zimbabweans were massacred. Many more were tortured, maimed or raped and displaced as refugees. No death certificates were issued. Surviving children of victims were denied birth certificates. Communities were starved, undeveloped or underdeveloped. Gukurahundi was a military, intelligence and political operation to violently impose politicians and their hegemony after ZANU PF had failed to win the hearts and minds of the local communities in the 1980 general election. The macabre imagination of "gukurahundists" was that genocide would succeed where elections had failed. It was an extreme case of anticipatory rigging.

The linchpin and coordinator of the Gukurahundi operation was Mnangagwa, who, as Minister for State Security, was responsible for the CIO, the lead institution in the Gukurahundi operation.

Even with the continuation of the Rhodesian State of Emergency, under which the CIO led intelligence-gathering and functioned as a police force, and collaborated with apartheid South Africa to create pseudo-dissidents (apartheid forces who saw PF-ZAPU as a springboard for the ANC's Umkhonto weSizwe guerrillas to launch attacks in South Africa) and deployed One Brigade in Matabeleland led by Chiwenga, the military still found it necessary to establish the Fifth Brigade, a special force trained in North Korea, to deal with Joshua Nkomo, PF-ZAPU and the Ndebele in Matabeleland. Mugabe's bond with the military and Mnangagwa was sealed in the Gukurahundi years, and that was used to repose him in power for 37 years, until the same military deposed him on 15 November 2017.

The unresolved Gukurahundi issues, with respect to truth and justice and the fear of being held accountable or personally liable, were, for Mnangagwa, Chiwenga and Perence Shiri, a major motivation for the November 2017 coup. Parenthetically, and this is a story yet to be told in full, the most uncompromising and radical implementers of the November 2017 military coup, who spearheaded the coup and insisted on Mugabe's ouster, were not former ZANLA officers but were ex-ZIPRA-Mberengwa ZDF commanders from the Midlands, who had been warehoused and protected by Mnangagwa during the Gukurahundi purges that swept out mainstream ex-ZIPRA leaders as well as rank and file from the army and the CIO. Since the coup, the ex-ZIPRA-Mberengwa commanders have not shown much of their ZIPRA or ZAPU roots but have come out as creatures of regionalism and tribalism in Mnangagwa's circle of cronies.

Former Vice-President, Phelekezela Mphoko, a former ZIPRA commander, told me in confidence about the loading of the 15 November military coup, in some considerable detail, a week before the fact and said that he had fully briefed President Mugabe about it and had urged him to take urgent counter measures to no avail. For reasons which even history might fail to unravel, Mugabe did not believe that Mnangagwa, and especially Chiwenga, would lead a military coup against him. Even after 15 November 2018, in the build-up to the 18 November "People's March" in Harare in support of the coup, Mugabe still believed that he could work things out with Chiwenga.

In fact, the two had been discussing having a "Most Holy Sacrifice of the Mass" at State House on 20 November 2017. Communication from Chiwenga suggested that he wanted Mugabe to remain in office and as President at least until the ZANU PF congress in December 2017, when he would hand over the baton to Sidney Sekeremayi, Mugabe's preferred successor. Chiwenga was inclined or well disposed to serve Mugabe as long as the alleged "criminals surrounding him" had been accounted for and removed from ZANU PF and the government and thrown in jail or killed. It is precisely for this reason that Mugabe's "Asante Sana" address to the nation on 19 November 2017 did not have even a hint that he was preparing to resign. Quite the contrary: the "Asante Sana Moment" was vintage Mugabe in his element, at a trying time. Mnangagwa and his allies had been made to believe that Mugabe would use the speech to resign, as per the resolutions of a hurriedly convened makeshift Zanu PF central committee meeting held earlier that day in Harare. That meeting had given Mugabe an ultimatum to resign by midday on 20 November 2017. Mugabe did not resign in his "Asante Sana" speech because he had reached an understanding with Chiwenga that he was not the target of the military coup and that he would remain as Commander-in-Chief of the Zimbabwe Defence Forces, and Head of State and Government.

But Chiwenga was not in full control of "Operation Restore Legacy", whose real movers and shakers were the ex-ZIPRA-Mberengwa commanders who made it clear to Chiwenga that Mugabe had to go, otherwise there would be blood on the floor in which Chiwenga's own position would not be guaranteed. In the circumstances, Mugabe was ousted from power against Chiwenga's better judgement, on the insistence of the ex-ZIPRA-Mberengwa commanders, ironically claiming to be getting even with Mugabe over Gukurahundi while bidding for Mugabe's Gukurahundi instigator and enforcer-in-chief, Emmerson Mnangagwa.

A swallowed ZAPU

On the back of Gukurahundi and on the eve of the expiry of the entrenched clauses of the Lancaster House Constitution – which provided for the reserved seats for whites in Parliament, a bicameral house and protection of property, all which required unanimous support in the legislature to be law – the military moved to humiliate Joshua Nkomo and PF-ZAPU by facilitating a Unity Accord on 22 December 1987.

The essence of the Accord was to swallow PF-ZAPU and to eliminate it once and for all as a potent electoral threat to ZANU PF. Under the Accord, Nkomo played second fiddle to Mugabe. This led to the entrenched marginalisation of Matabeleland.

Within ZANU PF, it is alleged that the Nkomo and Mugabe signed the Accord to save lives. This is ludicrous propaganda. To save what lives after the massacre of over 20,000 people in Matabeleland and parts of the Midlands provinces, and the displacements and destruction of the livelihoods of millions?

From the standpoint of "the system", the key to the Unity Accord which was seen as a master-stroke was clause number 6 of the agreement which said:

> That ZANU (PF) shall seek to establish a one-party state in Zimbabwe.[22]

Through a pen and a piece of paper, "the system" eliminated PF-ZAPU as an electoral opponent, in the guise of a Unity Accord, at a time when one-party-state regimes in Africa and around the world were beginning to fall in the face of the rise of a new international order, whose multiparty seeds were sprouting everywhere.

The 1987 Unity Accord cemented the role of the military as the centre of social engineering in Zimbabwe and dealt the biggest blow to the development of pluralism, inclusive politics and the development of a culture of free-and-fair elections in the country. While efforts to use the Unity Accord to introduce a legislated one-party state failed, owing to the winds of pluralism that were sweeping across the region in the wake of the collapse of the Berlin Wall and the fall of the Iron Curtain, the military's push for monopoly politics succeeded to create a *de facto* one-party state under which the military's hand was strengthened.

The death of PF-ZAPU in 1987 put democracy in Zimbabwe into a long coma. PF-ZAPU was in an unassailable position to match ZANU PF history for history, claim for claim, and even to come out better about the liberation struggle and patriotism. PF-ZAPU was the only political formation that had the best chance to sink the roots of multi-party politics and competitive elections in Zimbabwe permanently. The fact that the Unity Accord between PF-ZAPU and ZANU PF committed the parties to establishing a one-party state in the country was tragic and explains much of what has gone wrong with electoral politics in Zimbabwe today.

The MDC challenge

Between 1980 and 2000, securocrats, led by military commanders through JOC, directed and dominated political discourse in Zimbabwe under the banner of consolidating national independence and nation-building. This was derailed by the entry of the Movement for Democratic Change (MDC), which introduced the discourse on democracy and human rights and put it at the centre of mainstream politics. The MDC discourse, which coincided with the implementation of Zimbabwe's radical land-reform programme, challenged and rattled military commanders over their entitlement ideology and their negation of human rights and the importance of free, fair and credible elections.

---

[22] *See* the full text of "The Unity Agreement", *The Herald*, Harare, 23 December 1987.

By 1999, the effects of the army's operation in the DRC, the pay-out demands of the veterans of the liberation war, the 1997 currency crash, the economic cost of an unimplemented ESAP (Economic Structural Adjustment Programme), simmering tribal tensions, the growing demands for a new constitution and growing dissension with ZANU PF, were all conspiring to take a toll on Mugabe, who had been rattled by the 1998 food riots, as his power base started to crack.

The Lancaster House Constitution in general, and particularly Constitutional Amendment No. 7, under which Mugabe had gained what were effectively imperial executive powers, had lost legitimacy. ZANU PF's hegemonic influence was dissipating. The Zimbabwe Congress of Trade Unions (ZCTU), a ZANU PF creation and ally, was breaking away and networking with civil-society organisations, especially the student movement and intellectuals, to midwife a new political party, the MDC under Tsvangirai's leadership. The MDC's challenge was that, while Zimbabwe had attained independence in 1980, it was yet to attain democracy. The MDC was later to assert that the struggle for democracy in Zimbabwe had started in 2000 following the party's formation in 1999. This message resonated with workers, intellectuals, student groups, the business community, professional associations, NGOs, community-based organisations and the donor community, but not with peasants and veterans of the liberation struggle.

Mugabe and the military were shaken to the core and responded by setting up a Constitutional Commission, which reviewed the Lancaster House Constitution and recommended a new Constitution, the "Godfrey Chidyausiku draft Constitution". As a strategy for regaining lost ground in the popular stakes, Mugabe and the military subjected the Chidyausiku draft Constitution to a referendum but, in a strategic move that indicated that they did not support the draft Constitution, ZANU PF declined to campaign for or against it in the February 2000 referendum.

The MDC campaigned against the draft Constitution, incorrectly claiming that it extended and entrenched Mugabe's executive powers when it in fact split executive powers between a president and a prime minister, unlike the 2013 Constitution that retained the executive presidency. The referendum held in February 2000 rejected the draft Constitution and, supported by well-organised white commercial farmers who opposed land expropriation-without-compensation clauses in the draft, the MDC won the "No" vote and was instantly born as a major electoral force, four months before the June 2000 general election in which it performed exceedingly well. ZANU PF won by only three out 120 seats.

Formidable as it has been, especially in its early years, the MDC challenge has nevertheless not contended with Zimbabwe's "Machiavellian Moment".[23] This is a moment when a republic becomes unstable and must come to terms with the institutional roots of its instability to defend its founding ideals and enduring values. In this sense, a Machiavellian Moment is when a troubled society, as Zimbabwe is and has been since 2000 – and precariously so since the November 2017 military coup – must revisit its founding principles, values and ideals and realign them with its failing institutions or risk disintegrating.

---

[23] Jonathan Moyo, "Zim trapped in Machiavellian Moment", *The Zimbabwe Independent,* Harare, 27 April 2018.

The way out of such a moment requires a Machiavelli (a Philosopher) and a Prince (a King or leader with a philosophy or ideology), working in a symbiotic relationship in the vein of a Philosopher-King propounded by Plato in his Republic.[24] Having a Machiavelli without a Prince, or a Prince without a Machiavelli, necessarily triggers a Gramscian interregnum (see page 52) with morbid consequences, such as were most recently experienced in Zimbabwe with the military coup on 15 November 2017, the army atrocities in Harare on 1 August 2018 and across urban areas between 14 and 28 January 2019. A Machiavellian Moment is cruel when neither a Machiavelli nor a Prince is available.

Since 2000, the country's constitutional, institutional and political edifice has been crumbling under the weight of the unfulfilled expectations of a restless population based on the founding values and ideals of the country's liberation struggle, whose quintessential stated purpose was the restoration of the civil, political and socio-economic rights of the indigenous population.

At issue by 2000 was that the gains of independence had not included the enjoyment of civil and political rights, notably freedoms of assembly, association and expression, nor had they included socio-economic rights, particularly in land redistribution and economic empowerment. The MDC challenge emerged in 1999 as an expression of the former, while in 2001 the fast-track land-reform programme sought to address the latter as the pillars of a new Zimbabwe. Some 18 years later, that new Zimbabwe or "new dispensation", envisaged by the MDC challenge from 1999, and the fast-track land-reform programme and economic empowerment from 2001, has not been born; the old society, challenged by both, has been dying, albeit slowly and painfully, with lots of nasty things in between.

Zimbabwe's Machiavellian Moment, whose roots were sunk between 1999 and 2001, is now virtually two decades old. It has been cruelly long, and the expectation was that the 2018 general election would be the critical election to address it, but that was not to be because of the November 2017 military coup that pushed Zimbabwe deeper into a Gramscian interregnum.

A complicating factor with the MDC's challenge ahead of what could have been the party's historic performance in the 2018 general election was its ill-advised, unwise and rather shocking support for the November 2017 military coup. After making a lot of noise about the need for security-sector reforms to confine the army to the barracks and out of politics, the MDC support for the November 2017 military coup amounted to a kiss of death, and it showed MDC leaders as more concerned about being accommodated by ZANU PF than about replacing the ruling party to foster real political and socioeconomic change in Zimbabwe.

By ousting Mugabe in a military coup in cahoots with ZANU PF, the army had dug a grave for itself and ZANU PF. All that the MDC needed to do was to ensure that both the army and ZANU PF were buried in their own grave. The opportunity was historic. Instead, MDC leaders and most, but not all, of their civil-society associates jumped into the grave to rescue both the army and ZANU PF by entertaining the ruse of a GNU; and later, when the dangled GNU did not materialise, MDC leaders entertained the phoney promise of a free-and-fair general

---

[24] Plato, *The Republic* (New York: Simon & Schuster, 2010).

election in a military state after the coup. The naivety of MDC leaders, in their belief that the military would organise a free-and-fair election under the so-called new dispensation, was breathtaking.

There was no objective or rational basis for the MDC to expect the army to let go through the ballot box on 30 July 2018 the political power it had violently grabbed by the barrel of the gun on 15 November 2017. Having been sold a GNU dummy to get it to support an unconstitutional coup, the MDC should have understood that a free-and-fair general election in July 2018 was not possible after the 15 November 2017 military coup.

Since its formation in 1999, the MDC had focused on the need for a new democratic constitution as its rallying call. A major plank of the Global Political Agreement (GPA) under which the Inclusive Government, or Government of National Unity (GNU), between ZANU PF and the MDC formations was formed in 2009, was a commitment by the GPA parties to crafting a new democratic Constitution during the life of the GNU.

A major constitutional reform that emerged from public views gathered by a committee set-up for that purpose was the reform of the security sector to render it apolitical, subordinate to civilian authority, and subject to the Constitution. The new Constitution, with these security-sector reforms, was adopted in 2013 through a referendum. By then, the army, under Chiwenga, had silently taken over ZANU PF and was running the party's election campaign, which was supposed to be Mugabe's last in terms of the 2008 pact he had reached with Chiwenga and Mnangagwa.

A consideration, whose implication must weigh heavily on the MDC, is how the November 2017 coup was carried out under the one Constitution that had institutionalised security-sector reforms to keep the army out of politics. What this means is that, in 2013, Zimbabwe got a new democratic Constitution without a new Zimbabwe: a telling example of the African disease of having constitutions without constitutionalism.

The military–political complex that used Mugabe as its spokesperson for 42 years sought to present his ouster as a revolutionary, military-assisted transition, signalling a new dispensation, when that was far from the reality. It was quite the contrary: the military used its ouster of Mugabe to reinvent itself and reassert its 42-year-old control of ZANU PF and its quest for total control of the State.

By supporting the November 2017 military coup, the MDC gave the army an undeserved gate pass for a great escape, to the detriment of the much-needed transition from an old to a new Zimbabwe, given that the ZDF used the escape to steal the 2018 presidential election from the MDC.

Legalising the illegal

In Zimbabwe, public figures across the full spectrum of the public sphere are notorious for being in favour of what they are against and for being against what they are in favour of. This contradiction, which is based on the pervasive treatment of feelings as facts in public discourse, informed the various reactions to the military coup in and outside Zimbabwe.

On 18 November 2017, three days after the military coup, opposition political parties, civil-society organisations, SADC countries and diplomatic missions in Zimbabwe embraced the military coup only because it had toppled Mugabe and "dealt with Grace" (Mugabe's wife, who was alleged to have been bent on succeeding her husband). Yet the military coup was patently unconstitutional. This was ironic, not least because the same groups had since 2000, and especially since 2008, bemoaned the involvement of the military in politics and called for major security-sector reforms that were enshrined in the country's new Constitution in 2013 but which were flagrantly violated by the coup-makers on 15 November 2017.

One of the major highlights of the coup, on the back of the 18 November 2017 "Mugabe Must Go" march in Harare, was a "constitutional" case that was fast-tracked in the High Court by Justice George Chiweshe, an army judge seconded to the judiciary.[25] The applicants in the case, Joseph Evurath Sibanda and Leonard Chikomba, sued: as first respondent, the President of Zimbabwe, Robert Mugabe, in his official capacity; the Minister of Defence (Sydney Sekeramayi, as second respondent); the Commander of Defence Forces of Zimbabwe (General Constantino Chiwenga, as third respondent); and the Attorney-General (as fourth respondent).

In an amusing founding affidavit, the applicants made all sorts of outlandish and ridiculous averments. Their main submission was that:

> The Defence Forces of Zimbabwe intervened because there had been an effective civilian coup, by G40, as the President of the country was no longer able to execute his functions, which were now being done by unelected individuals around him. In particular, the unelected first lady was now running Government business to the country's prejudice. The economy had also ground to a halt by reason of that circumstance.

Without any evidence given by the applicants and without giving any reasons, Chiweshe legalised the illegal on 24 November 2017 by ruling that the military intervention on 15 November 2017 was constitutional and that the dismissal of Emmerson Mnangagwa on 6 November 2017 as Vice-President of Zimbabwe had been "unlawful". Mugabe, who had by then resigned as President, was cited but not represented in the case in which Chiweshe made the following shocking ruling:

> Whereupon after reading documents filed of record and hearing counsel, it is declared by consent that:
>> The actions of the Defence Forces (Zimbabwe Defence Forces of Zimbabwe [*sic*]) in intervening to stop the take-over of first respondent's (Mugabe's) constitutional functions by those around him are constitutionally permissible and lawful in terms of Section 212 of the Constitution of Zimbabwe in that:
>
> 1. a. They arrest first respondent's abdication of constitutional function, and
>   b. They ensured that non-elected individuals do not exercise executive functions which can only be exercised by elected constitutional functionaries.
>
> It is consequently ordered that:
>
> 2. The actions of the Defence Forces being constitutionally valid, second respondent has the right to take all such measures and undertake all such acts as will bring the desired end to its intervention.

---

[25] See Case HC 10820/17 in the High Court of Zimbabwe.

On the same day, 24 November 2017, on which Mnangagwa was inaugurated as President following the military coup, the same court and the same judge made another astonishing judgment in a case in which Mnangagwa, citing as the respondent an unknown and in fact non-existent "Acting President of the Republic of Zimbabwe", given that Phelekezela Mphoko should have been acting but was in hiding outside the country, asked the High Court to set aside his dismissal by President Mugabe on 6 November 2017.

Mnangagwa's averments mirrored the application by Joseph Evurath Sibanda and Leonard Chikomba. He alleged that Mugabe had failed to uphold his constitutional duties and functions as President as provided in s90 of the Constitution by allegedly abdicating his responsibilities and powers of Cabinet to his wife Grace and the G40, who he said had instigated his removal from office as Vice-President on 6 November 2017. The nonsensical averments in Mnangagwa's affidavit make \sad reading, more so given that he's a trained lawyer.

Again, without relying on any evidence and without giving any reason, Chiweshe purported to make a judgment by consent and wrote:[26]

> **Whereupon after reading documents filed of record and hearing counsel, it is declared by consent that:**
>
> 1. **The dismissal of the applicant by Robert Gabriel Mugabe, the then President of Zimbabwe, from the office of Vice-President of Zimbabwe on 6 November 2017, is null and void and, accordingly, of no force or effect.**
>
> 2. **There shall be no order as to costs.**

The two cases that were fast-tracked in the morning of 24 November 2017 raised many issues, including the *locus standi* of the respective applicants and whether the High Court had jurisdiction, or was the appropriate forum, to hear matters that should either be heard by the Constitutional Court or be confirmed by it for the orders to be legally valid.

Section 167(2)(d) of the Constitution states that:

> **Subject to this Constitution, only the Constitutional Court may –**
> **determine whether Parliament or the President has failed to fulfil a constitutional obligation.**

The claims that Mugabe had abdicated his duties to his wife Grace and the so-called G40, and that his dismissal of Mnangagwa on 6 November 2016 amounted to a failure to discharge his constitutional duties, could only be heard and determined by the Constitutional Court, not by the High Court, given the provisions of s167(2)(d) of the Constitution. Chiweshe, an army judge, had no jurisdiction to hear the two cases.

But if, for some obscure reason, the High Court did have jurisdiction to hear the two matters that came before Chiweshe on 24 November 2017, just before Mnangagwa was sworn in, then Chiweshe's orders should have been subject to s167(3) of the Constitution, which provides that:

> **The Constitutional Court makes the final decision whether an Act of Parliament or conduct of the President is constitutional, and must confirm any order of constitutional invalidity made by another court before that order has any force.**

---

[26] Ibid.

It is common cause that Chiweshe's 24 November 2017 High Court orders, corruptly alleged to have been by consent, when Mugabe did not consent and could not have consented, were not and have not been confirmed by the Constitutional Court. As such, they have no force of law, to this day.

The decision in the unprecedented order by Chiweshe legalising the illegal coup was later endorsed by Chief Justice Malaba when he ruled, sitting alone in his Chambers, without hearing Mugabe, that the former President had "resigned freely and voluntarily" on 21 November 2017.

In the case, the applicants – Liberal Democrats, Revolutionary Freedom Fighters, Vusumuzi Sibanda, Linda Masarira and Bongani Nyathi – applied for direct access to the Constitutional Court to bring an application against Emmerson Mnangagwa, Constantino Chiwenga, the Zimbabwe Defence Forces, the Speaker of Parliament and Robert Mugabe. The applicants averred in their papers that Mugabe's purported resignation on 21 November 2017 was neither free nor voluntary but was a direct result of the actions taken by the army on 14 November 2017, evidenced by the presence of military vehicles in the streets of Harare between 14 and 21 November. The applicants further submitted that the impeachment motion in Parliament was specifically intended to aid and abet the army's takeover of power and that Mnangagwa's inauguration as President on 24 November was illegal and unlawful.

Malaba sat in his Chambers to decide whether the applicants had established a case to be granted access to the Constitutional Court in the interest of justice, and, if not, the recourse for the applicants was to take their matter to the High Court. On the day, and for some unexplained reason, the applicants did not attend the Chamber hearing, and were thus in default. Instead of issuing a default judgment to dismiss the application for direct access to the Constitutional Court, Malaba proceeded to consider whether the applicants had any prospects of success in the Constitutional Court if they were granted the access they sought. In the process, Malaba ruled that Mugabe had resigned on 21 November 2017 freely and voluntarily, and cited, as evidence for this, Mugabe's letter of resignation addressed to the Speaker of Parliament. *The Herald* newspaper quoted Malaba making the following incredible remarks in his chambers:

> The former President's written notice of resignation speaks for itself. It sets the context in which it was written. He candidly reveals the fact that he had communicated with the Speaker of Parliament at 13:53 Hours. In the communication, the former President expressed to the Speaker his desire to resign from the office of President. The Speaker must have advised him that for the resignation to have the legal effect of bringing his presidency to an end, it had to be communicated to him by means of a written notice. A written notice of resignation addressed to the Speaker and signed by the President, on the face of it, meets the first requirement of constitutional validity. … What the former President said in the written notice of resignation is the best evidence available of the state of his mind at the time. … Not only does the former President declare in the written notice that he made the decision voluntarily, he gives reasons for doing so in clear and unambiguous language. He said he was motivated by the desire to 'ensure a smooth, peaceful and non-violent transfer of power that underpins national security, peace and sustainability'. There is no doubt, the Chief Justice said, that Mr Mugabe

ensured that his resignation from office was in strict compliance with the letter and spirit of Section 96(1) of the Constitution.[27]

It is shocking and unprecedented that Malaba sought to apply conventional rules of textual interpretation as tools for assessing Mugabe's state of mind when he allegedly wrote the resignation letter on 21 November 2017 not only to conclusively determine that Mugabe "voluntarily" and "freely" wrote the letter but to also describe the letter as "the best evidence of his [Mugabe's] state of mind at the time". This was absurd, shameful and unworthy of a chief justice in a modern, constitutional democracy.

There's more than enough evidence in the public domain that Mugabe did not want to resign but was coerced and put under duress to write the letter following threats, including from Jacob Mudenda, that if he did not do so, he would be impeached, prosecuted and would lose his status and benefits. In fact, there is evidence that the letter was drafted for him.

On 19 November 2017, as the military coup was intensifying, a "Special Session of the ZANU PF Central Committee" was held at the party's headquarters in Harare, amid confusion as to who had convened it and what capacity they had to convene it. Among other deliberations, the meeting made the following resolutions on Mugabe which expose Malaba as Mnangagwa's political judge with no regard to facts or the law:[28]

> **Resolution 8.0**
> That Cde Robert Gabriel Mugabe be and is hereby recalled from the position of President and First Secretary of ZANU PF forthwith.
>
> **Resolution 9.0**
> That Cde Robert Gabriel Mugabe resign forthwith from the position of President and Head of State and Government of the Republic of Zimbabwe, and if a resignation has not been tendered by midday 20th November 2017, the ZANU PF Chief Whip is ordered to institute proceedings for the removal of the President in terms of Section 97 of the Constitution of Zimbabwe (No. 20).

There is no need for the advice of a rocket scientist to be able to tell that the above two resolutions are what forced Mugabe's resignation, especially after he had ignored the ultimatum to resign from the position of President and Head of State and Government of the Republic of Zimbabwe by midday 20 November 2017. For Malaba to then claim that Mugabe resigned freely and voluntarily beggars belief.

As if going into Mugabe's mind was not preposterous enough, Malaba went further to consider whether the actions taken by the military between 14 and 21 November 2017 were legal. In an astonishing development, with deleterious implications on the rule of law and the integrity of the judiciary in Zimbabwe, Malaba relied on a seriously flawed judgment of a lower court and concluded that "the question of the lawfulness of the military action of 14 and 15 November 2017 was determined by the High Court" and that the applicants could not "seek to have the

---

[27] "Mugabe resigned freely, rules Chief Justice", *The Herald*, 17 July 2018, https://www.herald.co.zw/mugabe-resigned-freely-rules-chief-justice

[28] Resolutions of the ZANU PF Special Session of the Central Committee held at the Party Headquarters in Harare, 19 November 2017, pages 3–4.

question of the constitutionality of the military action enquired into by the Court whilst the order of the High Court determining the same issue is extant".

This was shocking, given s167(3) of the Constitution which states that "the Constitutional Court makes the final decision whether an Act of Parliament or conduct of the President is constitutional, and must confirm any order of constitutional invalidity made by another court before that order has any force". Chiweshe's High Court order legalising the coup was not extant but a nullity, and remains a nullity, not only because the High Court had no jurisdiction on the matter, but also because, if the High Court did have jurisdiction, the order was not confirmed by the Constitutional Court in terms of s167(3) of the Constitution.

But Malaba was not yet done, as he was apparently determined to sanitise the coup sitting alone in his Chambers when he was supposed to either grant or decline applicants' direct access to the Constitutional Court. Instead, he decided to tackle the issue of whether the military had influenced the impeachment motion in Parliament and whether Mnangagwa had assumed the presidency constitutionally. He found both to have been in order, without hearing any arguments and when the issues were not before him.

Malaba scandalously handled the application by Liberal Democrats, Revolutionary Freedom Fighters, Vusumuzi Sibanda, Linda Masarira and Bongani Nyathi for direct access to the Constitutional Court to bring an application against Emmerson Mnangagwa, Constantino Chiwenga, the Zimbabwe Defence Forces, the Speaker of Parliament and Robert Mugabe. What was scandalous was that he unilaterally, sitting alone in his Chambers and without hearing any arguments, dealt with the merits of a case whose applicants had wanted to place before the full bench of the Constitutional Court had they been granted the direct access they sought.

It is instructive that Malaba did this on 16 July 2018, a mere fourteen days before the 2018 presidential election. The way in which Malaba dealt with the case was manifestly political and scandalous, given that it had implications for how the Constitutional Court would handle petitions on the 2018 presidential election. Chiweshe's proposition that Mugabe had consented to the military coup and Malaba's proposition that Mugabe had freely and voluntarily written his resignation letter are not only outrageous but also demonstrate beyond doubt that the judiciary fell to the coup and became captured in a humiliating manner that damages the reputation of the bench, as well as putting Zimbabwe right in the basket of banana republics.

This development should have been enough to send clear signals to the MDC, before they decided to participate in the 2018 general election, that the judiciary would not be found on the side of impartiality, fairness, justice, constitutionalism and the rule of law in any dispute involving the 2018 general election.

An arrested transition

A fallacy peddled by the Junta to justify its illegal military ouster of Mugabe in November 2017 was that the coup was a "transition" to a "new dispensation": in other words, Mugabe's ouster was a military-assisted democratic transition. Apart from having been brazenly unconstitutional, as the publicly available "Coup Minutes" recorded by George Charamba on behalf of Constantino Chiwenga show, the November military coup was an illegal power grab exclusive to ZANU PF, with no public content besides its unconstitutionality.

As pointed out earlier in this chapter, when Chiwenga met Mugabe the day after the coup on November 16, he presented a two-page list of grievances with seven talking points, six of which were about succession politics in ZANU PF in favour of Mnangagwa and veterans of Zimbabwe's liberation war who claim to be the country's stockholders; one grievance was about security of tenure for the ZDF "command element" and their fear of future prosecution for various treasonous acts, including the November 2017 coup.

In the circumstances, it is a fallacy to claim that a coup motivated by ZANU PF succession politics, job-security concerns of the ZDF "command element", and the fear that the opposition would win the 2018 general election, all in violation of the Constitution of Zimbabwe, represented a democratic transition assisted by the military. In fact, the coup, which was not a popular uprising by any stretch of the imagination, represented an arrested or blocked transition.

The self-serving references to the well-subscribed Harare demonstration of 18 November 2017, which some embarrassed opposition and civil society quarters had used to justify their initial support of the Junta insurrection, cannot erase the evidence of who organised that demonstration and why.

It is now known beyond disputation that the demonstration was organised by Chiwenga from a Harare hotel to sanitise the coup by making it appear to be a "popular uprising", after some key opposition and civil-society activists had been kidnapped by soldiers and taken to Chiwenga's hotel room, where he gave some of them whisky and all of them money for consultancy fees to hire kombis and mobilise their supporters, telling them that he wanted "a demonstration against Mugabe to force him to resign".

The false propaganda that Chiwenga wanted to threaten a "Gaddafi-like lynching" of Mugabe, was music to the ears of the activists whose mantra had always been that "Mugabe must go". There are also now various ZANU PF documents, including minutes from various organs of the embattled party, which show beyond doubt that it was the ZDF that led the mobilisation for the 18 November 2017 demonstration in Harare.

This does not mean that, once the demonstration was organised, the demonstrators were aware of who the organisers were, or that they even cared about that. When the Junta ensured that the coup government was entirely made up of ZANU PF functionaries, after making false promises of a GNU as part of its mobilisation tricks for the demonstration, it was effectively confirming that the military action was not a political transition but an illegal military power grab to settle a leadership succession dispute within ZANU PF.

Only malcontents would claim that a leadership succession contest, especially one settled by a military coup, is a transition to a new democratic dispensation. The military coup was an aberration that represented an arrested transition. It was possible for a genuine transition to happen had, for example, the coup been done by middle-rank ZDF officers, the younger and professional generation, motivated by national and human interests against the old-guard in the "command element" who have a corrupt entitlement ethos and who arrogantly view themselves as the exclusive stockholders of Zimbabwe's liberation struggle. Prior to the coup, and this is what really triggered it, Mugabe had resolved to enable generational renewal, which would have led to a genuine political transition and to a new dispensation in ZANU PF, government and society.

Mugabe's belated generational renewal was resisted – to the point of staging a military coup to oust him – by those who betrayed him, especially Mnangagwa and Chiwenga, who had worked with or under him for up to 52 years, but especially since the infamous "Mgagao Declaration" in 1975 and throughout the independence period, and particularly during Gukurahundi and the State of Emergency between 1980 and 1990; as well as during Murambatsvina in 2005 and the army electoral coup in 2008.

The coup-makers felt that Mugabe had overstayed without a succession plan to guarantee the security of his Gukurahundi instigator and chief enforcer, Emmerson Mnangagwa and his Gukurahundi commanders such as General Constantino Chiwenga and Air Marshal Perence Shiri. Besides having mutual interest in protecting ill-gotten wealth, the primary reason that Mnangagwa and Chiwenga had joined forces to depose Mugabe was the fear of Gukurahundi consequences on their criminal liability.

Personal considerations and the fear of ZANU PF losing the 2018 general election featured prominently in the reasons that the so-called command element gave for the November 2017 military coup. The demands that the commanders made on Mugabe, and their justifications, are well documented in the Coup Minutes. In two very long sentences that reveal their rationale for the military coup, the Army's "command element" included concerns about ZANU PF being defeated in the 2018 general election:

> **Broadly, the CDF [Commander of the Zimbabwe Defence Forces, General Chiwenga] explained the rationale behind the Operation stressing that this was not a military take-over of Government but a time-bound Operation meant to extricate the President of Zimbabwe and Commander-in-Chief of the Zimbabwe Defence Forces from negative elements who encircled and had developed tentacles around him, thereby over threatening his legacy and interfering with the proper execution of his duties as leader of the Ruling Party, Zanu-PF, and as President of the Republic of Zimbabwe. Explaining that the Command Element had had several meetings with the President at which it had repeatedly expressed grave concern over this negative development, especially on the defence and the upholding of the ideals and vision of the National Liberation Struggle; on his Legacy and symbolism as the only surviving leader from that epochal Struggle; as the founding father of the Zimbabwe Nation; *on the electability of the ruling ZANU-PF Party in the impending 2018 Harmonised Elections* and, on the preservation and reproducibility of the whole ethos of the National Liberation Struggle as the dominant, enduring and governing idea in and for Zimbabwe, the CDF requested both the Chief Secretary and Chairman of the Civil Service Commission to help with a quick return to normalcy in respect of the functioning of the three pillars of the State, namely the Executive, the Legislature and the Judiciary.[29]**

---

[29] See Appendix: "The Coup Minutes", 15 November 2017, page 2.

Continuing with the theme of ZANU PF losing the 2018 general election, the Coup Minutes show that the "Command Element" reminded Mugabe of the 2008 election fiasco and told him that the army had to intervene to prevent what happened to UNIP (United National Independence Party) in Zambia (when it was voted out of power) from happening to ZANU PF, noting that:

> More worrisome were the divisive, manipulative and vindictive acts by the same cabal [that had allegedly encircled Mugabe] *which threatened the electability of ZANU PF in the impending 2018 Harmonised Elections, thus raising the spectre of an electoral defeat which harkened to the 2008 Electoral Crisis and more broadly, to a similar fate suffered by Zambia's founding UNIP in the early 1990s.*[30]

Further demonstrating that the fear of ZANU PF losing the 2018 was a major rationale for the November 2017 military coup, army commanders are recorded in the Coup Minutes as having told Mugabe that they had to take action because they had received worrying feedback about ZANU PF's electoral prospects from over 2,000 retired army officers they had embedded in communities across the country:

> … the Party [ZANU PF] risked creating conditions for the rise of 'independent' candidates in the forthcoming National Elections drawn from its embittered members, thereby dividing its vote to its own detriment and against its own electoral prospects. Feedback from the over 2 000 Commissars comprising retired senior officers from the Army already embedded in communities across the country pointed to worrisome, widespread disaffection and malaise within the Party, against its leadership, its decisions and management style. … The Operation by the Military was thus meant to reinstate the *bona fide* party processes for legitimate outcomes.[31]

Last on the Army's *election phobia* as a major rationale for the November 2017 military coup, the "Command Element" is captured in the Coup Minutes as having told Mugabe, who was by then virtually under house arrest, that the military intervention became necessary given the failure by Mugabe's government to implement the party's 2013 election manifesto:

> Noting the unfulfilled promises made in the 2013 Harmonised General Elections, the Command Element expressed fears that ZANU PF faced another election without evidence of real economic recovery by way of completion of flagship projects, or pointers to the general amelioration of socio-economic conditions of an expectant voting populace.[32]

Even from a cursory reading of the Coup Minutes, the pervasive rationale for the November military was clearly the fear by the "command element" that ZANU PF was facing electoral defeat. In this connection, the military ouster of Mugabe, seven months before the end of his term and before the next general election was due, sent a clear and ominous message against a free-and-fair general election in 2018. The writing was on the wall that the army was simply not going to allow it.

---

[30] Ibid., page 7.
[31] Ibid., page 8.
[32] Ibid., page 10.

No legitimacy without free and fair elections

As the old order has been slowly bleeding to death while the new has been struggling to be born, it has become quite clear that the birth of a new dispensation in Zimbabwe is being arrested by the country's lingering illegitimacy trap.

The means for legitimately getting into, staying in, and getting out of political office in Zimbabwe, in government and mainstream political parties, have remained intractably contested since 1980. Just about all holders of elective public office in politics, especially but not only at the level of the presidency, are illegitimate. The problem has been so pervasive that it has found expression even in appointed offices in the civil and security services. It is notable that key members of the ZDF "command element" that staged the November 2017 military coup had outlived their tenure and were thus in the command illegitimately.

Following the illegal military ouster of Mugabe in November 2017 and Tsvangirai's death in February 2018, Zimbabwe's two major parties in parliament, ZANU PF and the MDC, have been consumed by the fires of illegitimacy.

But this is not new. Illegitimacy has been the bane of Zimbabwean politics. While there are important foundational differences between ZANU PF and the MDC with regard to their ideologies, illegitimacy is common to and entrenched in both of them, with a resultant undemocratic culture of violence, entitlement, division and anointment.

On the one hand, for the MDC, the splits of 2005, 2012 and 2018 have basically destroyed the unity of the party, while leaving intact its founding values of democracy, human freedoms and the rule of law, which are now enshrined in the Bill of Rights in the 2013 Constitution. On the other hand, for ZANU PF, the party's founding values of self-determination, sovereignty and socio-economic rights, such as land reform and economic empowerment, have also found expression in the new Constitution, but virtually all of ZANU PF's political practices and disdain for civil and political rights – based on the stockholder mentality – have become outdated and unconstitutional.

The disintegration of ZANU PF and the overthrow of Mugabe have reduced that party to an ideologically bankrupt Junta outfit – whose leaders are associated with horrific human rights abuses – with a thin social base.

Although the coup took place with only seven months left before the next constitutionally due general election, the coup-makers behaved as if they had just won an election or the country had just undergone a revolution or uprising to warrant a root change of government policies, personnel, laws and institutions. Yet the coup did not have a visionary socio-economic blueprint for the country. It was a military coup with no plan beyond a power grab.

A forgotten but still relevant mantra asserted by African nationalists to rally the masses against colonialism and to mobilise the youth to join the armed liberation struggle was NIBMAR: "No Independence Before Majority (African) Rule".[33] The overarching and most important NIBMAR demand for independence, as it is for democracy and legitimacy today, was about

---

[33] Walter Darnell Jacobs, "Rhodesian Independence After the Fearless", *World Affairs*, 131(3), 1968, 162–176.

the right to vote under the banner of "one man, one vote". This demand was based on the fundamental and enduring principle that those who govern must have the consent of those whom they govern.

Central to this principle is the understanding that the means for getting into power, staying in power, and getting out of power must be decided by the people, and it is for the people to set up a government of the people. This is what democracy is all about. The people must elect their government in a free and fair election. It is in recognition of this principle that, for the first time since independence, the new Constitution adopted in 2013 enshrines free, fair and regular elections as a fundamental and thus justiciable political right under s67(1), which provides that:

> **Every Zimbabwean citizen has the right –**
> **(a) to free, fair and regular elections for any elective public office established in terms of this Constitution or any other law; and**
> **(b) to make political choices freely.**

The new Constitution facilitates the enjoyment of the political right to free, fair and regular elections by entrenching the right to vote under s67(3) which stipulates that:

> **Subject to this Constitution, every Zimbabwean citizen who is of or over eighteen years of age has the right –**
> **(a) to vote in all elections and referendums to which this Constitution or any other law applies, and to do so in secret.**

As such, the NIBMAR clarion call is now a justiciable right to vote that is enjoyed by every Zimbabwean. The authorities, through ZEC, have a constitutional duty to organise free, fair and regular elections in which every Zimbabwean must have a right to vote.

It is politically significant that the Bill of Rights in the new Constitution entrenches free, fair and regular elections, coupled with the right to vote, as justiciable rights. Ordinarily, elections are the only legitimate means of getting into power, staying in power and exiting from power. In this connection, an election is dialogical: it is a political and a legal concept. Put differently, an election is a rule-bound political process which is a legal event. The mark of a stable and vibrant democratic society is its ability to organise and hold contested elections that are free, fair and regular, and in which every Zimbabwean is enabled to participate.

Despite this constitutional imperative adopted in the 2013 Constitution, Zimbabwe's 2018 harmonised general elections, especially the presidential plebiscite, were neither free nor free, and were "regular" only in the calendar sense and in that they reproduced the same regular irregularities that have come to define Zimbabwe's captured electoral practice.

ZEC's collation, compilation and transmission of the result of the presidential election using a different route with a different destination from the one prescribed in s37C(4) of the Electoral Act was in contravention of s67 of the Constitution of Zimbabwe in that it denied voters their political rights, including the right to free-and-fair elections.

As in other African countries that are going through arrested political transitions from authoritarian to democratic rule, free-and-fair elections, in which citizens fully enjoy the right to vote, remain an elusive dream in Zimbabwe. While most countries in Africa have formally discarded one-party-state governance and adopted multi-party politics, virtually all of them have done so without institutionalising and consolidating democracy.[34]

As far as free-and-fair elections are concerned, Africa is in the cusp of a Gramscian interregnum in which its old authoritarian trappings of one-man and one-party-state rule are dying a very slow death, while the promise of a new democracy is taking too long to be born.[35] This inter-regnum was vividly and violently demonstrated in Zimbabwe's 2018 presidential election, whose promised new chapter, wrapped in the rhetoric of a new dispensation, turned out to be a familiar script from the old book of electoral fraud and violence such as witnessed on 1 August 2018, two days after the election and one day before the result of the presidential election was announced.

In the run-up to Zimbabwe's 2018 general election held on 30 July, hopes were high that the 11th poll post-independence would be of historic significance as only the country's second critical election out of ten (including two referendums) held since 1980. While horrific incidents of violence had characterised the 1985, 1990, 2000 and 2008 elections, none of the nine were as critical as that of 1980.

The 2018 election was expected to be as critical as the 1980 election because it was set to be a transitional year in which Mugabe would pass the baton to a successor to lead the transition not only from the old nationalist guard steeped in the liberation struggle to the new generation of millennials, who had become known as Generation 40,[36] but also a transition from the old Lancaster House Constitution enforced in 1980 to a new Constitution adopted in 2013.

Although the optics were that Mugabe would be ZANU PF's presidential candidate as per the party's decision at its 2014 congress, the reality was that a congress had been called for December 2017 at which the plan was to elect Sydney Sekeramayi as Mugabe's successor to face the electorate in a critical 2018 election.[37] Political scientists define a critical election as one in which an older coalition dies and a new one is born.

A critical election is one where there is a realignment of dominant political views, moral sentiments, and people's aspirations regarding their expectations of leadership, the emerging constitutional and policy issues as well as their ethnic and demographic bases of power, such as generational dynamics. The *locus classicus* in the study of critical elections is Key's seminal essay, "A Theory of Critical Elections", published in 1955.[38]

Zimbabwe's 1980 poll was a critical election that ushered in the Patriotic Front (PF) coalition, which brought ZAPU and ZANU (or more accurately ZIPRA and ZANLA) as liberation movements with a mission to stop the war in Rhodesia, which Abel Muzorewa had failed to do, and build a new and united nation, which did not happen because of Gukurahundi atrocities and the attempt to establish a one-party state, which was resisted by the 1990 election under Edgar Tekere's ZUM challenge.

---

[34] For a comprehensive review and critical analysis of the evolution of electoral politics and democratic transitions in Africa since 1990, see Jamie Bleck, & Nicolas van de Walle, *Electoral Politics in Africa Since 1990* (Cambridge: Cambridge University Press, 2018).

[35] Antonio Gramsci, "Between Past and Present", in *Prison Notebooks (Selections 272–76)*, translated by Joseph Buttigieg (New York: Columbia University Press, 1992).

[36] Jonathan Moyo, "Zanu-PF: An introspection", *The Zimbabwe Independent,* Harare, 6 November 2015.

[37] Owen Gagare, "Mexico Declaration: Mugabe's Waterloo", *The Zimbabwe Independent,* Harare, 11 May 2018.

[38] Valdimer Key Jr, "A Theory of Critical Elections", *The Journal of Politics* (Southern Political Science Association) 17 (1), 3–18, 1955.

Since 2000, as the fallacy of the 1987 Unity Accord was becoming self-evident, the Patriotic Front coalition started dying as a new patriotism emerged on the back of the MDC challenge together with the gains of the fast-track land-reform and economic-empowerment programmes propelled by a new generation, largely within ZANU PF, that was dominated by Zimbabwe's millennials.

These gains, along with Zimbabwe's new demographics, in which Zimbabweans between the ages of 18 and 49 years make up some 64% of the electorate, promised a new coalition ahead of the 2018 general election. This coalition supported the indigenisation and empowerment agenda, was opposed to the politics of entitlement entrenched by the old guard, favoured pluralism, merit-based human-resources policies, the balanced allocation of national resources, market-sensitive economic policies, modernisation and industrialisation through technologically driven high-end solutions, and globalised international relations through STEM (Science, Technology, Engineering, Mathematics) education and STEM skills. This agenda was ideologically appealing across the political divide and thus had the ingredients to spark a new coalition based on new politics.

The political expression of the agenda would have been the 2018 poll as a critical election. The old guard, who had coalesced around General Constantino Chiwenga, with Emmerson Mnangagwa as the political figurehead and the Zimbabwe National Association of the National Liberation War Veterans Association (ZNLWA) as the barking dogs, would have none of the passing of the baton to the younger generation through Sydney Sekeramayi as the transitional leader. After failing to persuade Mugabe, the old guard staged a military coup on 15 November 2017 and ousted Mugabe and his government, seven months before the 2018 general election was constitutionally due.

The military coup put paid to the prospects of a critical presidential election in 2018, an election which would have endowed its winner with the necessary legitimacy to turn the page in Zimbabwe to enable the country to break the Gramscian interregnum for the old Zimbabwe to die and new Zimbabwe to be born.

Chapter 3

THE RIGGING SYSTEM

"THE system must know the result, especially of the presidential election, before civilians, including those at Zimbabwe Electoral Commission (ZEC), get it," said the senior CIO securocrat who called me in the early hours of 31 July 2018 to tell me that Nelson Chamisa had won the presidential election with 66% of the vote to Mnangagwa's 33%.

The securocrat explained that it was important for "the system" to know the result ahead of civilians in order to manage the situation and know where and how to intervene, if necessary. Depending on the outcome of the election in question, an intervention might require "the system to manage the environment where the result can provoke demonstrations or any form of instability, or might require changing the result where a different outcome is desired."

In the case of the 2018 presidential election, "the system" sought to know the result ahead of civilians to both alter the result that had gone against Mnangagwa and to manage the environment by pre-empting demonstrations that Defence House, the head office of the Ministry of Defence, feared would follow the alteration, and with it the delay, of the result.

The background to this is best explained by understanding the involvement of the Joint Operations Command (JOC) in Zimbabwe's electoral politics over the years. This is because, as pointed out in Chapter 2, JOC has over the years come to represent "the system".

In the case of the 2018 presidential election, JOC operated through the following components that are exposed in this chapter as critical parts of the "the rigging system":

- **Defence House**: This is the head office of the Ministry of Defence. It was headed by Vice-President and Minister of Defence, Rtd General Constantino Chiwenga. Defence House directed the election operation, as the second phase of the November 2017 military coup which removed the late former President Robert Mugabe. ZEC liaised and reported to Defence House, which was the overall coordinator of the 2018 rigging process. In relation to the 2018 harmonised elections, particularly the presidential poll, the operational arm of Defence House was the Military Intelligence Department (MID) and other military structures.

- **CIO**: Of all JOC components, the CIO (Central Intelligence Organisation) has over the years evolved as the lead organisational instrument through which "the system" intervenes to manage or influence electoral outcomes. It conducts its own pre-election surveys and compiles its own results to ensure whatever necessary interventions are done effectively and on time.

- **The Data Recovery Centre**: Because the CIO is a vast organisation with multiple and complex structures and functions as an intelligence organisation, one of its key arms with a specific focus on election management is its Information Technology (IT) Department and its associated Data Recovery Centre based at Chaminuka

Building in Harare. Through the IT Department and the Centre, the CIO uses its network of agents and informants across the country to gather information and to conduct specialised opinion surveys on elections to forecast and predict likely electoral outcomes for planning and intervention purposes. Significantly, in the 2018 presidential election, the Centre housed a computer system that monitored and mirrored the main server at ZEC.

- **Chiltern Trust**: This is one of the many shadowy companies owned by the CIO for covert operations that are off-budget. In the 2018 presidential elections, the Chiltern Trust was responsible for ZEC's accreditation of election and polling officers, election and polling agents, local and foreign election observers and local and foreign media. In terms of the Constitution of Zimbabwe and the Electoral Act, the accreditation is specifically a ZEC function not meant to be delegated to a third party.

- **Africom Zimbabwe**: This is a company owned by the Zimbabwe Defence Forces (ZDF) through Ferhaven Investments. It was setup in 1995 as a provider of Internet, mobile network and computer network services, among other information technology functions. In the 2018 presidential election, and at the behest of Defence House, Africom managed, monitored and serviced ZEC's computer network at its national command centre in Harare. It is still working on the computerisation of Zimbabwe's electoral system on behalf of ZEC.

- **ZEC**: The logistical execution of the rigging system at ZEC was undertaken first and foremost through its Chairperson Justice Priscilla Chigumba, who liaised with Chiwenga and Defence House, and executed through its operations division, part of which is located at the CIO's Hardwicke Building in Harare. According to ZEC, the operations division is "responsible for the core function of the Commission, that is, the actual conduct and management of elections and referendums, election logistics, voter education and publicity campaigns and image promotion". The division is headed by a Deputy Chief Elections Officer and four key departments fall under it: Polling and Training, Public Relations, Voter Education, and Election Logistics.

- **Constitutional Court**: Chief Justice Luke Malaba was a key player in the process, having not only shown his predilection to rule in favour of Mnangagwa at the Pretoria Sheraton Hotel in Pretoria, South Africa, ahead of Chamisa's Court challenge, but also in the manner in which he blocked Chamisa's subpoena for the ZEC server and how he inexplicably ignored the MDC leader's chief election agent, Jameson Timba's unimpeached evidence in his supporting affidavit that ZEC failed to discharge its statutory obligation to display the constituency returns, V23Bs, in the verification and determination of the result of the presidential election, as required by s110(3)(d) of the Electoral Act.

These seven components – together with the control of the whole electoral process by Mnangagwa and his allies throughout the process, including at polling stations – outlined above constituted the operational core of the 2018 rigging system, as further explained below. First, more about the definition of "the system" and its context and meaning in relation to the conduct of elections in Zimbabwe.

The system

When I was Minister of Information in 2015, I had a charged conversation with George Charamba, then permanent secretary in the ministry, now a deputy chief secretary in the Office of the President and Cabinet and the minute-taker of the November 2017 coup meetings, whose sum and substance was to reveal what senior civil servants in Zimbabwe mean by "the system". The conversation, which was carried in an interview I had with Zimbabwe's *Standard* newspaper published on 7 February 2016, went as follows:[39]

> Minister, Minister, shouted Charamba. I am very, very worried.
>
> The commanders have been asking me what's going on with you and the whole system is concerned about you minister. I'm being asked a lot of hard questions about the BBC (HardTalk) interview.[40] Who organised it? How did they come here? Things would have been okay if the interview had ended there, but then it was transcribed, and the script was published in *The Herald*. They want to know who did that because it is only done for the president and nobody else.
>
> Then Charamba said, 'Minister, the system does not trust you at all. Now the commanders are angry with me. They are saying why am I not stopping you. It's like, it's my job to stop you'. 'Stop me from what?' I asked Charamba agitatedly. Stop you from doing what you are doing minister and you know what you are doing.
>
> When Charamba realised that I was getting very frustrated and even annoyed with his narrative, he then said, Minister, the system is asking if Moyo is not supporting VP Mnangagwa to succeed, so who then is he supporting? Why is he trying to prevent VP Mnangagwa? That makes him dangerous and he must be stopped.

It is clear that by "the system" Charamba meant army commanders, whose other name since the 15 November 2017 is the "command element", previously known by the more inclusive name of JOC.

JOC as "the system"

As explained in Chapter 2, JOC – the Joint Operations Command – is a colonial relic as a structure and the instrument of Zimbabwe's *de facto* ruling authority. It is the most critical instrument of the Government of Zimbabwe, from a decision-making and operational point of view.

Ordinarily, JOC is taken to be a conglomeration of the commander of the Zimbabwe Defence Forces (ZDF) and the heads of the army, air force, police, intelligence, and the prisons. But this categorisation does not quite capture what JOC is in functional terms.

JOC was created before independence to spearhead the brutal Rhodesian settler regime war against Zimbabwean freedom fighters in the country and in neighbouring frontline states.

---

[39] "Mugabe succession: Jonathan Moyo bares it all", *The Standard*, 7 February 2016, https://www.thestandard.co.zw/2016/02/07/mugabe-succession-jonathan-moyo-bares-it-all

[40] BBC HardTalk interview with Jonathan Moyo, https://www.bbc.co.uk/programmes/n3csy4q7 18 May 2015

It is an indictment of the post-independence political and military leadership that a colonial instrument created by the racist Rhodesian regime to brutalise freedom fighters was retained by the same liberators in independent Zimbabwe for oppressive purposes that have turned out to be worse than those of the Rhodesians who established it.

The repressive role of JOC after independence in 1980 took root in the early years of independence during the Gukurahundi atrocities. Outside that moment of madness, JOC has been the state's instrument of choice to checkmate and suppress the opposition, civil society and citizens in-between and during elections, while also functioning as the filter of government policies, decisions and actions.

Structurally, JOC brings together not only security chiefs, but also security ministers responsible for defence, home affairs and national security, as well as security departments, notably the immigration department and the office of the Registrar-General, which used to organise and conduct elections before the establishment of ZEC.

But even more telling, JOC is decentralised to operate at provincial and district levels. As such, there is the national JOC in Harare, in 10 provincial JOCs and in 63 district JOCs. Most of the agenda or work of the national JOC is derived from the decentralised JOCs which are the most active, given that politics happens at the local level. Typically, JOC's operational side, made up of officials, meets weekly on Thursdays and reports to the politicians on Fridays. National JOC reports to the president and ministers who make up the security cluster, provincial JOC to the minister of state for provincial affairs and provincial departmental heads, and district JOC to the district administrator and district departmental heads.

In reality, from an information and action point of view, the JOC's structure and process is by far better organised and more focused than that of Cabinet. To make matters worse for Cabinet, JOC deliberations at national, provincial and district levels are confidential and not accessible to ministers, save for items that national JOC may direct security ministers to report to Cabinet. This reality is what makes JOC the *de facto* ruling authority in Zimbabwe. Yet JOC, as an informal body, has no legal standing and is thus not accountable to any authority with a legal standing.

JOC is not accountable to Cabinet because, in fact, it is above Cabinet, since its deliberations are confidential, and it is not accountable to Zimbabwe's elected representatives in Parliament. Yet JOC makes fundamental decisions in its own right and acts on those decisions, but it cannot be sued, nor can it sue, because it is not a legal person and hides behind its key parental ministries, none of which take any responsibility for its operational activities, some of which involve gross violations of human rights such as killings, torture, rape and abductions. There is no single case of atrocities committed in Zimbabwe since independence that has not involved JOC or a component thereof.

The dark history of JOC includes the Gukurahundi genocide, the plunder of minerals in the Democratic Republic of Congo (DRC), Operation Murambatsvina, the 2008 presidential election run-off atrocities, the Chiadzwa diamonds plunder, and command agriculture looting. In the same vein, individuals have been murdered, tortured or abducted, and high-profile cases include: the maiming of the late Godfrey Majonga; the abduction and disappearance of Rashiwe Guzha, Patrick Nabanyama, Cain Nkala and Itai Dzamara; the bombing of the *Daily*

News printing press; harbouring Rwandan genocide fugitives; the torture of Jestina Mukoko; the murder of Solomon Mujuru; the 1 August 2018 Harare Massacre; and the January 2019 atrocities. In all these and other related cases, there has been no accountability whatsoever because JOC elements are a law unto themselves and have enjoyed unparalleled impunity since the Gukurahundi days.

The staggering story of JOC is breathtaking, made worse by the fact that Zimbabwe's *de facto* ruling authority, which is JOC, operates outside the law and is *ipso facto* above the law.

This aberration was a major focus of political and constitutional reform in the Global Political Agreement (GPA) negotiated between ZANU PF and the MDC formations in 2009. The parties agreed to replace JOC with the Zimbabwe National Security Council. In this regard, the Zimbabwe National Security Council Act (No. 2 of 2009) was enacted and gazetted on 4 March 2009 under General Notice 19/2009.

The Act was the first attempt since independence to bring JOC under the law. Unfortunately, it failed, because JOC would have none of it. The legislation ceased to exist when the GPA terminated on 22 August 2013. During the subsistence of the Act, JOC continued to meet and operate as if there was no Act, while resisting meeting under the Act because of its opposition to Morgan Tsvangirai, who was Prime Minister, and to the MDC formations, which were seen as a threat to national security despite being part of the government.

The CIO in JOC during elections

The CIO plays a critical role in the Zimbabwean state – from intelligence-gathering, collation, coordination and analysis of information to supporting law enforcement, national security, military, economic and foreign-policy objectives – but its role often goes beyond these and other associated covert actions, particularly when it comes to politics and elections.

Since independence in 1980, the CIO, also known as the President's Department, has been the lead intelligence organisation in the state's meddling in electoral politics on behalf of ZANU PF. It has done this by scanning the political and campaign environments, assessing political parties and candidates, and conducting election surveys on the likely performance of parties and candidates. Most importantly, the CIO, especially since 2000, has actively sought to influence not just the electoral environment, but also the mechanics and the actual results of elections themselves.

The senior CIO securocrat, who told me about the result of the presidential election on 31 July 2018 and who has been with the organisation since 1980, said the service is now always deeply involved in elections to gather anticipatory intelligence to detect, identify and warn of emerging issues and outcomes. He said that although the strategy of anticipatory intelligence is one of the intelligence community's foundational missions, it is usually used during elections to manipulate the electoral environment and processes to determine or influence election results using state resources and machinery. The CIO has developed infrastructure and a tried-and-tested *modus operandi* to manipulate and rig elections in various ways, depending on the circumstances of a given election.

Before every election, the CIO deploys its expansive formal and informal personnel – who include specialised officers, field operatives and informants – to collect, analyse, coordinate, process and disseminate information on elections within a closed circle. It also uses other security and government structures to gather information and to conduct its election operations. Crucially, the CIO deploys and embeds its intelligence officers within ZEC structures where they work as seconded staff, whose loyalty is first and foremost to the CIO.

Having scanned the environment, the CIO then conducts its own surveys – usually a series of them – before the elections almost until the voting day to detect trends, events and changing conditions, on the basis of which it predicts election results. Together with JOC, the CIO did this, even for the 1980 elections.

The CIO uses its national, provincial and district structures to conduct the surveys. In doing this, the CIO also enlists the services of professionals from outside its system to do the surveys or to replicate its own surveys for purposes of managing the political environment.

For example, the *Zimbabwe Independent* newspaper reported in March 2008, based on the intelligence service's survey which the newspaper had obtained, that the CIO had warned before the 29 March 2008 presidential election that President Mugabe would fail to win an outright majority vote, or would even lose the election altogether, owing to ZANU PF's divisions that were boiling on the back of the economic and social crisis that engulfed the country at the height of the meltdown and hyperinflation that year.[41]

In a pre-election intelligence survey report, which the *Zimbabwe Independent* had obtained, the CIO projected that Mugabe would get 49,2% of the vote if he did well – which was not enough to claim an outright victory, given the 50% + 1 vote statutory threshold needed to win a presidential election. The CIO was, however, later put under immense pressure by its political principals and ended up revising its forecast to put Mugabe initially at 52,3% and eventually at 56%, which were thumb-sucked figures. After the counting, recounting and the verification of the result, which took over a month and triggered a political crisis, ZEC announced a result on 2 May 2008 showing that Tsvangirai had won 47,9% of the vote with Mugabe getting 43,2%, thereby necessitating a run-off, which ZEC set for 27 June 2008.

In its survey, the CIO had initially predicted that Simba Makoni, an independent candidate, would get 21,5% of the vote, before it later revised this down to 13%. In the end, Makoni got 8,3% of the vote.

Meanwhile, the *Zimbabwe Independent* had also reported in early April 2008 that the CIO survey was similar in form, content and detail to an election report released the week before by University of Zimbabwe lecturer Joseph Kurebwa, prompting suggestions that it was actually the same document produced through collaboration between him and the CIO in an attempt by the intelligence service to use the academic to justify its manipulation and rigging of the election. Kurebwa is now a Commissioner at the Zimbabwe Human Rights Commission.

---

[41] "Mugabe to 'steal' polls", *Zimbabwe Independent*, 27 March 2008, https://www.theindependent.co.zw/2008/03/27/mugabe-to-steal-polls/

The CIO national elections surveys are done in order to advise "the system" on how ZANU PF and its local, parliamentary and presidential election candidates are likely to fare in an election. The CIO surveys also give "the system" an indication of whether any interventions would be needed to manage the environment or to affect (change) any election result in the harmonised election.

If the surveys project the ZANU PF president, parliamentary and local government candidates to win, "the system" leaves things at that and continues to manipulate the environment to ensure that the projected results are in fact realised. If, however, the surveys project a ZANU PF loss, then "the system" pulls out all the stops to avert the foreseen defeat to ensure a victory for ZANU PF.

The anticipatory intelligence gathered by the CIO through its surveys is also used to manage the political and security situation in the country. The operational presumption is that "the system" must get and know the election results before civilians, including those at ZEC, to be in a position to manage the result and the ensuing situation, rather than to react to the result after the fact. The rationale is that if "the system" waits to get the election results at the same time as the civilians, it would not have the time and the required strategic advantage or opportunity to intervene, should the situation demand an intervention, whether to change the result or to deal with political and security contingencies that might arise.

The virtual collapse of JOC ahead of 2017 coup

Following the November 2017 military coup, in the run-up to – and during – the 2018 election, the CIO was no longer enjoying its strategic position within JOC, nor enjoying the influence within JOC that it had cultivated over the years predating Zimbabwe's independence in 1980.

After the 2013 general election, and in the build-up to the November 2017 military coup, cracks bedevilled JOC as the security chiefs became entangled in ZANU PF's factions, with some supporting Joice Mujuru and others supporting Mnangagwa. By 15 November 2017, JOC had become dysfunctional. Riddled with factionalism, it was no longer cohesive. This was dramatically highlighted by the "Command Element" in an entry in its "Coup Minutes" which made this startling observation:

> His Excellency the President and Commander-in-Chief was informed of a serious attack on Inter-Agency Cohesion within the National Security Establishment by the aforementioned cabal [the so-called G40 kingpins] which appeared to have influenced key departments of National Security. *The impact had been the virtual collapse of the National Joint Operations Command (JOC)* through which issues relating to National Security were dealt with collectively, and jointly presented to the Head of State. This vital structure had given way to narrow departmental reports and debriefings which not only misrepresented the overall National Security situation, but also provided a conduit for briefings to the Commander-in-Chief that were based on self-serving falsehoods and character assassinations calculated to settle vendettas. The obtaining selective access to the Commander-in-Chief had undermined the spirit of intelligence-sharing and collegiality which all along had underpinned the institution of the National Joint Operations

Command. On this score, the Command Element blamed the Police Commissioner General, Cde Augustine Chihuri, and the former Director-General of the Central Intelligence Organisation (now Minister of Justice, Legal and Parliamentary Affairs), Rtd General Happyton Bonyongwe.[42]

There was no JOC to speak of after the coup and seven months before the 2018 harmonised general election. The hierarchy of the CIO and the police were not singing the coup song that ZDF commanders were singing. In fact, the CIO and the police were opposed to the coup and the leadership of the two organisations were seen by the coup-makers as part of, or at least sympathetic to, the so-called G40.

The structure of the 2018 rigging system

The void created by the virtual collapse of JOC, and particularly the CIO's loss of power and influence after the November 2017 military coup, was filled by Defence House, as seen in Diagram 5, which illustrates the key components of the rigging structure. A new *ad hoc* and thus informal structure emerged for purposes of executing the 2018 presidential election as a military operation to obtain the result that was consistent with the strategic objectives of the coup. The key components of the structure, excluding the Constitutional Court which became involved after the election, are as outlined earlier in this chapter. Taken together, the components defined the structure of the 2018 election-rigging system.

---

[42] See Appendix: "The Coup Minutes", 15 November 2017, page 17.

DIAGRAM 5
APEX OF THE 2018 RIGGING STRUCTURE

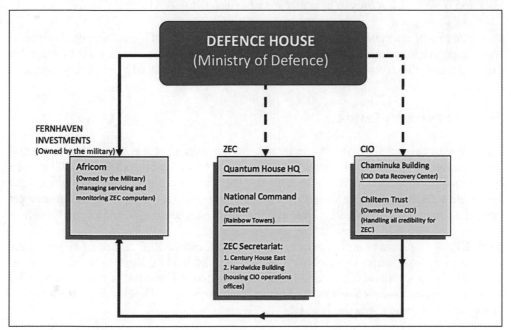

Some further elaboration about Africom, the CIO's Data Recovery Centre and Chiltern Trust is in order. This is to help the understanding of the orgy of illegality that surrounded the conduct of the 2018 presidential election and the manipulation of its result.

Africom Zimbabwe

For the 2018 harmonised general election, and in particular with respect to the 2018 presidential election, at the behest of Defence House, ZEC assigned the responsibility for managing, servicing and monitoring its multiple computer servers to Africom.

As already mentioned, Africom is owned by the ZDF through Fernhaven Investments, a holding company controlled by the military and used as its investment arm. Africom was established in 1995 as an Internet service provider which also at its inception provided data, mobile-network services and computer-network services. Initially it was based at Block 3 Tendeseka Office Park in Eastlea, along Samora Machel Avenue in Harare. Now it is located at Number 99 Churchill Avenue in Gunhill, Harare.

The services that Africom offered to ZEC for the 2018 presidential election covered the gamut of end-to-end ICT solutions, including cyber-security solutions, access management, risk and compliance management, encryption, DLP (data-loss prevention), unified threat management, firewalls, antivirus and web-filtering solutions. It was contracted to computerise the electoral system. For purposes of the 2018 presidential election, Africom also prioritised the networking and management of the servers at the ZEC national command centre.

What this means is that a military company effectively had unlimited access to the election data in ZEC's custody. How and why ZEC engaged Africom is a matter of huge constitutional concern and public interest. In a post-coup environment, it cannot be right that a military company is found to be in bed with a constitutional electoral body that has a constitutional duty and obligation not only to be transparent but also to be seen to be transparent.

It is quite clear that a major reason why ZEC did not and could not come clean on its server at its national command centre in Harare is that, among other considerations, some of which are outlined below, the server was being managed, monitored and serviced by a military company.

The Data Recovery Centre

As pointed out above, the CIO's instrument for election engagement is its IT Department and Data Recovery Centre located within the Computer Services Bureau, where the CIO uses its own structures supported by JOC – to bring together the Police Internal Security Intelligence (PISI) and Military Intelligence Department (MID) – to monitor the electoral process from voter education, voter registration, voting, vote-counting and result declaration and announcement.

The CIO's IT Department and computer network monitors the ZEC computer system at the national command centre at Rainbow Towers and at Mahachi Quantum Building, corner Jason Moyo Street in Harare, through its system located at Chaminuka Building, the CIO headquarters commonly known as "Red Bricks" because of the red brickwork of the building, along Simon Muzenda Street in Harare.

The CIO's IT Department and Data Recovery Centre monitors the ZEC systems and enables the intelligence organisation to run the show, to know what is going on, or even to influence what is going on and its outcomes as "the system" may desire. Using its labyrinth of structures, the CIO sees in advance the voting patterns and trends to be able to predict election results with reasonable probability. This facility and capacity gives the CIO an opportunity to inform the President ahead of the official release of the results about the situation and the arithmetic of the results so that the President, in consultation with the military commanders and security advisers, can decide what to do: whether to concede if the President has lost, or whether to fight back to reverse and nullify the result through manipulation and rigging, as happened in 2018, as it had in 2008.

Chiltern Trust

Apart from its own direct involvement through its network of operatives, embedded staff at ZEC and its IT system which mirrors and monitors ZEC computers, the CIO has a vast network of off-budget companies some of which, like Chiltern Trust, are involved in Zimbabwe's electoral system.

In 2018 ZEC assigned its accreditation function to Chiltern Trust, a CIO entity, under murky and opaque circumstances that are inconsistent with ZEC's constitutional obligation to conduct elections transparently. Through Chiltern Trust, ZEC accredited 3,377 electoral personnel, including commissioners, permanent staff and seconded staff who were operating at election centres across the country. The Trust also vetted and accredited candidates and election agents, as well as the following categories of foreign and local observers and foreign and local press:[43]

CATEGORIES	TOTAL
Foreign Observers	1,007
Local Observers	11,019
Foreign Press	202
Local Press	740
TOTAL	12,968

Vetting in intelligence circles is considered a critical process, as it gives personal information about people and insight into who they are and what they do. Through vetting, individuals are background-checked and screened to ensure that they meet the set criteria for accreditation. In this case, the CIO's interest, through Chiltern Trust, was to ensure to the extent possible that accredited individuals in the various accreditation categories prescribed were acceptable to Defence House and ZANU PF, and that "the system" was able to monitor any of the accredited individuals throughout the election, as persons of interest.

If executed according to the book, vetting and accreditation constitutes a vital part of counter-intelligence, which is apparently one of the reasons why the CIO became involved in managing

---

[43] ZEC, *Zimbabwe 2018 Harmonised Elections Report*, page 56.

ZEC's accreditation function through Chiltern Trust. In carrying out the exercise, Chiltern Trust, acting on behalf of the CIO under the control of Defence House, considered mainly these factors: applicant's personal background, history, past behaviour and experiences, relationships, affiliation to political parties and organisations, and political views.

There is no suggestion or argument here that people should not be vetted, save to say that the vetting should be transparent and done by a lawful entity in accordance with the law in an accountable constitutional manner. Chiltern Trust is not a lawful entity envisaged in s40I of the Electoral Act or s239(i) of the Constitution of Zimbabwe.

By clandestinely getting involved in the electoral process, Chiltern Trust formed part of the state infrastructure and secret weapons that were used in the 2018 presidential election to subvert the democratic will of the people. The fact that Chiltern Trust is a company outside the transparent ambit of the state or government makes the arrangement particularly sinister, not least because there's no accountability whatsoever. The process is a gross violation of the privacy of people who, in good faith, apply to ZEC for accreditation to report on or participate in or observe a general election in the belief that their application for accreditation is processed above board and in accordance with the law.

The case of Chiltern Trust is made worse by the Trust's dodgy past arising from its involvement in previous disputed elections and in the controversial saga of Nikuv, in which the 2013 elections were clouded by allegations of manipulation, allegedly done with the help of that shadowy Israeli intelligence-linked company, which was paid millions of United States dollars before the 2013 elections.

In 2003, Chiltern Trust was embroiled in the failed CIO plot to frame the late MDC founding leader, Morgan Tsvangirai, the party's then Secretary-General, Welshman Ncube, and the late Renson Gasela, an MDC functionary, with allegations that they had conspired to assassinate President Mugabe.

In the plot to frame the trio, Chiltern Trust was used by the CIO as a conduit to make payments through CBZ Bank and ZB Bank (formerly Zimbank) to a dodgy international Israeli consultant, Ari Ben-Menashe, through his political consultancy, Dickens & Madison between 30 November 2001 and 5 August 2002. The plot was later exposed in the courts when Tsvangirai and his co-accused MDC leaders were charged with treason, for which they were acquitted.

In the circumstances, the fact that ZEC used CIO's Chiltern Trust to discharge its accreditation responsibility was improper, illegal, unconstitutional and scandalous.

The servers

The foregoing discussion of the 2018 rigging system is particularly important regarding the question of the ZEC server, which contained the result of the presidential election that showed Chamisa with 66% of the vote and Mnangagwa with 33%. I have pointed out in the preceding chapters that ZEC's bare denial in Chamisa's ConCourt case that it did not have any server on which it kept the result of the 2018 presidential election was false and not supported by any evidence, and inconsistent with its constitutional obligation not only to be transparent but also to be seen to be transparent.

Mnangagwa himself – as President, presidential candidate, and the one respondent with everything to lose in the ConCourt case – virtually confirmed the existence of the server in his opposing papers, which ZEC claimed did not exist. And more tellingly, the involvement of Africom, a military company, was precisely to computerise the electoral process and network the system with respect to the capturing and processing of voting data at ZEC's national command centre. It is ZEC that roped in Africom to computerise the system and run its multiple servers, fully knowing that the company's purpose was to set up a voting and results database.

It was dishonest for ZEC to deny the existence of the server or servers to give the impression that, in this day and age, Zimbabwe's electoral body does not have a computerised system for capturing, storing and processing voting data. ZEC averred in its opposing papers in the ConCourt case that it had used an Excel spreadsheet only as calculator to add the result of the presidential election from election returns it was using. Where did ZEC store the voting data from the returns it claimed to have, which were used by "a group of people, in excess of twenty, punching in what was identified as V11 data into an Excel spreadsheet" over two days? Was this voting data stored on USB flash drives? On CD-ROMs? It is hard to believe that ZEC wants the world to think that it has no computer capacity to store election results.

ZEC had a main server with election results and it was linked to other multiple servers operated by the electoral body. Diagram 6 depicts ZEC's main server at its national command centre, as networked by Africom, and mirrored by the CIO's IT Department and Data Recovery Centre.

DIAGRAM 6
RIGGING SERVERS

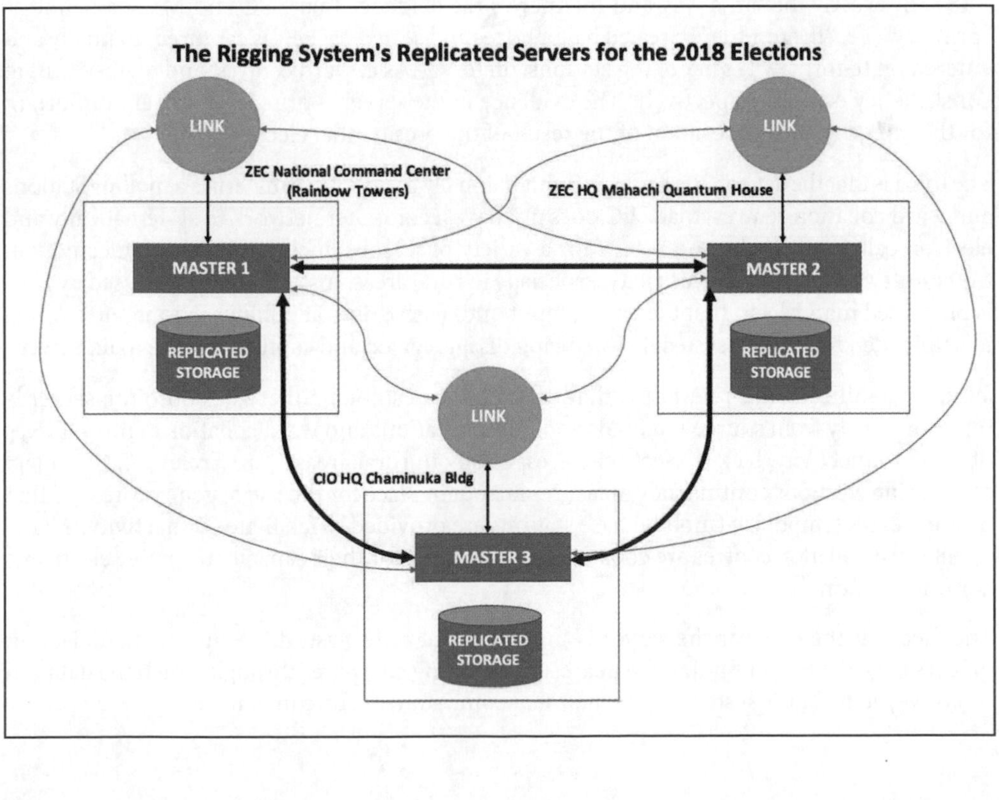

The Rigging System's Replicated Servers for the 2018 Elections

A lot was made by ZEC in its opposing papers in Chamisa's ConCourt case about the server, the main argument being that, even if a server was there and was used, there was no issue, supposedly because the data it contained proved nothing at all. To amplify this stance, four points emerged about ZEC's position whose import is to dismiss the relevance and importance of the server:

The first is that, while Zimbabwe has Biometric Voter Registration (BVR), it does not have an Electronic Voting System (EVS) which automatically and electronically captures the result of an election as voters cast their votes.

But this point is irrelevant. The fact that Zimbabwe does not have an EVS does not mean that it cannot have a computer server that stores and processes election results. The difference is that, where there is an EVS, the result is captured electronically, whereas where voting is manual, the capturing is manual.

If you can use an Excel spreadsheet to process an election result, as ZEC claims to have done to determine the result of the 2018 presidential election, surely you can also use a server not only to process but also to store the result securely?

The second, and Malaba made a meal out of this point during the ConCourt hearing as well as in both his preliminary and full judgments, is that the server is not primary evidence, that there is no primary evidence in the server, that primary evidence is the residue, which is in the sealed ballot boxes and sealed election packets, as provided under s70(4) of the Electoral Act.

This is a baseless and self-indulgent argument which betrays ignorance of both the electoral process and electoral law. The fact of the matter, backed by electoral law, is that the data on the result of the presidential election in the server is captured manually and entered at source – that is, at polling stations, ward centres and constituency centres on to forms V16 and V18 – in exactly the same way and manner as the evidence that ZEC and Malaba define as "primary": i.e. "the residue" in sealed ballot boxes and sealed packets is captured manually and entered on to forms V11s at polling stations, on to V23As at ward centres, and on to V23Bs at constituency centres, respectively. The evidence in the server is primary, and very important for the integrity and aggregation of the result of the presidential election.

The third is that the data on the server is input manually from source materials at polling stations and ward collation centres, that ZEC does not have a computer network to systematically and electronically process election results for a variety of reasons, including poor connectivity in the country and the lack of electricity, especially in rural areas. Instead, the system used by ZEC is processed manually in that the data is input onto flash drives at polling stations, after which it is uploaded into ZEC's system before being disaggregated and captured by the main server.

What is significant and relevant is that the election-result data that goes onto the server is input manually from source materials and polling stations and ward collation centres. Issues of poor connectivity, lack of electricity – especially in rural areas – are irrelevant. It is a fact that during elections contingency measures are put in place for the use of generators, and that in some cases temporary (mobile) base stations are provided to facilitate connectivity. All the 1,958 ward collation centres are chosen and designated for their capacity to enable electronic communication.

The fact that the data for the server is initially input onto flash drives means that election officers have the task of finding the nearest functioning computer through which the data can be conveyed to ZEC's systems at the national commander centre in Harare.

Fourth, as emphatically stated by Malaba at page 45 of his "fully dressed judgment", is the point that ZEC kept making in its opposing papers in Chamisa's ConCourt case:

> **The law of elections does not have a provision requiring the electronic transmission of polling station returns to, and storage in, a server.**[44]

Further, at page 101, Malaba emphatically declares that:

> **In Zimbabwe the counting and transmission of the results is wholly manual. The process involves counting of all the ballots at the polling station in the presence of election agents of candidates who participated in the election. A polling station return, the V11 Form, is completed and countersigned by the election agents. The import of ss 64-65B of the Act is that they lay down the processes and procedures for the counting of votes, securing of the voting material and transmission of the polling station returns together with the election residue.**[45]

The claim that the law of elections in Zimbabwe does not have a provision requiring the electronic transmission of polling station returns to, and storage in, a server is a misrepresentation arising from the use of the word "requiring". The correct position is that notification of election results, through electronic transmission, is indeed provided for, under s67 of the Electoral Act. ZEC's 2018 *Electoral Officers Manual,* read with Statutory Instrument 21 of 2005 (Electoral Regulations), as amended, **provides** for the electronic transmission of polling station returns to, and storage, in a server. This is done through the prescribed forms V16 and V18, respectively, for the result of the presidential election. Notably, in the 2013 presidential election, ZEC had transmitted results to the national command centre electronically, including by fax and SMS. The transmission of the presidential election results in 2018 was done in the same way.

Diagram 7 is the prescribed form through which a polling station electronically notifies ZEC's national command centre in Harare of the result of the presidential poll.

DIAGRAM 7:
FORM V.16

ELECTORAL ACT [*CHAPTER 2:13*]
PRESIDENTIAL ELECTIONS: TELEGRAM, TELEFASCIMILE OR ELECTRONIC
MAIL NOTIFYING THE RESULT OF POLL

_____

To the Chief Elections Officer, Harare.
Form the constituency elections officer for the constituency of ....
....
date ....code word.. stop
Counting of votes completed stop..received a total of
....votes stop ....received a total of
....votes stop..received a total of
....votes stop
There were.. rejected papers stop
The percentage poll was...End of message.

---

[44] Judgment No. CCZ 21/19, *Nelson Chamisa and 24 Ors v Emmerson Mnangagwa*, page 45.
[45] Ibid., page 101

The electronic notification of the result of a presidential election in terms of form V16, shown above, is followed or accompanied with the actual breakdown of the result in terms of form V18, shown on Diagram 8:

DIAGRAM 8:
FORM V.18

ELECTORAL ACT [CHAPTER 2:13]
PRESIDENTIAL ELECTIONS: RESULT OF POLL

_____

To: The Chief Elections Officer, Harare
From: The constituency elections officer for the constituency of ....

....

....

In confirmation of my telegram/telefacsimile/electronic mail of notification of the result of the poll dispatched to you on ...., the details of the counting are as follows:

FIRST COUNT
1. Name of candidate .... received ....votes
2. Name of candidate .... received ....votes
3. Name of candidate .... received ....votes
4. Name of candidate .... received ....votes
5. Name of candidat...................................... received ....votes

SECOND COUNT
1. Name of candidate .... received ....votes
2. Name of candidate .... received ....votes
3. Name of candidate .... received ....votes
4. Name of candidate .... received ....votes
5. Name of candidate .... received ....votes
There were.. spoilt ballot papers.
The percentage poll was* ....
Dated at ....
                                        Constituency elections officer

*Divide the number of votes cast by the number of votes on the roll and multiply the result by 100.

Diagram 9 is taken from ZEC's *Electoral Officers Manual for 2018 Harmonised Elections*.[46] Notably, original copies of the V11 are affixed outside the polling station, given to each candidate or polling agent present at polling station, sealed in the ballot box and sent to the relevant ward collation centre. Copies are sent to the relevant constituency centre, district

---

[46] ZEC, *Electoral Officers Manual for 2018 Harmonized Elections*, https://www.zec.org.zw/final/files/ZEC%20Election%20Officers%20 Full%20Manual.pdf, page 43.

command centre, provincial command centre and national command centre. Whereas the originals are transmitted physically, the copies are not, and cannot rationally be, sent physically but by telegram/telefacsimile/electronic mail along with forms V16 and V18.

DIAGRAM 9
DISTRIBUTION OF V11 FORMS

Original version of this form must be produced and they must be distributed as follows:

PRESIDENTIAL ELECTION	NATIONAL ASSEMBLY ELECTION	LOCAL AUTHORITY ELECTION
Affix original outside of polling station	Affix original outside of polling station	Affix original outside of polling station
Provide original to each candidate or polling agent present at polling station	Provide original to each candidate or polling agent present at polling station	Provide original to each candidate or polling agent present at polling station
Seal original in the ballot box	Seal original in the ballot box	Seal original in the ballot box
Send original return to: • Ward Collation Centre and copies to: • Presidential Constituency Centre, • District Command Centre • Provincial Command Centre, and • National Command Centre	Send original return to: • Ward Collation Centre and copies to: • National Assembly Constituency Centre, • District Command Centre • Provincial Command Centre, and • National Command Centre	Send original return to: • Ward Collation Centre and copies to: • Constituency Command Centre, • District Command Centre • Provincial Command Centre, and • National Command Centre

Given the foregoing, it cannot be true – as claimed by ZEC and asserted by Malaba in his 137-page judgment released on 7 November 2019 – that the voting data in the server is not primary evidence or that it has no legal standing.

Key players in the rigging system

The *ad hoc* rigging structure used in the 2018 presidential election had key players, the rigging team, whose identification is necessary to shine a spotlight on who was who in the manipulation of the result of the presidential election and the subversion of the will of the people.

I have explained that the rigging system was led from Defence House, the head office of the Ministry of Defence, from where it got its policy guidance, financial and logistical support, as well as political protection. Led by Rtd General Chiwenga, as Vice-President and Minister of Defence, the principals included: Rtd General Sibusiso B. Moyo, the link to Fernhaven and Africom, the military companies he has been extensively involved with, including as Africom board chairman; General Anselem Sanyatwe, who commanded the Presidential Guard that spearheaded the November 2017 military coup and which was involved in the 1 August 2018 Harare Massacre; General Thomas Moyo, Commander of the Military Intelligence Department (MID); and General Engelbert Rugeje, who was ZANU PF's national commissar in charge of the party's election campaign.

At ZEC, Priscilla Chigumba was the high-level link with and contact for Defence House, with direct and unrestricted access to Chiwenga, whom she found to be a hands-on and reliable leader she could depend on to get things done in a volatile and high-stakes rigging assignment, especially regarding mobilising financial and material resources for the electoral body.

As a retired army officer, Utoile Silaigwana, ZEC's acting Chief Elections Officer, was in the general but not specific loop. Silaigwana was an ever-willing rigging accomplice, incapable of saying "no", in defence of ZEC's constitutional duty and mandate. His loyalties were firmly with Defence House.

Within the CIO, Isaac Moyo, the Director-General and a Mnangagwa loyalist, was nominally involved and was keen to be more involved, but he did not enjoy the confidence of Defence House nor of the relevant operatives within the CIO itself, who resent his links with Mnangagwa and involvement in the November 2017 military coup. The CIO director in the Information Technology Department was a key part of the rigging system, not least because the Data Recovery Centre falls under his supervision.

All players considered, the key operative who was the centre and mainstay of the rigging system, and around whom the rest of the hands-on operatives coalesced, was Mavis Matsanga, an active CIO Divisional Intelligence Officer (DIO), first seconded to ZEC in 2008. Fully embedded in ZEC, Matsanga is the Chief Information Security Officer at ZEC in the all-important operations division.

This division is in charge of ZEC's main function as an electoral body in that it deals with "the actual conduct and management of elections and referendums, election logistics, voter education and publicity campaigns and image promotion". As mentioned earlier, the division is headed by a Deputy Chief Elections Officer and has four departments: Polling and Training, Public Relations, Voter Education, and Election Logistics.[47]

Having clocked twelve years experience at ZEC, Matsanga knows the operational side of ZEC inside out, and she details her job description on LinkedIn, as follows:[48]

> **My responsibilities [at ZEC] include: participating in the national logistics of elections, logistics of ballot paper and other election material and organisation, coordinating and conducting election observer accreditation, attending to queries from the field and many other operation matters in the field.**

It is illustrative that Matsanga's LinkedIn job description dovetails neatly with ZEC's description of the responsibility of the operations division that performs the core function of the Commission: you describe Matsanga's job, you describe the responsibility of ZEC's operations division.

---

[47] https://www.zec.org.zw/pages/departments
[48] *See* https://zw.linkedin.com/in/mavis-matsanga-89a47938

As an embedded active CIO operative under the guise of a seconded official, Matsanga's CIO credentials and real work at ZEC is known only to and by Chigumba, the ZEC chairperson, as it was known to her predecessor, Justice Rita Makarau. To put Matsanga's job at ZEC bluntly: it is to manage and rig elections for ZANU PF under the command of the CIO. In the 2018 harmonised elections, Matsanga was deputised by one Chivasa, a retired military operative, seconded to ZEC by the ZDF specifically to rig elections. As if to underscore his pivotal role in the manipulation of the result of the 2018 presidential election, Chivasa's full names and identity are a closely guarded secret at ZEC and within the rigging system.

The brazen operation to audaciously rig the result of the 2018 presidential election by inventing an unlawful route and destination for the collation, compilation and transmission of the result, through operational liaison with Africom for server networking and servicing, with Chiltern Trust for the accreditation function and the CIO's Data Recovery Centre for the result monitoring and manipulation, was logistically organised, coordinated and led by Mavis Matsanga, as ZEC's Chief Information Security Officer in the operations division, and as an active CIO embed controlled by Defence House on behalf of, or in the name of, JOC.

Malaba and the server

On evidence, the significance of the ZEC server that contained the result of the 2018 presidential election showing Chamisa with 66% of the vote and Mnangagwa with 33% is that it triggered the constructive rigging of the election by ZEC at the instigation of Defence House. To understand and appreciate this consideration, it is important to recall a fundamental and indisputable matter of fact stated by ZEC itself in its Report on the 2018 harmonised elections. Under paragraph 4.6.2 of its Report, dealing with the collation, compilation and transmission of presidential and national assembly returns from ward collation centres, ZEC reports that:

> Results for the Presidential and the National Assembly elections were transmitted using different routes from the ward collation centre. While the destination for the National Assembly election results was the constituency centre, the Presidential results were forwarded to the district centre for onward transmission to the National Command Centre in Harare. Verification was done at each point by checking the accuracy of every collation return and whether it was properly completed. If not, corrections would be effected by use of polling station source documents (V11s).[49]

From the ward collation centre, ZEC transmitted results of the presidential and national assembly elections using different routes with different destinations. The destination for the national assembly results was the constituency centre, whereas the presidential results were forwarded to the district centre for onward transmission to the national command centre in Harare. As detailed in Chapter 2, ZEC's use of different routes with different destinations to transmit presidential and national assembly elections violated the peremptory provisions of s37C(4) of the Electoral Act in a major way and, *ipso facto*, voided whatever result of the presidential election it declared and announced, thereafter.

---

[49] ZEC, *Zimbabwe 2018 Harmonised Elections Report*, page 67.

At page 76 of his fully dressed judgment released on 7 November 2019, Chief Justice Malaba notes with emphasis the route and destination of transmitting the result of the presidential election peremptorily prescribed in the Electoral Act and says:

> The ward elections officer is then enjoined to provide a copy of the completed ward return to every candidate, election agent and observer who requests one. He or she must also ensure that a copy of the ward return is displayed prominently outside the ward centre, so that all members of the public who wish to do so may inspect it and record its contents. Immediately after causing a copy of the ward return to be displayed outside the ward centre, the ward elections officer *must cause the return, certified by himself or herself to be correct, to be transmitted to the constituency centre for the constituency in which the ward is situated* [emphasis added].

> Any reference to a constituency centre or a constituency elections officer shall be construed in respect of the Presidential election as reference to a Presidential constituency centre or a Presidential constituency elections officer.[50]

Malaba's wording uses "must" where the Electoral Act uses "shall". The import of Malaba's "must" is that ZEC has no power or authority to vary the route and destination for transmitting the result of the presidential election from ward collation centres to constituency centres. The results of the presidential and national assembly elections must be transmitted from ward centres using the same route with the same destination.

Given that ZEC violated the law regarding this matter, the question must be asked: what motivated or prompted ZEC to transmit the result of the presidential election using a different route with a different destination from that used for the national assembly election?

The answer is blowing in the wind. Through Mavis Matsanga, the CIO's Data Recovery Centre and Africom's management of the server at ZEC's national command centre, Defence House got to know early before civilians, including ZEC civilians, that Chamisa had garnered 66% of the presidential election vote while Mnangagwa had managed only 33%. A radical, brazen and audacious decision was made to intercept at 1,958 ward centres the result of the presidential election recorded in 1,958 V23As reflecting 10,985 V11s from polling stations and to re-route it away from constituency centres and transmit it to district election offices for onward transmission direct to the national command centre in Harare. This re-routing was a military operation, and not done transparently.

The server was crucial in making this happen. It would not have been possible for "the system" to know that Mnangagwa had dismally lost to Chamisa without the server. It is precisely for this reason that the server is the most important and the best evidence to show that there was shockingly bold and massive rigging of the result of the presidential election by the rigging system. The blocking and denial of access to the server by Malaba was a gross injustice, bordering on premediated criminal conduct.

---

[50] Judgment No. CCZ 21/19, page 76.

Indeed, the server is the best evidence of the motive behind ZEC's invention of different routes and different destinations for the transmission of the results of the presidential and national assembly elections from ward collation centres, the former going via district election offices and direct to the national command centre in Harare, the latter going to constituency centres.

The server backs up the dictum of the senior CIO securocrat who has repeatedly told me since the early hours of 31 July 2018 that "the system must know the result of the presidential election before civilians, including ZEC civilians" in order to know where, how and when to intervene one way or another. On the basis of the server, "the system" decided to intervene on 31 July 2018 at the level of 1,958 ward collation centres and did so by commandeering the V11s and V23As to disharmonise the harmonised election, and used an illegal route for transmitting them to the national command centre in Harare, which was turned into an illegal giant polling station.

On this, ZEC's Report on the 2018 harmonised elections declares:

> **For validation of receipt of results, a parallel system was used to transmit and collate the presidential election results. The results were taken to the national command/collation centre physically by the District Elections Officers** *where they were captured and collated on a results collation template at the National Collation Centre* [emphasis added].[51]

There is no electoral law that empowers ZEC to snatch V11s and V23As from 1,958 ward centres and drag them to Harare for capturing and collation at the national command centre. In his ConCourt application, Chamisa described this "capturing and collation" of results at ZEC's national command centre vividly:

> **On the 1st of August 2018 twenty third respondent [ZEC] started what it called a verification process and which it asked Messrs Komichi and Timba to witness.** *The process involved a group of people, in excess of twenty, punching in what was identified as V11 data into an Excel spreadsheet. For close to two days that process continued.*[52]

The unavoidable impact of ZEC's use of a different route with a different destination for the transmission of the result of the presidential election from the ward centres was to nullify the evidentiary value of election residue in sealed ballot boxes and to render meaningless the result of the presidential election that Chigumba declared and announced on 3 August 2018. Tellingly, Chigumba's declaration violated s110(3) of the Electoral Act, whose requirements regarding the declaration and announcement Malaba highlights as follows at page 77 of his fully dressed judgment:

---

[51] ZEC, *Zimbabwe 2018 Harmonised Elections Report*, pages 67–68.
[52] Paragraph 5.1 of Nelson Chamisa's affidavit in his Constitutional Court challenge (CCZ42/18).

Immediately after receiving all the constituency returns transmitted to him or her, the Chief Elections Officer is required to verify them, having given reasonable notice to each candidate or to his or her chief election agent of the time and place at which the returns are to be verified.

At the time and place notified for the verification of the constituency returns, and in the presence of such candidates, their chief election agents and such accredited observers as are present, the Chief Elections Officer shall display each constituency return to those present. He or she shall, upon request, allow a candidate or the chief election agent of a candidate to make notes of the contents of each constituency return.

When the Chief Elections Officer has completed the verification of the constituency returns, he or she shall, in the presence of the candidates or their chief election agents and such accredited observers as are present, add together the number of votes received by each candidate as shown in each constituency return.

After the number of votes received by each candidate as shown in each constituency return has been added together, the Chairperson of the Commission or, in his or her absence, the Deputy Chairperson or, in his or her absence, a Commissioner designated by the Chairperson shall, where there are two or more candidates, forthwith declare the candidate who has received more than half the number of votes cast to be duly elected as President of the Republic of Zimbabwe with effect from the date of such declaration.[53]

Alas, ZEC did not have, and could not have had, the required V23Bs, the presidential constituency returns. This is because the use of a different route and destination for the result of the presidential election meant that ZEC could not have the presidential constituency returns from presidential constituency centres, which ZEC systematically avoided as a destination. In fact, rather than verifying and determining the result of the presidential election using presidential constituency returns, or V23Bs, ZEC used provincial returns or V23Cs.

The collation and verification of the Presidential election results were completed on the 3rd of August 2018. The voter turnout for the 30th of July 2018 Presidential elections was *85%*. *The Chief Elections Officer who was the Returning Officer for the election completed the V23D Form which is a record of results as collated at national level.* The results were subsequently announced by the Chairperson of the Zimbabwe Electoral Commission on that same day in accordance with the provisions of the law. *A copy of the V23D Form was signed by political party agents and observers present; they were given a copy each* [emphasis added].[54]

The process described by ZEC as having been done to verify and determine the result of the presidential election declared and announced by Chigumba on 3 August 2018 was wholly illegal. The V23D form that ZEC completed as a record of results as collated at the national level was not a collation of 210 constituency returns, the V23Bs, but a collation of 10 provincial returns, known as V23C forms.

---

[53] Judgment No. CCZ 21/19, page 77.
[54] ZEC, *Zimbabwe 2018 Harmonised Elections Report*, page 72

Below is a sample of the V23C form, the provincial return:

FORM V23C (PROVINCIAL RETURN)

ELECTORAL REGULATIONS CONSOLIDATED 2018

Form V.23C
(Collation at Provincial Command Centre)

COLLATION AT PROVINCIAL COMMAND CENTRE

Section 37(C)(4)(b)(i) of the Electoral Act [*Chapter 2:13*]

Name of Province	

Collation of Presidential returns in respect of Presidential election

	Name of candidate	Name of candidate	Name of candidate	Name of candidate	Name of candidate	Name of candidate	Votes rejected
	1.	2.	3.	4.	5.	6.	
Name of constituency							
1.							
2.							
3.							
4.							
5.							
6.							
Total votes received							

Declaration by Provincial Elections Officer

I hereby certify that the above is a correct statement of the collated results Presidential constituency centres.

Full names of Provincial Elections Officer	
Signature of Provincial Elections Officer	
Date	
Name of witness	
Signature of witness	

Declaration by candidates/ election agents

I hereby confirm that this return is a correct statement of the collated results of the Presidential returns from the Presidential constituency centres.

	Name	Name of political party	Independent candidate	Designation	Date	Signature
1.						
2.						
3.						
4.						
5.						

Distribution of Presidential constituency return:

The Provincial return for the Presidential elections must be dispatched to the Chief Elections Officer at the National Command Centre.

[Form inserted by s.i 87 of 2013]

As provincial returns, V23Cs are completed and declared by Provincial Election Officers. There are 10 such returns. Once they are received by the Chief Elections Officer at the national command centre in Harare, the 10 V23C forms from the country's 10 provinces are collated and compiled at ZEC's national command centre in Harare into form V23D, which is shown below:

FORM V23D (NATIONAL COMMAND CENTRE RETURN WITH INITIAL PRESIDENTIAL ELECTION RESULT)

Electoral Regulations Consolidated 2018

ELECTORAL REGULATIONS CONSOLIDATED 2018

Form V.23D

COLLATION AT NATIONAL COMMAND CENTRE
OF RETURNS FROM PRESIDENTIAL CONSTITUENCY CENTRES

Section 110 of the Electoral Act [*Chapter 2:13*]

Collation of returns from Provincial Command centres

	Name of candidate	Name of candidate	Name of candidate	Name of candidate	Name of candidate	Name of candidate	Votes rejected
	1.	2.	3.	4.	5.	6.	
Name of province							
1.							
2.							
3.							
4.							
5.							
6.							
7.							
8.							
9.							
10.							
Total votes received							

Declaration by Chief Elections Officer

I hereby certify that the above is a correct statement of the collated results for the Presidential elections from the Provincial Command centres.

Full names of Chief Elections Officer	
Signature of Chief Elections Officer	
Date	
Name of witness	
Signature of witness	

Declaration by candidates/ election agents

I hereby confirm that this return is a correct statement of the collated results of the Presidential election.

	Name	Name of political party	Independent candidate	Designation	Date	Signature
1.						
2.						
3.						
4.						
5.						

Form substituted by s.i 87 of 2013]

Quite clearly, Form V23D is not the constituency return, or V23B, described in s110(3)(d) of the Electoral Act. In terms of s37C(4)(f)(i) of the Act, form V23D is an initial result of the presidential election, not the final result which can only be determined and verified on the basis of presidential constituency returns which are specified in s110(3) of the Act as follows:

(3) Subject to this Part, Part XIII shall apply, with any changes that may be necessary, to an election to the office of President (any references to a constituency centre or a constituency elections officer being construed as references to a presidential constituency centre or a presidential constituency elections officer respectively), other than sections 66, 67 and 68, for which the following provisions are substituted –

(a) after the number of votes received by each candidate as shown in each polling-station return has been added together in terms of section 65(3)(i) and the resulting figure added to the number of postal votes and special votes received by each candidate, the constituency elections officer shall forthwith –

(i) record on the constituency return the votes obtained by each candidate and the number of rejected ballot papers in such a manner that the results of the count for each polling station are shown on the return; and

(ii) display the completed constituency return to those present and afford each candidate or his or her election agent the opportunity to subscribe their signatures thereto; and

(iii) transmit to the Chief Elections Officer by hand through a messenger the constituency return or a copy thereof certified by the constituency elections officer to be correct;

(b) immediately after arranging for the constituency return to be transmitted in terms of paragraph (a)(iii), the constituency elections officer shall affix a copy of the constituency return on the outside the constituency centre so that it is visible to the public;

(c) immediately after receiving all the constituency returns transmitted in terms of paragraph (a)(iii), the Chief Elections Officer shall verify them, having given reasonable notice to each candidate or to his or her chief election agent of the time and place at which the returns are to be verified;

(d) at the time and place notified for the verification of the constituency returns referred to in paragraph (c) and in the presence of such candidates, their chief election agents and observers as are present, the Chief Elections Officer shall display each constituency return to those present and shall, on request, allow a candidate or chief election agent of a candidate to make notes of the contents of each constituency return;

(e) when the Chief Elections Officer has completed the verification of the constituency returns under paragraph (d) the Chief Elections Officer shall, in the presence of such persons referred to in paragraph (d) as are present, add together the number of votes received by each candidate as shown in each constituency return;

(f) subject to paragraph (h), after the number of votes received by each candidate as shown in each constituency return has been added together in terms of paragraph (e), the Chairperson of the Commission (or, in his or her absence, the Deputy Chairperson or, in his or her absence, a Commissioner designated by the Chairperson) shall –

(i)   where there are two candidates, forthwith declare the candidate who has received the greater number of votes to be duly elected as President of the Republic of Zimbabwe with effect from the day of such declaration; or

(ii) where there are more than two candidates, forthwith declare the candidate who has received more than half the number of votes to be duly elected as President of the Republic of Zimbabwe with effect from the day of such declaration; or

(iii) where there are more than two candidates, and no candidate has received more than half the number of votes, forthwith declare that a runoff presidential election shall be held on the date fixed by the President in terms of section 38(1)(a)(iii) (that is to say, a fixed date not less than twenty-eight and not more than forty-two days after the polling day or last polling day, the case may be, of the original election):

Provided that the Electoral Court, on the application of the Commission, may for good cause extend the period.

ZEC did not follow the procedure stipulated in s110(3) of the Electoral Act. Instead, ZEC invented its own verification process through which it displayed only some V11s and V23As but not the necessary V23Bs, which are the presidential constituency returns. The unimpeached evidence on this is in the affidavit by Chamisa's chief election agent, Jameson Timba, who averred in paragraphs 13 and 14 that:

> On the 1st of August 2018, I was invited by ZEC to verify *constituency returns* for the presidential election. On arrival at National Results Centre where ZEC was collating results for the presidential election on the basis of data from all ward returns, that is *Form V23a* accompanied by *polling station returns (i.e. Form V11)*, these forms were laid before me by Mr. Murenje, the ZEC Director of Elections and Training.
>
> *Mr. Murenje did not present to me the constituency return (that is Form V23B)* [emphasis added].[55]

Form V23B, which ZEC did not display and which is not mentioned in the ZEC Report on the 2018 harmonised elections, is the presidential constituency returns that must be used to verify and determine the result of the presidential election in terms of s110 of the Act. The presidential constituency return, or the V23B, is precisely the return referred to by Malaba at page 77 of his fully dressed judgment.

Given the provisions of s110(3) of the Act cited above, and given Timba's unimpeached evidence, against the backdrop of the different route and different destination that ZEC used from ward centres to collate, compile and transmit the result of the 2018 presidential election, it is abundantly clear that the Commission did not verify and determine the result of the presidential election in accordance with s110(3) of the Electoral Act, on the basis of form V23B, shown in Diagram 12.

---

[55] *See* Jameson Timba's Supporting Affidavit, pages 178–182.

FORM V23B (CONSTITUENCY RETURN FOR DETERMINING FINAL RESULT OF PRESIDENTIAL ELECTION)

ELECTORAL REGULATIONS CONSOLIDATED 2018

Form V.23B
(Presidential Constituency Centre)

COLLATION AT PRESIDENTIAL CONSTITUENCY CENTRE

Section 37(C)(4)(b)(i) of the Electoral Act [*Chapter 2:13*]

Name of constituency	
Name of Province	

Collation of ward returns in respect of Presidential election

	Name of candidate	Name of candidate	Name of candidate	Name of candidate	Name of candidate	Name of candidate	Votes rejected
	1.	2.	3.	4.	5.	6.	
Name of ward							
1.							
2.							
3.							
4.							
5.							
6.							
Total votes received							

Declaration by Presidential Constituency Officer

I hereby certify that the above is a correct statement of the collated results at Presidential constituency centre.

Full names of Presidential Constituency Elections Officer	
Signature of Presidential Constituency Officer	
Date	
Name of witness	
Signature of witness	

Declaration by candidates/ election agents

I hereby confirm that this return is a correct statement of the collated results at Presidential constituency centre.

	Name	Name of political party	Independent candidate	Designation	Date	Signature
1.						
2.						
3.						
4.						
5.						

Distribution of Presidential constituency return:

The Presidential constituency return is to be distributed as follows:
1.   Affix copy outside constituency centre.

2.   Provide copy to each election agent and observer present at polling station.

3.   Send copy to the Provincial Elections Officer.

4.   Send copy to the Chief Elections Officer.

[Form substituted by s.i 87 of 2013]

Timba's unchallenged evidence that ZEC displayed only V11s and V23As but not V23Bs is the best evidence that corroborates the effect of ZEC's use of a different route with a different destination to transmit the result of the presidential election from ward centres to the national command centre in Harare. The effect was that ZEC could not possibly have had presidential constituency returns, V23Bs, hence Timba's evidence that ZEC did not display V23Bs as required under s110(3)(d) of the Electoral Act.

It is not by accident or innocent negligence that Malaba's fully dressed judgment is embarrassingly silent about Timba's unimpeached evidence. The silence is part of the rigging system's orgy of deceit, driven by a conspiracy to rig the 2018 presidential election. The canvas of the conspiracy includes Malaba, who dismissed Chamisa's ConCourt application at the Pretoria Sheraton hotel in South Africa on the weekend of 10 August 2018, even before seeing and hearing the arguments in the case.

Equally embarrassing for Malaba is that, having delayed issuing it without any apparent good cause, his fully dressed judgment, released on 7 November 2019, did not take judicial notice of ZEC's Report on the 2018 harmonised elections tabled before Parliament by Justice Minister, Ziyambi Ziyambi, on 27 June 2019 in terms of s241 of the Constitution of Zimbabwe. Malaba had a judicial duty to familiarise himself with the constitutionally mandated report, given that it was precisely and entirely about a momentous matter that he was adjudicating over.

Had Malaba taken judicial notice of ZEC's Report, as he ought to have done, he would have realised that, by its own account in fulfilment of its constitutional obligation under s241 of the Constitution, on 31 July 2019, just hours after the conclusion of the 30 July 2019 harmonised elections and the counting of votes at polling stations and ward centres, ZEC intentionally, and therefore criminally, violated the peremptory provisions of s37C(4) of the Electoral Act by inventing a different route and different destination for the collation, compilation and transmission of the result of the 2018 presidential election. The different route and different destination were substantially contrary to the prescribed route and destination as to necessarily void the result of the presidential election announced by Priscilla Chigumba on 3 August 2019.

Had Malaba taken judicial notice of the ZEC Report, he would not have reached the conclusion at page 47 of his fully dressed judgment, or would have been at least circumspect about it:

> There was evidence of ambivalence in the applicant's mind as to the grounds on which he wanted the Court to determine the question of the validity of the Presidential election. The substance of the relief sought in para 1(i) of the order sought shows that the case the applicant was alleging, and on the proof of which the order would be granted, was the failure by the Commission to deliver free, fair and credible harmonised elections, including the Presidential election. The ground was that the harmonised elections were not conducted in accordance with the law.
>
> The applicant alleged, and would have had to prove, that the Commission through its officers had committed irregularities, or the Commission had failed to act against the commission of electoral malpractices by others where it was under the duty to act. The allegation was that as a result of the commission

of irregularities or the omission to act against the commission of electoral malpractices by others the Commission failed to deliver free, fair and credible harmonised elections. The appropriate relief upon a finding of the facts alleged by the applicant would have been a declaration of invalidity of the whole election process and the setting aside of the Presidential election result.[56]

The reason that ZEC invented a different route with a different destination for the collation, compilation and transmission of the result of the 2018 presidential election is because the rigging system had noticed from the server that the result that had been captured in the server was overwhelmingly in favour of Chamisa and against Mnangagwa; "the system" had decided to intervene to change the result before civilians could know it. Otherwise there was primary evidence, in the form of the server, that Chamisa had won the presidential election and was entitled to be declared and announced as the winner.

If Malaba had not blocked the subpoena on the server, the ConCourt would have known that Chamisa had indeed won the presidential election, and that "the system" had stolen the victory by getting ZEC to invent a new and illegal route and destination for the collation, compilation and transmission of the result of the presidential election. Having blocked the subpoena on the server, Malaba was not entitled to conclude that there was a contradiction between Chamisa's prayer to be declared by the ConCourt as the winner of the presidential election on the one hand and, on the other, his submission that the presidential election was littered with irregularities and that ZEC did not conduct it lawfully. Quite clearly, ZEC's invention of a different route and different destination to collate, compile and transmit the result of the presidential election – and everything that happened thereafter – was indeed littered with irregularities and was unlawful, such that any result declared and announced on the basis of the illegal route and destination was void. But the same cannot be said about the result that was captured in the server before the illegal route and destination were invented and followed. This is why Chamisa subpoenaed the server.

Therefore, contrary to Malaba's self-indulgent assertion in his fully dressed judgment, there was no contradiction between Chamisa's justified prayer to be declared and announced as the winner of the 2018 presidential election based on the result captured in the server and his justified submission that the invented route and destination was littered with irregularities and illegal conduct by ZEC, with the inevitable consequence of voiding any result based on the illegal route and destination.

---

[56] Judgment No. CCZ 21/19, page 47.

Chapter 4

THE V FORMS

AFTER midnight on voting day, 30 July 2018, reports and messages from election agents, polling agents and election observers had started circulating that Nelson Chamisa had defeated Emmerson Mnangagwa by a landslide. These messages were given impetus by copies of V11s that started circulating, especially on social media platforms, showing that Chamisa had done exceedingly well, even in rural constituencies.

This caused panic within "the system" at Defence House, as the chatter that Mnangagwa had lost grew in currency, based on the V11s that were circulating on social media platforms. ZEC, especially its Chairperson, Priscilla Chigumba, and military officers deployed within ZEC, came under pressure from security operatives assigned to be their gatekeepers. The pressure triggered an unprecedented hullabaloo over V11s.

To understand the hullabaloo and why it was misplaced, it is necessary to unpack the legal definition, purpose and place of the "V" Forms in the electoral process. Under the First Schedule (Section 2) of Statutory Instrument 21 of 2005 as amended [The Electoral Regulations] provides for 25 V forms, 14 of which have since been repealed, leaving 11 that were operational in the 2018 presidential election. There are four V forms that are election returns.

V11 [The polling station return]

This originates at a polling station. Form V11 contains the results of a given election, in this case, a presidential election at a polling station. V11s are sent by the polling station Election Officer to the ward collation centre. In the 2018 election, there were 10,985 polling stations. As such, there were 10,985 V11s with the result for the presidential election. As will be shown later, it is important to mention here that it would be unreasonable to expect, as did ZEC and Chief Justice Malaba, that the verification and determination of the result of the presidential election at the national command centre can rationally involve the scrutiny and confirmation of the validity of a staggering 10,985 V11s by a group of 20 or so people, over two days.[57]

Once completed in terms of the law, Form V11 is distributed as follows: One original copy is affixed outside the polling station; each candidate, or his or her election agent present at the polling station, gets an original copy, as does each observer present; another original is sealed in the ballot box; **one original copy is sent to the ward collation centre**; and only duplicate copies are sent to the presidential constituency centre; provincial command centre and national command centre.

It is notable that an original copy of Form V11 is not sent to the national command centre but to the ward collation centre. In this regard, the ZEC *Electoral Officers Manual for 2018 Harmonised Elections* provides that:

---

[57] Form V11 is outlined in the First Schedule (Section 2) of Statutory Instrument 21 of 2005, as amended in Statutory Instrument 87 of 2013. [The Electoral Regulations]

Immediately after affixing a Polling-Station Return on the outside of the polling station, the Presiding Officer must personally transmit the Polling Station Return certified by himself or herself to be correct, specific Protocol Register extractions, Voter Statistics Tally Form, HR-Attendance Register and the sealed Ballot Box to the Ward Elections Officer.[58]

V23A [The ward return]

This originates from a ward collation centre. There are 1,958 wards in Zimbabwe, meaning there were 1,958 V23As for the 2018 presidential election. A V23A contains the results of an election, in this instance, the presidential election at a ward collation centre. The V23A records the results of a presidential election from all the polling stations in a ward. **In other words, a V23A is the total of the ward's V11s.**

As such, a V23A indicates which candidate won the ward, by detailing the total votes garnered by each candidate in the ward. The V23A for the presidential election is sent to the constituency centre by the ward elections officer.

The ward elections officer collates the ward results for the presidential, national assembly and local authority elections and uses the original V11 forms for each polling station to complete entries on the V23A forms for the three elections. Notably, for each polling station in that ward there must be one corresponding original V11 Form attached to the back of the V23A Form. The ZEC *Electoral Officers Manual* directs that:

> Under no circumstances is the Ward Elections Officer permitted to complete an entry for any polling station on the V23A Form without having on hand its original V11 Form! ...
> The original V23A Forms (for the Presidential, national assembly and Local Authority) along with all of their attached *original supporting documents* should be placed in appropriately marked envelopes for onward transmission to the Constituency Elections Officer.[59] [emphasis added]

Form V23A is outlined in the Electoral Regulations and provides that, upon its completion in terms of the law, it is distributed as follows:
- A copy is displayed outside the ward collation centre;
- A copy is given to the candidate or his or her election agent;
- A copy is provided to each election agent and observer present at the ward centre;
- A copy is sealed in the ballot box;
- And copies are sent to the presidential constituency centre, the national assembly presidential constituency, the provincial command centre, and to the Chief Elections Officer at the national command centre.

V23B [The constituency return]

This is originated by a constituency centre. A V23B has the results of an election, in this case, at a constituency. The V23B contains the results of the presidential election from all the wards in

---

[58] ZEC, *Electoral Officers Manual* page 44.
[59] Ibid., page 48.

---

a constituency. Put differently, a V23B is the total of the V23As from each of the wards that make up the constituency – to wit, a V23B is the sum of V23As in a constituency. For the presidential election, the V23B form is crucially important as it is the return that is used to verify and determine the final result used to declare and announce the winner of the election in terms of s110 of the Electoral Act.

The ZEC *Electoral Officers Manual* emphatically directs that:

> The Constituency Elections Officer must verify that each and every original V23A Form has its required original V11 Forms attached. If any such forms are missing or are deemed to be copies, then these must under no circumstances be accepted!
> …
> The Constituency Elections Officer may only complete the V23B Form after receiving the original V23A Forms along with all their relevant original V11 Forms attached. Under no circumstances is the Constituency Elections Officer allowed to complete an entry for a ward's Collated Return on the V23B Constituency Collation Form if he/she does not have the original V23A Form (along with ALL the relevant original V11 Forms) in his/her possession! The key thing to note here is that original Forms are required at every step in the process!

> After all the results of every Ward in that Constituency have been captured, only then are the Ward entries on the V23B Form deemed to be complete. The totals must be summed up thereafter, double-checked. Once that is done all that remains is for the Constituency Elections Officer and the relevant stakeholders to sign the V23B Form.

> The V23B Form is complete when it contains all the collated results for all the Wards in that Constituency. The relevant stakeholders (if present) must be requested to sign the completed V23B Form. Remember that at the back of every V23B Form, all the original V23A Forms with every one of their original V11 Forms must be attached.

> It is a serious violation of the prescribed results aggregation procedures if any original V23A or its V11 Forms are missing for any of the captured Ward entries on the V23B Form!
> …
> Note that the winner of the Presidential Election is not announced at the Constituency Command Centre – instead, the winner of the Presidential Election will only be announced later on at ZEC Head Office by the Chief Elections Officer.[60]

Zimbabwe has 210 constituencies. This means there are 210 V23Bs that contain the result of the presidential election. As will be demonstrated later, the verification and determination of the presidential election, in terms of s110 (3)(d) of the Electoral Act, is exclusively based on the V23B Form, the **constituency return**. EXCELGATE is about ZEC's total and deliberate failure to uphold the peremptory requirements of s110(3)(d) of the Electoral Act. Certified copies of V23Bs are sent by the Constituency Election Officer to the provincial command centre and to the national command centre.

---

[60] Ibid., pages 49–50.

Form V23B is the all-important presidential constituency return, referred to under s110(3)(d) of the Electoral Act, regarding the verification and determination of the result of the presidential election.

Once completed in terms of the law, Form V23B is distributed as follows:
- A copy is affixed outside the presidential constituency centre.
- The election agent and observer present at the presidential constituency centre is given a copy.
- And copies are sent to the Provincial Elections Officer at the provincial command centre and to the Chief Elections Officer at the national command centre.

V23C [The provincial return]

This originates from a provincial command centre. For the presidential election, a V23C has the total of the result of the presidential election of the constituencies in the province. Therefore, a V23C contains the total of the province's V23Bs. There are 10 V23C forms, given that Zimbabwe has 10 provinces. The V23Cs are used by the national command centre to determine the preliminary or initial result of the presidential election. V23Cs are sent by the Provincial Election Officer to the national command centre.

Upon its completion in terms of the law, Form V23C must be dispatched to the Chief Elections Officer at the national command centre.

V23D [The National Command Centre Return]

This return originates from the national command centre. Form V23D is a record of the total of the V23C Forms from the 10 provincial command centres. As already mentioned, the result of the presidential election in Form V23D is the **initial result of the presidential election** in terms of s37C(4)(f)(i) of the Electoral Act which provides that:

> the provincial returns (Form V23Cs) shall be collated to *obtain the initial results of the presidential election.*

Section 37C(4)(f)(ii) makes it abundantly clear that:

> **The final result of the presidential election shall, after reconciling the provincial returns with the polling station returns and presidential constituency returns referred in the provisos to paragraphs (b) and (d) respectively, be reflected in a return that distinctly reflects number of votes cast for each presidential candidate at every polling station, ward centre, presidential constituency centre and provincial command centre.**

The final result of the presidential election is and verified and determined in terms of s110(3)(d) of the Electoral Act, based on the presidential constituency return, Form V23B, which is the only return that distinctly reflects the number of votes cast for each presidential candidate at every polling station, ward centre, presidential constituency centre.

The Legal Framework of the V Forms

The Electoral Act provides for the V Forms, outlined above, under s64 [*V11 at polling stations*]; s65 [*V23A at ward collation centres*]; s66A [*V23B at constituency centres*] and s65B [*V23C at provincial command centres*] as follows:

V11 Form

s64   **Procedure after counting at polling station**

(1)   After the counting is completed the presiding officer shall without delay, in the presence of such candidates and their election agents as are present –

(a)   close and seal the aperture in the ballot box; and

(b)   make up into separate packets sealed with his or her own seal and with the seals of those candidates and election agents, if any, who desire to affix their seals –

(i)   the unused and spoilt ballot papers and counterfoils of the unused ballot papers placed together;

(ii)   the counterfoils of the used ballot papers, including the counterfoils of the spoilt ballot papers;

(iii) the register of assisted voters;

[Subparagraph amended by s. 29 of Act No. 6 of 2014]

(c)   record on the **polling-station return** the votes obtained by each candidate and the number of rejected ballot papers in such a manner that the results of the count for each ballot box are shown on the return; and

(d)   display the completed **polling-station return** to those present and afford each candidate or his or her election agent the opportunity to subscribe their signatures thereto; and

[Paragraph amended by s. 29 of Act No. 6 of 2014]

(d1) provide each candidate or his or her election agent with a copy of the completed **polling-station return**; and

[Paragraph inserted by s. 20 of Act No. 3 of 2012 and amended by s. 29 of Act No. 6 of 2014]

(e)   affix a copy of the **polling-station return** on the outside of the polling station so that it is visible to the public and shall ensure that it remains there so that all members of the public who wish to do so may inspect it and record its contents.

[Paragraph amended by s. 29 of Act No. 6 of 2014]

(2)   Immediately after affixing a **polling station return** on the outside of the polling station in terms of subsection (1)(e), the presiding officer shall personally transmit to the ward elections officer for the ward in which the polling station is situated –

(a)   the ballot box and packets referred to in subsection (1)(a) and (b), accompanied by a statement made by the presiding officer showing the number of ballot papers entrusted to him or her and accounting for them under the heads of used ballot papers, excluding spoilt ballot papers, unused ballot papers and spoilt ballot papers; and

(b) the **polling-station return** certified by himself or herself to be correct:

Provided that if, by reason of death, injury or illness, the presiding officer is unable personally to transmit the ballot box, packets, statement and polling station return under this subsection, a polling officer who was on duty at the polling station shall personally transmit these, and in that event any statement or certification required to be made by the presiding officer for the purposes of this section may be made by the polling officer concerned.

[Section as substituted by s. 46 of Act No. 17 of 2007 and amended by s. 29 of Act No. 6 of 2014]

V23A Form

s65   Procedure on receipt of polling-station returns at ward centre

(1)   Either before or as soon as possible after receiving **polling-station returns** transmitted in terms of section 64, a ward elections officer shall give reasonable notice in writing to –
(a) each candidate or his or her chief election agent; and
(b) each political party whose party-list candidates are contesting the election in the ward; and
(c) such observers as can readily be contacted;
of the time when the ward elections officer **will verify and collate the polling-station returns at the ward centre** and count the postal votes.

(2)   At the time notified in terms of subsection (1) and in the presence of such candidates, election agents and observers as are present, the ward elections officer shall –
(a) display each **polling-station return** to those present; and
(b) verify each **polling-station return** by ensuring that it purports to be duly certified by the presiding officer of the polling station concerned; and
(c) on request, allow any candidate, election agent or observer to make notes of the contents of any **polling-station return**.

(3)   When the ward elections officer **has displayed and verified the polling-station returns in terms of subsection (2)**, he or she shall add together the number of votes received by each candidate as shown in each **polling-station return** and record the result on a ward return.

(4)   Having recorded the results of **the polling-station returns** in terms of subsection (3), the ward elections officer, in the presence of such candidates, election agents and observers as are present, shall –
(a) verify the postal ballots in accordance with sections 78, if they have not already been verified; and
(b) count the postal votes and record separately on the ward return the number of such votes received by each candidate; and
(c) enter on the **ward return** the total number of votes received by each candidate, including postal votes; and
(d) close and seal the aperture in the postal ballot box.

(5)   Section 63 shall apply, with any necessary changes, to the counting of the postal votes in terms of subsection (4)(b).

(6) The ward elections officer shall –

    (a) provide a copy of the completed **ward return** to every candidate, election agent and observer who requests one; and

    (b) ensure that a copy of the **ward return** is displayed prominently outside the ward centre so that all members of the public who wish to do so may inspect it and record its contents.

(7) Immediately after causing a copy of the **ward return** to be displayed outside the ward centre, the ward elections officer shall cause **the return**, certified by himself or herself to be correct, to be transmitted to the constituency centre for the constituency in which the ward is situated.

        [Section substituted by s. 30 of Act No. 6 of 2014]

V23B Form

65A Procedure on receipt of ward returns at constituency centre

(1) Either before, or as soon as possible after, receiving ward returns transmitted in terms of section 65, a constituency elections officer shall give reasonable notice in writing to –

    (a) each candidate or his or her chief election agent; and

    (b) each political party whose party-list candidates are contesting the election in the constituency; and

    (c) such observers as can readily be contacted;

    of the time when the constituency elections officer will verify and collate the ward returns at the constituency centre and declare the results of the constituency election.

(2) At the time notified in terms of subsection (1) and in the presence of such candidates, election agents and observers as are present, the constituency elections officer shall –

    (a) display each **ward return** to those present; and

    (b) verify each **ward return** by ensuring that it purports to be duly certified by the ward elections officer concerned; and

    (c) on request, allow any candidate, election agent or observer to make notes of the contents of any **ward return**.

(3) When the **constituency elections officer has displayed and verified the ward returns** in terms of subsection (2), he or she shall add together the number of votes received by each candidate as shown in each **ward return** and –

    (a) record the totals on a **constituency return**; and

    (b) in terms of section 66, declare the result of the election in the constituency.

(4) The constituency elections officer shall –

    (a) provide a copy of the completed **constituency return** to every candidate, election agent and observer who requests one; and

    (b) ensure that a copy of the **constituency return** is displayed prominently outside the constituency centre so that all members of the public who wish to do so may inspect it and record its contents.

(5) Immediately after causing a copy of the **constituency return** to be displayed outside the constituency centre, the constituency elections officer shall cause the return, certified by himself or herself to be correct, to be transmitted to the provincial command centre for the province in which the constituency is situated.

        [Section inserted by s. 22 of Act No. 3 of 2012 and substituted by s. 30 of Act No. 6 of 2014]

V23C Form

65B Procedure on receipt of constituency returns at provincial command centre

(1)   Either before, or as soon as possible after, receiving constituency returns transmitted in terms of section 65A, a provincial elections officer shall give reasonable notice in writing to –

(a) each candidate or his or her chief election agent; and

(b) each political party whose party-list candidates are contesting the election in the province; and

(c) such observers as can readily be contacted;

of the time when the **provincial elections officer will verify and collate the constituency returns at the provincial command** centre and declare which of the party-list candidates have been duly elected for the province.

(2)   At the time notified in terms of subsection (1) and in the presence of such candidates, election agents and observers as are present, the provincial elections officer shall –

(a) display each **constituency return** to those present; and

(b) verify each **constituency return** by ensuring that it purports to be duly certified by the constituency elections officer concerned; and

(c) on request, allow any candidate, election agent or observer to make notes of the contents of any **constituency return**.

(3)   When the **provincial elections officer has displayed and verified the constituency returns** in terms of subsection (2), he or she shall add together the number of votes received by each candidate as shown in each constituency return and –

(a) record the totals on a **provincial return**; and

(b) ascertain, in accordance with section 45J and the Eighth Schedule, the party-list candidates who are to be declared duly elected in terms of that section.

(4)   The provincial elections officer shall –

(a) provide a copy of the completed **provincial return** to every candidate, election agent and observer who requests one; and

(b) ensure that a copy of the **provincial return** is displayed prominently outside the constituency centre so that all members of the public who wish to do so may inspect it and record its contents.

(5)   Immediately after causing a copy of the **provincial return** to be displayed outside the provincial command centre, the provincial elections officer shall cause the **return**, certified by himself or herself to be correct, to be transmitted to the national command centre.

[Section inserted by s. 30 of Act No. 6 of 2014]

From the above description of the legal procedure for the counting and verification of votes at polling stations, ward collation centres, constituency centres and provincial command centres, two key issues standout.

First, is that a V11 is legally a **polling station return**, a V23A is a **ward return**, a V23B a **constituency return**, a V23C a **provincial return** and a V23D a **national command centre return**.

Second, and this is very important to keep in mind in relation to the collation, compilation and transmission of the result for the presidential election which ZEC violated in the 2018 harmonised election, V11s from 10,985 polling stations are collated and verified at 1,958 ward collation centres. The result of that collation and verification is contained in 1,958 V23As that are collated and verified at 210 constituency centres and the results are recorded in 210 V23Bs. The 210 V23Bs are collated and verified at 10 provincial command centres, and the results recorded in 10 V23Cs. In turn, the 10 V23Cs are collated and verified at the national command centre and recorded in a V23D Form, which contains only the initial result of the presidential election.

Critically, these Electoral Act procedures are detailed in s64 regarding V11s; s65 on V23As; s66A about V23Bs, and s65B concerning V23Cs; they should be read with s37C(4)(a) and (b) and s37(4)(d) which have important provisos. Section 37C (4)(a) and (b) stipulates that:

(4)   The Commission shall ensure that the results of the presidential, national assembly and local authority elections are collated, compiled and transmitted in the following manner—

   (a)   with respect to local authority elections, polling-station returns gathered from every polling station within a ward shall be transmitted to the appropriate ward centre in a return distinctly indicating the results obtained in each polling station relating to those elections;

   (b)   with respect to—

      (i)   presidential elections, polling-station returns gathered from every polling station within a ward shall be transmitted to the appropriate ward centre for collation at that centre, the results of which collation shall be embodied in a return ("presidential election ward return") distinctly indicating the results obtained in each polling station relating to that election; and

      (ii)   national assembly elections, polling-station returns gathered from every polling station within a ward shall be transmitted to the appropriate ward centre for collation at that centre, the results of which collation shall be embodied in a return ("national assembly election ward return") distinctly indicating the results obtained in each polling station relating to those elections:

      Provided that duplicate copies of the polling-station returns gathered from every polling station within a ward for the purposes of subparagraph (i) and (ii) shall also be transmitted through the appropriate ward centre directly to the national command centre.

The proviso of s37C(4) means that each of the 1,958 ward centres sends directly to ZEC's national command centre duplicate copies of every polling station return (V11 Form) containing the respective results of the presidential election and the national assembly election to the national command centre. This is even before the return reaches the ward collation centre where the polling station returns (V11s) are collated and verified. This is very important to understand, as it shows that the national command centre receives the result of the presidential election and the national assembly election virtually in real time, based on polling station returns (V11s) in advance of their collation and verification at ward centres.

Section 37C (4)(d) provides that:

> …gathered from every presidential constituency centre shall be transmitted to the provincial command centre for collation at that centre, the results of which collation shall be embodied in a return ("provincial return for the presidential election") distinctly indicating the results obtained in each constituency relating to those elections.

> Provided that duplicate copies of the presidential constituency returns gathered from every presidential constituency centre shall also be transmitted directly from the provincial command centre concerned to the national command centre.

The proviso under s37C(4)(d) means that the Constituency Election Officer directly sends to the national command centre only **duplicate copies** of the presidential constituency return (V23B) Form. This is done in advance of sending the certified copy of the presidential constituency return (V23B) that is used for collation and verification of the result of the presidential election in terms of s110(3)(d) of the Electoral Act.

Chapter 5

TRANSMISSION OF HARMONISED ELECTION RESULTS

WHEN it comes to the integrity of the collation, compilation and aggregation of the results of the local government, parliamentary and presidential elections that define Zimbabwe's harmonised general election, what matters the most is how the results are transmitted to and between electoral centres. The best way of putting this is that, in order to ensure the integrity and credibility of the results, transmission is everything. For this reason, the route and destination of the transmission are prescribed by electoral law.

ZEC is not at liberty to transmit the result of any of the three elections in any way it may choose to. The route by which the results of the elections must be transmitted, and the destination for the transmission, are provided in peremptory language under s37C of the Electoral Act.

At the core of the rigging of the result of the 2018 presidential election is the established fact that, under the command of the military, ZEC invented a different route and different destination for the collation, compilation and transmission of the result of the presidential election from ward centres to the national command centre in Harare, via district election offices. This fact is admitted by ZEC in its official Report on the 2018 harmonised elections tabled in Parliament on 27 June 2019, in accordance with s241 of the Constitution of Zimbabwe, and posted on the ZEC website on 15 August 2019. In the Report, ZEC announces that:

> **4.6.2 Presidential and National Assembly Returns**
> **Results for the presidential and the National Assembly elections were transmitted using different routes from the ward collation centre.** *While the destination for the National Assembly election results was the constituency centre, the Presidential results were forwarded to the district centre for onward transmission to the National Command Centre in Harare.* **Verification was done at each point by checking the accuracy of every collation return and whether it was properly completed If not, corrections would be effected by use of polling station source documents (V11s)** [emphasis added].[61]

ZEC did not have the power or authority to use "different routes from the ward collation centre" for the transmission of the results for the presidential and national assembly elections, each with its own destination. This was in blatant violation of the mandatory transmission of the results for the presidential and national assembly elections that has one route and one destination for both elections. The one route and one destination for the transmission of the results for the presidential and national assembly elections is detailed in 37C of the Electoral Act, as reproduced below, with emphasis added to illustrate the important point:

---

[61] ZEC, *Zimbabwe 2018 Harmonised Elections Report*, page 67

37C Electoral centres and transmission of results to and between electoral centres

   (1) The Commission shall designate a place –

      (a) to be the national command centre from which it controls all elections conducted in terms of this Act;

         (i) a presidential election conducted within the province; or

         (ii) an election of party-list members of Parliament conducted within the province; or

         (iii) an election of members of the provincial council established for the province;

      (c) within each constituency, to be the presidential constituency centre for the purposes of a presidential election conducted within the province;

      (d) within each constituency, to be the constituency centre for the purposes of an election of members of the national assembly conducted in the constituency;

      (e) within each ward, to be the ward centre for the purpose of an election of councillors to the local authority concerned.

           [Subsection substituted by s. 12 of Act No. 6 of 2014]

   (2) The Commission may designate the same place to be a constituency centre, a district centre, a ward centre and additionally, or alternatively, a presidential constituency centre.

           [Subsection amended by s. 12 of Act No. 6 of 2014]

   (3) The Commission may designate its head office or any other place to be the national command centre.

   (4) The Commission shall ensure that the results of the presidential, national assembly and local authority elections are collated, compiled and transmitted in the following manner –

      (a) with respect to local authority elections, polling-station returns gathered from every polling station within a ward shall be transmitted to the appropriate ward centre in a return distinctly indicating the results obtained in each polling station relating to those elections;

      (b) with respect to –

         (i) **presidential elections, polling-station returns gathered from every polling station within a ward shall be transmitted to the appropriate ward centre for collation at that centre, the results of which collation shall be embodied in a return ("presidential election ward return")** distinctly indicating the results obtained in each polling station relating to that election; and

         (ii) national assembly elections, polling-station returns gathered from every polling station within a ward shall be transmitted to the appropriate ward centre for collation at that centre, the results of which collation shall be embodied in a return ("national assembly election ward return") distinctly indicating the results obtained in each polling station relating to those elections:

           Provided that duplicate copies of the polling-station returns gathered from every polling station within a ward for the purposes of subparagraph (i) and (ii) shall also be transmitted through the appropriate ward centre directly to the national command centre; and

(c) after collation of the results of –
  (i) **presidential election at each ward centre, presidential election ward returns gathered from every ward centre within a constituency shall be transmitted to the appropriate presidential constituency centre for collation at that centre, the results of which collation shall be embodied in a return ("presidential constituency return")** distinctly indicating the results obtained in each ward within that constituency relating to that election;
  (ii) national assembly elections at each ward centre, national assembly election ward returns gathered from every ward centre within a constituency shall be transmitted to the appropriate national assembly constituency centre for collation at that centre, the results of which collation shall be embodied in a return ("national assembly constituency return") distinctly indicating the results obtained in each ward within that constituency relating to those elections; and

(d) after collation of **the results of the presidential election at each presidential constituency centre, presidential constituency returns gathered from every presidential constituency centre shall be transmitted to the provincial command centre for collation at that centre,** the results of which collation shall be embodied in a return ("provincial return for the presidential election") distinctly indicating the results obtained in each constituency relating to those elections;

  Provided that duplicate copies of the presidential constituency returns gathered from every presidential constituency centre shall also be transmitted directly from the provincial command centre concerned to the national command centre; and

(e) after collation of the results of the national assembly elections at each national assembly constituency centre, national assembly constituency returns gathered from every national assembly constituency centre shall be transmitted to the provincial command centre, where –
  (i) the result of the national assembly election in the province in question will be embodied in a return ("provincial return for the national assembly elections") distinctly indicating the results obtained in each constituency relating to those elections; and
  (ii) the results of the election for the party-list candidates for the province in question will be determined in accordance with section 45I on the basis of the provincial return for the national assembly elections, and be embodied in return ("provincial return for elections of party-list candidates") distinctly indicating the results obtained for the Senate, national assembly and provincial council party-list seats; and

(f) after the collation of **the results of the presidential election at each provincial command centre, provincial returns for the presidential election gathered from every provincial command centre shall be transmitted to the national command centre,** where –
  (i) **the provincial returns shall be collated to obtain the initial results of the presidential election; and**
  (ii) **the final result of the presidential election shall, after reconciling the provincial returns with the polling station returns and presidential constituency returns referred to in the provisos to paragraphs (b) and (d) respectively, be reflected in a return that distinctly reflects number of votes**

> cast for each presidential candidate at every polling station, ward centre, presidential constituency centre and provincial command centre; and
>
> (g) after the compilation of the provincial return for the national assembly elections and the provincial return for elections of party-list candidates at each provincial command centre, the provincial returns for the national assembly elections and elections of party-list candidates shall be gathered from every provincial command centre and transmitted to the national command centre.
>
> [Subsection substituted by s. 12 of Act No. 12 of 2014]
> [Section inserted by s. 10 of Act No. 3 of 2012]
> [Part VIIIA inserted by s. 28 of Act No. 17 of 2007]

The mandatory transmission route and destination of the results for both the Presidential and National Assembly elections is reflected in **Diagram 13**:

DIAGRAM 13

MANDATORY ROUTE & DESTINATION FOR TRANSMITTING PRESIDENTIAL ELECTION RESULTS IN TERMS OF S37C(4) OF THE ELECTORAL ACT

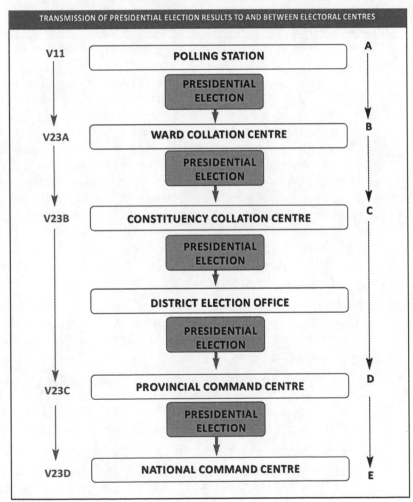

To fully appreciate the total import of ZEC's violation of the prescribed transmission route and destination of the 2018 result for the presidential election, it is necessary to read s37C of the Electoral Act with s110 which deals with "the determination and declaration of the result of election to office of President".

110   Determination and declaration of result of election to office of President

(1)   Where only one candidate for President is validly nominated at the close of the day on which a nomination court sits in terms of section 38(1)(a), the Chairperson of the Commission (or, in his or her absence, the Deputy Chairperson or, in his or her absence, a Commissioner designated by the Chairperson) shall declare such candidate to be duly elected as President without the necessity of a poll.

[Subsection amended by s. 39 of Act No. 6 of 2014]

(2)   Where two or more candidates for President are validly nominated, a poll shall be taken in each constituency for the election of a President.

(3)   Subject to this Part, Part XIII shall apply, with any changes that may be necessary, to an election to the office of President (any references to a constituency centre or a constituency elections officer being construed as references to a presidential constituency centre or a presidential constituency elections officer respectively), other than sections 66, 67 and 68, for which the following provisions are substituted –

(a)   after the number of votes received by each candidate as shown in each polling-station return has been added together in terms of section 65(3)(i) and the resulting figure added to the number of postal votes and special votes received by each candidate, the constituency elections officer shall forthwith –

(i)   record on the constituency return the votes obtained by each candidate and the number of rejected ballot papers in such a manner that the results of the count for each polling station are shown on the return; and

(ii)   display the completed constituency return to those present and afford each candidate or his or her election agent the opportunity to subscribe their signatures thereto; and

(iii)   transmit to the Chief Elections Officer by hand through a messenger the constituency return or a copy thereof certified by the constituency elections officer to be correct;

(b)   **immediately after arranging for the constituency return to be transmitted in terms of paragraph (a)(iii), the constituency elections officer** shall affix a copy of the constituency return on the outside the constituency centre so that it is visible to the public;

(c)   **immediately after receiving all the constituency returns** transmitted in terms of paragraph (a)(iii), the Chief Elections Officer shall verify them, having given reasonable notice to each candidate or to his or her chief election agent of the time and place at which the returns are to be verified;

(d)   **at the time and place notified for the verification of the constituency returns** referred to in paragraph (c) and in the presence of such candidates, their chief election agents and observers as are present, the Chief Elections Officer shall **display each constituency return to those present and shall, on request, allow a candidate or chief election agent of a candidate to make notes of the contents of each constituency return;**

(e) when the Chief Elections Officer has completed **the verification of the constituency returns** under paragraph (d) the Chief Elections Officer shall, in the presence of such persons referred to in paragraph (d) as are present, **add together the number of votes received by each candidate as shown in each constituency return;**

(f) subject to paragraph (h), **after the number of votes received by each candidate as shown in each constituency return has been added together in terms of paragraph (e), the Chairperson of the Commission (or, in his or her absence, the Deputy Chairperson or, in his or her absence, a Commissioner designated by the Chairperson) shall –**

   (i) **where there are two candidates, forthwith declare the candidate who has received the greater number of votes to be duly elected as President of the Republic of Zimbabwe with effect from the day of such declaration; or**

   (ii) where there are more than two candidates, forthwith declare the candidate who has received more than half the number of votes to be duly elected as President of the Republic of Zimbabwe with effect from the day of such declaration; or

   (iii) where there are more than two candidates, and no candidate has received more than half the number of votes, forthwith declare that a runoff presidential election shall be held on the date fixed by the President in terms of section 38(1)(a)(iii) (that is to say, a fixed date not less than twenty-eight and not more than forty-two days after the polling day or last polling day, the case may be, of the original election):

   Provided that the Electoral Court, on the application of the Commission, may for good cause extend the period;
   [Paragraph amended by s. 39 of Act No. 6 of 2014]

(g) subject to this section, if a runoff presidential election is required to be held –

   (i) only the two candidates who received the highest and next highest numbers of valid votes cast at the previous election shall be eligible to contest the election; and

   (ii) the election shall be held in accordance with this Act or, in case any situation arises that may be peculiar to such election, in the manner prescribed;

   (iii) after the number of votes received by each candidate at a presidential runoff election as shown in each constituency return has been added together in terms of paragraph (e), the Chairperson of the Commission (or, in his or her absence, the Deputy Chairperson or, in his or her absence, a Commissioner designated by the Chairperson) shall forthwith declare the candidate who has received the greater number of votes to be duly elected as President of the Republic of Zimbabwe with effect from the day of such declaration:

Provided that if the two candidates receive an equal number of votes, Parliament shall, as soon as practicable after the declaration of the result of that election, meet as an electoral college and elect one of the two candidates as President by secret ballot and without prior debate;

[Subparagraph amended by s. 39 of Act No. 6 of 2014]

(h) a declaration by the Chairperson of the Commission (or, in his or her absence, the Deputy Chairperson or, in his or her absence, a Commissioner designated by the Chairperson) under paragraph (f) or (g)(iii) shall be made not later than –

(i) five days after the polling day or last polling day, as the case may be, in the presidential election or runoff presidential election concerned; or

(ii) where a recount has been ordered in terms of section 67A, five days after the completion of the recount:

Provided that the Electoral Court may, on application by the Commission, for good cause extend the ten-day period;

[Paragraph amended by s. 39 of Act No. 6 of 2014]

(i) a declaration by the Chairperson of the Commission (or, in his or her absence, the Deputy Chairperson or, in his or her absence, a Commissioner designated by the Chairperson) under paragraph (h) [shall] be final, subject to reversal on petition to the Electoral Court that such declaration be set aside or to the proceedings relating to that election being declared void;

[Paragraph amended by s. 39 of Act No. 6 of 2014]

(j) the Chairperson of the Commission (or, in his or her absence, the Deputy Chairperson or, in his or her absence, a Commissioner designated by the Chairperson) shall as soon as possible after he or she has declared the result of an election to the office of President in terms of paragraph (i), publish such result by notice in the *Gazette* and in such other manner as he or she considers necessary to give sufficient publicity to the result, which notice shall also, in the event that the candidate in question has obtained more than half of the votes at the election, give the full name of the person duly elected as President of the Republic of Zimbabwe and the day with effect from which he or she was so elected.

[Paragraph amended by s. 39 of Act No. 6 of 2014]

(4) Subject to this Part, Parts XIV, XIVA and XV, shall apply, with any changes that may be necessary, to an election to the office of President, any references to a constituency centre or a constituency elections officer being construed as references to a presidential constituency centre or a presidential constituency elections officer respectively.

(5) In accordance with section 94 of the Constitution, a person elected as President assumes office when he or she takes, before the Chief Justice or the next most senior judge available, the oath of President in the form set out in the Third Schedule to the Constitution.

[Subsection substituted by Part VI of Schedule to Act No. 3 of 2016]

[Section substituted by s. 29 of Act No. 3 of 2012]

Crucially important to note is that s110 is about constituency returns, the V23Bs. **Diagram 14** depicts the link between s37c and s110 of the electoral Act:

DIAGRAM 14

TRANSMISSION & DETERMINATION OF THE RESULT FOR THE PRESIDENTIAL ELECTION GIVEN SECTIONS 37C & 110 OF THE ELECTORAL ACT

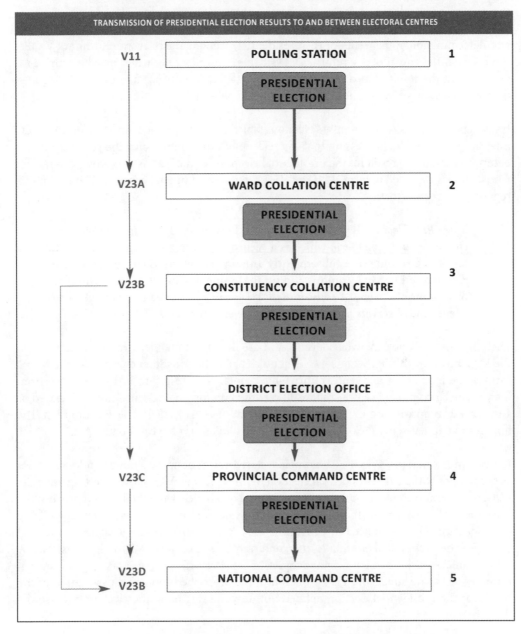

It is clear that the determination of the result for the presidential election, transmitted through one and the same route and destination as the parliamentary election under s37C of the Electoral Act, is verified and determined in terms of s110 of the Act. Section 110(3)(a)(iii) provides that the Constituency Elections Officer shall:

transmit to the Chief Elections Officer by hand through a messenger the constituency return or a copy thereof certified by the constituency elections officer to be correct.

Important to note in this regard is the fact that the only relevant election return for this purpose is the constituency return, that is to say Form V23B. It is important to underscore this, given the misplaced deafening cacophony about V11s made by ZEC and Chief Justice Malaba during Chamisa's ConCourt case. V11s are not the relevant returns in the verification and determination of the result for the presidential election. The relevant returns are V23Bs, the presidential constituency returns. V11s come into play only when or where there's a query about the result of a particular V23B. The aggregation procedure of V23Bs requires that original copies of V11s and V23As be attached behind each V23B.

In its Report on the 2018 harmonised elections tabled before Parliament on 27 June 2019, ZEC misleadingly gives the impression that the relevant election returns for the verification and determination of the result for the presidential election are the V23Cs, the provincial return, whose total is recorded in form V23D, at ZEC's national command centre in Harare. In this regard, ZEC reports that:

> *The Chief Elections Officer who was the Returning Officer for the election completed the V23D form* which is a record of results as collated at national level. The results were subsequently announced by the Chairperson of the Zimbabwe Electoral Commission on that same day in accordance with the provisions of the law. *A copy of the V23D form* was signed by political party agents and observers present; they were given a copy each.[62]

There is absolutely nothing whatsoever anywhere in s110 of the Electoral Act that refers to the V23D form. Nothing. Section 110 is about V23Bs, the constituency returns. The V23D form is a national command centre return which contains the results recorded on V23Cs from the provincial command centre. The result recorded on form V23D must not be declared or announced because it is only an initial result in terms of s37C(4)(f)(i) of the Electoral Act. The final result stipulated in s37C(4)(f)(ii) is determined in terms of s110(3) of the Act.

It is common cause that Priscilla Chigumba declared and announced Emmerson Mnangagwa as the winner of the 2018 presidential election on the basis of a V23D form. Putting aside the fact the declaration and announcement were based on an illegal and thus invalid process, the use of from V23D to declare the final result of the presidential election was itself unlawful. The result declared and announced by Chigumba on 3 August 2018 had no legal basis. The final result for the presidential election is only, and only, based on form V23B, the constituency return, on the back of which original copies of ward returns (V23As) and polling station returns (V11s) are attached. ZEC's violation of the prescribed route and destination of the result for the presidential election defined not only the rigging of the election but also the theft thereof.

---

[62] ZEC, *Zimbabwe 2018 Harmonised Elections Report*, page 72.

Chapter 6

SEVERING THE SERVER

AFTER midnight on voting day, 30 July 2018, widespread chatter that Nelson Chamisa had won the presidential election, and that ZANU PF parliamentary candidates were doing better than Mnangagwa, started spreading on social media platforms like a veld fire. The sources of this chatter were election agents, polling officers, election observers, police, CIO and army security details deployed at polling stations. Some of these sources circulated copies of V11s that showed Chamisa winning with huge margins at various polling stations across the country.

Unknown to the public is the fact that, at the same time (around midnight or so), the ZEC national command centre in Harare was also receiving **duplicate copies** of both the presidential election and the parliamentary election results from all the country's 10,985 polling stations.[63] Although this critical purpose is provided under s37C (4) of the Electoral Act, it is done by ZEC officials without being observed by election candidates or election agents or election observers. In other words, there is no transparency of the transmission by ward centres of duplicate copies of V11s with the results of the presidential election and national assembly election in the ward to the national command centre in Harare.

The question is, how are these 21,970 V11s (10,985 for the presidential election and another 10,985 for the national assembly election), transmitted to the national command centre in Harare? Could it be by both electronic and physical means?

ZEC and Chigumba maintained under oath that the result of the presidential election is by law transmitted only by physical means. Chief Justice Malaba agreed with them in his 137-page "fully dressed" judgment released on 7 November 2019, writing at page 101:

> *In Zimbabwe the counting and transmission of the results is wholly manual.*
> The process involves counting of all the ballots at the polling station in the
> presence of election agents of candidates who participated in the election. A
> polling station return, the V11 Form, is completed and countersigned by the
> election agents [emphasis added].[64]

But the submission by ZEC and Chigumba was a deliberate falsehood with no basis in fact or law. The falsehood was intentionally designed to hide the server in order to facilitate the massive rigging of the 2018 presidential election, which involved the hijacking of its result recorded in V11s and V23As from all ward centres and taken to ZEC's national command centre in Harare where the result was mixed with other V11s and V23As and input into an Excel spreadsheet to generate a result that could not possibly be legally valid. It is scandalous that Malaba associated himself with the falsehood that in Zimbabwe the counting and transmission of election results is wholly manual.

---

[63] And, in fact, unknown to election candidates, their agents, election observers and the media.
[64] Judgment No. CCZ 21/19, page 101.

The correct legal position is that Electoral law in Zimbabwe does indeed allow for election results to be transmitted electronically to the national command centre in Harare. It would be irrational for the transmission to be "wholly manual", as falsely claimed by Malaba in his "fully dressed" judgment.

To begin with, s67(1) and (2) of the Electoral Act, which deal with the "notification of result of election" provide that:

67 Notification of result of election

(1) As soon as the constituency elections officer has declared a candidate to be duly elected, he or she shall, without delay, notify the Chief Elections Officer, **by telegram, telefacsimile, electronic mail or such other means as may be prescribed**, of the names of the person declared duly elected, the day with effect from which he or she was declared elected, the number of votes received by the respective candidates and the number of rejected ballot papers.
[Subsection amended by s. 24 of Act No. 3 of 2012]

(2) The information referred to in subsection (1) **shall be confirmed by notice in writing** which is signed by the constituency elections officer and sent to the Chief Elections Officer by the first postal delivery after he or she was notified of the information in terms of subsection (1).
[Subsection amended by s. 24 of Act No. 3 of 2012]

Specifically, and as outlined in Chapter 3, contrary to the claims made by ZEC and Chigumba before the Constitutional Court, which were unsurprisingly endorsed by Chief Justice Malaba, Electoral Regulations made by ZEC in terms of the Electoral Act, which were confirmed and published by ZEC on 8 June 2018, **there is a provision for the transmission of the result of the presidential election to the national command centre by telegram, telefacsimile or electronic mail using Forms V16 and V18.** Form V16 is used for the electronic notification of the result of the presidential election, and Form V18 gives the breakdown of the result, in terms of the Electoral Regulations.[65] This puts paid to the claim by ZEC and Malaba that in Zimbabwe the transmission of election results "is wholly manual".

Considering the foregoing, and as ZEC sought to contain the wave of V11s on social media platforms that showed a huge win by Chamisa, the ZEC Commissioner who served as the body's spokesperson, Qhubani Moyo, said the following on 31 July 2018:

> **In the morning we were seeing certain trends that were trending on social media regarding how the elections have, you know, been progressing and who has won. But the actual results that we have received so far indicate a different trend altogether. The presidential election results are collated separately in their own V11 form, and they need to go to the wards and then the wards are the ones that are supposed to bring them here [to the national command centre]**

---

[65] See Statutory Instrument 21 of 2005, Electoral Regulations, 2005, SIs 21/2005, 182/2006, 13/2008, 32/2008, 44/2008, 82A/2008, 94/2008, 153/2009, 26A/2013, 68/2013, 69/2013, 87/2013, 88/2013, 89/2013. https://www.zec.org.zw/pages/electoral_regulations, Zimbabwe Electoral Commission, Harare, 8 June 2018, page 18.

physically in terms of the transmission process. ... **What is happening now is the process of transmission. Like I told you that the process of transmission is laborious and manual.** *We are not allowed to declare results on the basis of soft copies or anything that has been sent by scan.* **We need to get the physical copies from the presiding officers in the areas and some of the areas are very far ...** [emphasis added].[66]

There are two important observations to make from Commissioner Moyo's comments:

The first is that Moyo confirmed the legal position in s37C(4) of the Electoral Act that presidential V11s were sent to the national command centre from wards and had been received by 31 July 2018. However, he seemed to be unaware that the parliamentary results were also similarly sent in terms of s37C(4) of the Electoral Act. The question is, how were the presidential and parliamentary V11s sent from the wards to the national command centre? By making specific reference to **soft copies and scanned copies,** Moyo confirmed that the presidential V11s had been sent electronically to a central system, **which cannot be anything else but a server.** Significantly, he also confirmed that the presidential V11s sent from the wards, which are in fact duplicates and not original copies, would not be taken as official until the physical copies of the results were received.

What should be noted in this regard is that the physical copies of the result of the presidential election that are sent to the national command centre are not V11s from the wards but V23Bs from the constituencies. The physical and certified V23Bs, with original copies of V11s and V23As attached to them, are collated and verified at the national command centre to determine the result of the presidential election in terms of s110(3)(d) of the Electoral Act.

Therefore, soon after midnight on 30 July 2018, or at least in the wee hours of 31 July 2018, all the 10,985 polling stations had completed the counting of votes, and all the ward centres had received the V11s with the results of the presidential election and national assembly election, and sent them to the national command centre in Harare. At this time, "the system" knew who had won the presidential and parliamentary elections, and this information was in ZEC's central server at the national command centre, as well as at the CIO's Data Recovery Centre, which mirrors the ZEC server. This fact is important to keep in mind.

But, did ZEC have a central server?

This is a crucial question and it is important to establish the facts, based on the public record and on rational expectations. It is important to unpack the question upfront because ZEC and Chigumba claimed under oath that there was no server containing the result for the presidential election.

---

[66] Interview with Zimbabwe Election Commission (ZEC) Commissioner, Qhubani Moyo, South African Broadcasting Corporation Digital News, 31 July 2018. https://www.youtube.com/watch?v=sNIo_pGGbmo

According to the submissions they made in response to Chamisa's Constitutional Court presidential election result challenge, ZEC and Chigumba astonishingly used propaganda spin to claim that ZEC did not have a server. Under paragraph 32.1 of their opposing affidavit, Chigumba and ZEC claimed that:

> Transmission of results from polling stations, wards and constituencies is done manually. This is consistent with the provisions of s64(2) of the Electoral Act. The Electoral Commission had no server set up at the national command centre or anywhere else, on which results were sent and stored in real time as the applicant suggests.

Section 64(2) of the Electoral Act provides that:

(2) Immediately after affixing a polling station return on the outside of the polling station in term of subsection (1)(e), the presiding officer shall personally transmit to the ward elections officer for the ward in which the polling station is situated –

(a) the ballot box and packets referred to in subsection (1)(a) and (b), accompanied by a statement made by the presiding officer showing the number of ballot papers entrusted to him or her and accounting for them under the heads of used ballot papers, excluding spoilt ballot papers, unused ballot papers and spoilt ballot papers; and

(b) the polling-station return certified by himself or herself to be correct:

> Provided that if, by reason of death, injury or illness, the presiding officer is unable personally to transmit the ballot box, packets, statement and polling station return under this subsection, a polling officer who was on duty at the polling station shall personally transmit these, and in that event any statement or certification required to be made by the presiding officer for the purposes of this section may be made by the polling officer concerned.
> [Section as substituted by s. 46 of Act No. 17 of 2007 and amended by s. 29 of Act No. 6 of 2014]

Clearly, s64(2) of the Electoral Act does not help their submission because it is specifically about the transmission of results from a polling station to a ward. There is nothing in this provision that relates to the transmission of results to the national command centre, from a polling station or a ward or a constituency.

Under paragraph 32.3 of their opposing affidavit, ZEC, and Chigumba further claimed that:

> As he [Nelson Chamisa] has alleged the existence of a server, it is incumbent upon the applicant to prove his allegation.

This was astounding. Either there was or there wasn't a server, and it was irrational for ZEC and Chigumba to challenge Chamisa to prove ZEC had a server, if the position of ZEC was simply that there was no server. Why would ZEC, as a constitutional body with a duty to be transparent, ask a citizen who was a presidential candidate to prove whether ZEC had a server? If there was no server, no central system for data storage, where were the massive data from the presidential and parliamentary results, each with multiple candidates, contained in the 21,970 V11s received by ward centres kept? And, if that data was not kept on a server, where was it kept and how secure was it?

On 29 June 2017, a local daily newspaper in Harare had reported that:

> The Zimbabwe Electoral Commission (ZEC) is planning a second tender connected with the biometric voter registration (BVR) exercise, as it tries to contain the fallout over revelations that a central server containing voters' information would be managed by Israeli firm Nikuv International Projects, who are accused of rigging the last [2013] election in Zanu PF's favour. In the initial tender, ZEC had not said it would run two tenders, but a *NewsDay* exposé showed that the firm that won the [BVR] tender – Laxton Group of Companies – was uncomfortable with an arrangement where they just did the voter registration and another entity was responsible for storing data.[67]

Later the same day, the then ZEC Chairperson, Justice Rita Makarau, confirmed on the Voice of America (Studio 7 Radio) that the electoral body was indeed going to have two tenders and said:

> I want to make it clear that what we are buying, what we are going to use to register votes, we are buying this in two phases. The first phase, we have completed. This is where we bought the kits, which we are going to use to collect the data. After collecting that data, we are going to put it in a machine (central system), which will help us with cleaning the voters roll, issues like duplication. That machine we are going to use is the second phase of voter registration. This phase, we are yet to conduct.[68]

This statement by Makarau was significant in so far it established that, over and above its BVR system, ZEC needed a server for data storage and processing. The notion that an election body in the 21st century would organise and run an election without a server, was simply irrational and plainly preposterous.

About a week after Makarau confirmed that ZEC would run a second tender to procure a server, there was yet another twist. A weekly newspaper in Harare reported on 9 July 2017 that:

> The Zimbabwe Electoral Commission is set to stir another controversy after it emerged that the electoral body is likely to use an old server for the biometric voter registration (BVR) exercise ahead of next year's elections. ZEC awarded Laxton Group of Companies the tender to supply BVR kits but the company raised concerns that there were security risks related to the central system to store data, which would be sourced outside their tender agreement. ZEC has been flip-flopping on the acquisition of the crucial central system that will be used to store data with the commission's chairperson Rita Makarau making

---

[67] Blessed Mhlanga, "ZEC BVR blunder blows up", *NewsDay*, Harare, 29 June 2017.
[68] Justice Rita Makarau, Voice of America (VOA, Studio 7) 27

conflicting statements on the matter. She first claimed ZEC would have to go for a second tender before making an about turn, saying they already had their system in place. However, this paper has been informed that the United Nations Development Programme (UNDP) gave ZEC the central system, which was previously used by the Constitution Parliamentary Committee (COPAC) almost five years ago. A senior ZEC official who requested anonymity confirmed that the electoral body received the system from UNDP. … 'Yes, we might use that system but why are you trying to complicate these things', said a source within ZEC while trying to downplay the boob. 'You see, data is collected from the field and stored in a server. Just like your computer, you put data and [it is] stored in a server, which can be in the form of a hard drive or external hard drive, depending with the size and that is what this server is all about. There is no complication and there is no need to buy a new one each time you undertake a new project'.[69]

The position that ZEC already had a server in place had been effectively confirmed on Twitter on 8 July 2017 by ZEC Commissioner N Mushonga (@*Nmasivanda*) who tweeted that:

We register you, we save information in server, we print and you check if your name is there and we print the final voters roll, where does NIKUV come in?

Rather curiously, when the Laxton Group of Companies, which is Chinese, got the tender to supply the BVR kits, it expected to be awarded the second tender to supply the server which was necessary to store and process data on voter registration and election results.

On 29 September 2019, a daily newspaper in Harare published a revealing story about the BVR kits and their connection to a server anticipated by the Chinese company that supplied the kits, the Laxton Group. The story said:

Zimbabwe Electoral Commission (Zec) on Wednesday took delivery of the remaining 2 600 biometric voter registration (BVR) kits. … This comes after Zec launched the BVR exercise on September 18, four days after the date proclaimed by President Mugabe. The launch saw the setting up of 63 registration centres countrywide, utilising 400 kits received early September. The latest arrival of 2 600 kits will see Zec opening 10 000 registration countrywide.[70]

The 10,000 registration centres were created by 3,000 BVR kits, and these registration centres became 10,985 polling stations. There is a dark cloud over the extra 985 registration centres or polling stations. How were they created and which BVR kits were used to create them? There is an untold story about this, and the Chinese company, the Laxton Group, knows a lot about that story, as do the state security organs in "the system" that worked closely with this company which was desperate to supply the server for storing and processing data on the BVR exercise and election results.

[69] Obey Manayiti, "ZEC's BVR saga in new twist", *The Standard*, Harare, 9 July 2017.
[70] Farayi Machamire, "ZEC takes delivery of 2 600 BVR kits", *The Daily News*, Harare, 29 September 2017. See also Felex Share, "ZEC receives 2,600 BVR kits", *The Herald*, 3 October, 2017; and Farirai Machivenyika, "ZEC receives 400 BVR kits", *The Herald*, 9 August, 2017.

Soon after receiving the full complement of 3,000 BVR kits, questions emerged about the connection between the 3,000 kits and the 10,000 registration centres, the polling stations that the kits would create. How would the voter data for these 10,000 centres be stored and processed in a central system, the server? ZEC suddenly took a defensive and hostile posture about the server and, on 3 October 2017, the Zimbabwe Broadcasting Corporation reported that:

> The Zimbabwe Electoral Commission (ZEC) says it will guard jealously information on the voters roll and results to enable credible elections. This came out at a stockholder engagement between ZEC and political parties in Harare today. *According to the Commission, access to the server containing information on the voting process will be restricted to selected ZEC employees.* '*The server is a security area and all political parties will not be allowed to access it*', said ZEC Chairperson, Justice Rita Makarau [emphasis added].[71]

This is important to underscore, as it points to a predisposition on ZEC's part, which is against the transparency that is mandated by the Constitution. ZEC officially and publicly announced, as early as 3 October 2017, a little over a month before the November 2017 military coup that:

> …Access to the server containing information on the voting process will be restricted to selected ZEC employees. The server is a security area and all political parties will not be allowed to access it.

The unconstitutional position that **political parties cannot access the server containing information on the voting process** was repeated by ZEC, more emphatically, just before the 30 July 2018 harmonised elections when the electoral body released an official statement on 10 June 2018 in response to a number of concerns raised by the MDC-Alliance in which it said:

> The issue of access to the server is controlled in the same way as is the case with all institutions that keep custody of information of a security or confidential nature.[72]

As if this was not terrible enough, the electoral body arrogantly maintained that:

> Just like banks deny access to its servers, ZEC treats this as a security issue.[73]

Again, given that the Constitution requires ZEC to be transparent, under what law did ZEC adopt and assert this position of secrecy about its server with voting information?

It is an indictment of opposition political parties in Zimbabwe that this unconstitutional position taken by ZEC, an independent Chapter 12 Commission, has not been challenged. The position is contrary to s233(d) of the Constitution of Zimbabwe which provides that:

---

[71] "Parties not allowed to access servers: ZEC", @zbcnewsonline, 3 October, 2017. See also Blessed Mhlanga, "No access to servers – Zec", *NewsDay*, Harare, 4 October, 2017.
[72] Thandeka Moyo, "ZEC responds to MDC Alliance petition", *The Chronicle,* 11 June 2018.
[73] "ZEC Responses to MDC Alliance Electoral Reforms Demands", *The Sunday Mail*, 10 June 2018

The independent Commissions have the following general objectives in addition to those given to them individually –

(a).......
(b).......
(c).......
(d) to promote transparency and accountability in public institutions
(e).......
(f).......

More specifically, s239(a)(iv) on the functions of the Zimbabwe Electoral Commission enjoins the electoral body to:

> ... ensure that those elections and referendums are conducted efficiently, freely, fairly, *transparently* and in accordance with the law.

It would have been one thing had ZEC put in place guidelines under which political parties or election candidates might have accessed the server containing information on the voting process, but it was entirely another totally unacceptable thing for ZEC to decree that there would be no circumstances, not even court process, under which political parties or candidates could access the server information. The Constitution is clear that ZEC must conduct elections efficiently, freely, fairly, **transparently** and in accordance with the law.

Having taken an uncompromising, and unconstitutional position, that political parties cannot access the server containing information on the voting process, under any circumstances, ZEC proceeded with the second tender, after the one on the BVR kits, for a server to store and process BVR and voting data. The tender for the server was awarded in December 2017 to an American company based in New York called IPSIDY, Inc. The American company won the tender over the Chinese Laxton Group of Companies that had supplied the BVR kits and had assumed that it would get the tender for the voting information server because of its connection with the security establishment in the post-military-coup environment.

On 8 January 2018 *The Herald* newspaper reported that:

> The Zimbabwean Electoral Commission (ZEC) is at the centre of a storm after it reportedly manipulated and violated tender procedures when it awarded an American company a contract to supply Biometric Voter Registration (BVR) de-duplication hardware and software. The electoral body last month awarded a New York-based company, IPSIDY Inc, the tender to supply, install and configure the de-duplication equipment. In essence, de-duplication equipment and software is used to eliminate redundant or repeated copies of data in a biometric system. ... ZEC's decision to award IPSIDY Inc the contract has upset the Chinese company, Laxton Group Limited, which in June last year won the tender to supply BVR kits ahead of the polls. ... The company exposed ZEC for setting a tender requirement for a specific server – HP Enterprise ProLiant XL270d Gen9 – which forms part of an-all-in-one solution called Appollo 6500. The Appollo 6500 includes 2 servers. ... "However, during the

evaluation, the first respondent (ZEC) determined that i not longer required both servers but rather only one server.[74]

The Chinese company, Laxton Group Limited, took the tender award on appeal to the Administrative Court with ZEC as the first respondent, the State Procurement Board as the second, and IPSIDY Inc as the third. The Court ruled in favour of ZEC, and thus for the American company IPSIDY, Inc and against the Chinese company, Laxton Group Limited.[75]

In a surprising but revealing submission, the State Procurement Board told the Court that IPSIDY Inc should not have been awarded the tender to supply the server because, unlike Laxton Group limited from China, it was not security vetted. This submission was surprising because it was made by a state entity, whose legal duty was to ensure that the tender process followed the relevant procedures and the law in the first place. The submission by the State Procurement Board was also revealing as it showed that the securocrats, who were operating at Defence House, had taken their eyes off the ball in December 2017 when the tender for the ZEC was awarded to an American company without security vetting following the November 2017 military coup. This exposed the lie behind ZEC's mantra that the server is a security facility whose BVR data and voting information must not be accessed by political parties or election candidates.

Regarding the tender case, it is manifestly clear in reading Judgment No. AC4/18 by Justice H. Mandeya in the Administrative Court that the issue in dispute was the supply of the server to ZEC for use to store and process BVR data and voting information for the 2018 presidential election. Add to this that, ZEC already had in place a server it had acquired before it procured the 3,000 BVR kits, as confirmed by ZEC Commissioner in a tweet she posted on 8 July 2017, and another it got from the UNDP (United Nations Development Programme).

To the question posed by ZEC and Chigumba in their opposing affidavit, did ZEC have a server to store and process voting information, the empirical answer is a resounding and unqualified, **YES**.

The Cover-up

In the circumstances, the duplicate copies of the polling-station returns, V11s with the results of the presidential election and parliamentary election, that were gathered from all 10,985 polling stations that were situated within each of the 1,958 wards across the country, were **transmitted through the appropriate ward centre directly to the server at the national command centre. The results of the presidential election in the IPSIDY server showed Nelson Chamisa with 66% of the votes and Emmerson Mnangagwa with 33%.**

Diagram 15 below shows the flow of electronic transmission of results not only from election centres to the national command centre, but also to and from election centres between them.

---

[74] Felex Share, "ZEC in BVR tender storm", *The Herald*, 8 January 2018.
[75] Zvamanida Murwira, "Court upholds Zec decision", *The Chronicle*, 24 February 2019.

DIAGRAM 15

TRANSMISSION OF RESULTS BY ELECTRONIC MEANS

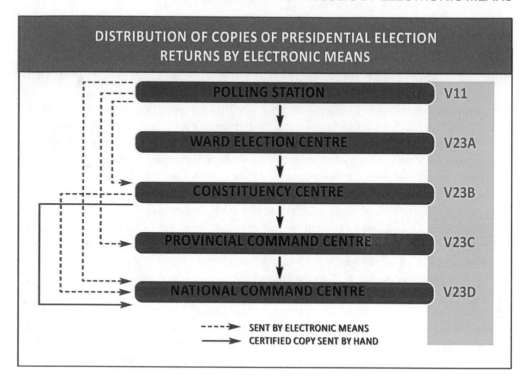

DISTRIBUTION OF COPIES OF PRESIDENTIAL ELECTION RETURNS BY ELECTRONIC MEANS

POLLING STATION	V11
WARD ELECTION CENTRE	V23A
CONSTITUENCY CENTRE	V23B
PROVINCIAL COMMAND CENTRE	V23C
NATIONAL COMMAND CENTRE	V23D

- - - -▶ SENT BY ELECTRONIC MEANS
————▶ CERTIFIED COPY SENT BY HAND

The results of the 2018 presidential election in the IPSIDY server, which were a true reflection of the duplicate copies of the V11s transmitted to the national command centre from 1,958 ward centres, caused panic among a few selected ZEC staff who had access to the voting data on the server. The panic was worse among the securocrats at Defence House who were running and supervising the server, as it had become a top security facility. There was pandemonium when information reached Mnangagwa and the military hierarchy.

A midnight order was given to the technical team, dominated by securocrats, and headed by Mavis Matsanga, to "correct" the server, while Chigumba and Moyo took charge of pushing back the growing and widespread word that Chamisa had won the 2018 presidential election by a landslide, as per the results that were in the server. In effect, an operation to rig the election was underway. The rigging was done by inventing a different route with a different destination for the collation, compilation and transmission of the result of the presidential from ward centres, away from constituency centres, to district election offices for onward transmission direct to the national command centre in Harare.

Around 8:00am on 31 July 2018, Chigumba sent WhatsApp messages to her key media contacts and some SADC diplomats, one of which was seen by this writer, claiming that celebrations of a Chamisa win were premature because **"ZEC's information was that Mnangagwa had won by 53%."** By noon that day, Moyo had upped the figure, telling some journalists that figures at the disposal of ZEC were showing **"Mnangagwa winning by 55%"**.

A particularly revealing if not scandalous WhatsApp message sent by Chigumba boasted that:

> They [MDC] don't have to agree. We will announce based on our own V11.
> We don't need any party's V11. It's just courtesy for us to ask them to verify.
> Agree or not, we announce.

Spirited efforts to correct the server came to naught. The IPSIDY server could not be corrected. Its hardware and software were impenetrable. The Chinese company, Laxton Group Limited, were having the last laugh with a "we told you to award us the server-tender, but you chose the Yankees" posture. The capacity of the JOC technical team was not up to scratch. Their attempt to hack the server ended up damaging it, and making it dysfunctional, without "correcting" the results of the presidential election. An order was given by the military hierarchy to sever the server and to find another option by all and any means necessary.

The server and its contents were severed and abandoned. From then on, the securocrats and ZEC took the astonishingly false view that there was no server at all. To make this bad situation worse, ZEC then set itself up as a giant polling station for the whole country and started gathering and collating duplicate polling station returns for the presidential election, V11s, to generate a new result of the election to enable Mnangagwa to win.

Rigging was in progress. As pointed out earlier, V11s are not collated, or verified, at the national command centre: rather, they are collated and verified at ward centres.

As ZEC started creating and processing polling station returns (V11s) at the national command centre, securocrats across the country started removing the V11s that had been posted outside polling stations to stop the media confirmation of reports of Mnangagwa's loss, that were spreading like a veld fire.

On the nights of 30 and 31 July 2018, unmarked vehicles, believed to belong to the ZDF, ZEC vehicles and ZRP vehicles were seen at different places across the country in various circumstances loaded with unprotected, unsealed, ballot boxes with marked ballot papers and election residue. Some of these were confronted by members of the public.

The European Observation Mission made the following finding:

> Counting was observed in a total of 52 polling stations. EU observers reported that they were able to follow the counting of ballots without undue restriction in the presence of party agents and citizens observers. Counting was generally well organised and meticulous, although very slow. Observers in Makonde, Hurungwe and other areas reported that in many rural polling stations gas lamps were missing and that polling staff used mobile phones and candles to complete the counting of ballots. Some problems in ballot reconciliation, in determining valid and invalid ballots, in completing the numerous originals of return forms and in packing election materials for the three elections were noted. EU observers reported that the results were not posted at the polling station, as required by law, in 10 out of the 52 polling stations observed.[76]

---

[76] EU EOM, *Zimbabwe Harmonised Elections 2018: Final Report*, October 2018, page 34.

On this sample, ZEC did not implement the legal requirement to post the V11s with the results of the presidential election outside 20% of the polling stations observed by the EU Observation Mission.

The EU EOM found that some party agents and CSOs (Civil Society Organisations) had reported that "polling station return forms, the V11s, were altered and return figures changed at ward and constituency collation centres".[77] But, even more telling, the evidence of the operation to alter the presidential result was reported by the EU Observation Mission in these graphic and shocking terms:

> **EU EOM observed ZEC officers in Makoni North completing V11 Forms two days after Election Day, even though polling staff and party agents were not present. They claimed this was due to the earlier lack of V11 Forms.[78]**

The fact that ZEC officers were this brazen in the alteration of election results shows beyond reasonable doubt that a sinister operation was indeed under way. The question that arises is simple: where did these V11s go? The answer is also simple: they went to the rigging effort.

Against this backdrop, "the system" intervened by getting ZEC to hijack the result of the presidential election recorded in the V11s from 10,985 polling stations and 1,958 ward centres by inventing an illegal route and destination for collating, compiling and transmitting them contrary to the prescribed manner. The hijacked result was taken to ZEC's national command centre in Harare, where it was mixed with other V11s and V23As and input into an Excel spreadsheet to produce a fake result of the presidential election. This was the direct effect of ZEC's invention of a different route with a different destination for the collation, compilation and transmission of the result of the presidential election. The invention and use of a different route with a different destination rendered any outcome, in the form of a result, necessarily void whatever the numbers.

The corruption of the server and its abandonment in favour of the hijacking of the result of the presidential election, and the collation and compilation of a different result at the national command centre through an Excel spreadsheet, prompted Morgen Komichi, as chairperson of the MDC-Alliance, whose presidential candidate was Nelson Chamisa, and Jameson Timba, who was Chamisa's chief election agent, to write a letter to ZEC, dated 2 August 2018, complaining about ZEC's use of an Excel spreadsheet and seeking access to the ZEC server as shown in that letter:

---

[77] Ibid., page 36.
[78] Ibid.

The Chairperson   02-08-2018
Zimbabwe Electoral Commission
Harare

DEAR MADAM

RE: **ACCESS TO ZEC SERVER**

We approach you in connection with a matter that has caused us grave concern, and which must be addressed before the announcement of the presidential results and addressed as a matter of urgency.

We are aware that the correct results of the elections have been inputted into the ZEC system and are in its server. Those results are a clear projection of the overwhelming winner of the presidential elections.

On the 2ⁿᵈ of August 2018 the legal Advisor to PRESIDENT NELSON CHAMISA had a conversation with certain ZEC officials at ZEC in connection with this matter of concern. A Mr Madzimure to whom Advocate Mpofu was referred to as the person best placed to address the concerns indicated that ZEC is 'running a parallel' data collection process. That parallel process includes an Excel spreadsheet on the one hand and a central server on the other. The process which the Election Agents are currently being asked to verify only relates to the Excel spreadsheet.

The use of the Excel spreadsheet is meant, in our considered view, to provide a basis upon which the presidential result is to be manipulated in that Excel inputs can be altered. It is of concern that, notwithstanding the existence of the parallel process, ZEC has only allowed access to the Excel spreadsheet process. We have been allowed to verify a ruse. That process is not auditable and cannot be verified. Whilst that forms the backdrop, the crux of the matter is that PRESIDENT NELSON CHAMISA is entitled to have access to the results on the server. He is entitled to verify them. He is entitled to audit how those results, received in real time and immediately after counting, compare with the results on the Excel spreadsheet.

We must however emphasize that the Excel spreadsheet results are themselves not yet fully out. We, however, have all the full results available and are clear on what we are talking about.

We point out that we had a meeting with the ACTING CHIEF ELECTIONS OFFICER, Mr Silaigwana at which impromptu meeting these issues were raised. Mr Silaigwana whilst claiming that there is no parallel process in existence was however, not prepared to state on his name and honour that there is no server involved in the election process. Indeed, it is unfathomable that there could be no central server and that an entire election could be run on an Excel spreadsheet. We will not allow ZEC to take us for fools. Further, Mr Silaigwana refused our request to have our experts confer with the ZEC experts over the issue. Obviously, there is something that he intends to hide. What he intends to hide in our view is that there is an ongoing process to manufacture results. Indeed, there exists authentic results that ZEC is prepared to hide from the electorate. That with respect is completely unacceptable.

We point out that you had advised the nation that the presidential election results would be announced at 12:30 on 1ˢᵗ August 2018. You were correct that this could be done for the following reasons:

(i)   The Presidential votes are counted ahead of the Parliamentary votes. You could not have results of Parliamentary Elections unless you also had results of the presidential elections.

(ii)   Once voting is complete results are immediately transmitted by radio or some such process to the national command centre. The forms will then follow by normal deliberate process and those are meant to verify results already received. You are obviously aware of the irregularities that attend to the manner in which the relevant forms were collected and that is an issue to be addressed on some other day.

(iii) All your actions point to an intention to 'manage' the results of the presidential election. The reason you have done so is quite clear.

You accordingly have these results and you have a constitutional obligation to ensure that the correct results are announced. The people of Zimbabwe are entitled to and demand no less.

In view of the foregoing, we call upon you to do the following:

i.   That you immediately allow us as PRESIDENT CHAMISA'S agents and the technical experts, access to the server so that we can audit same and reconcile those results with what is being inputted on the Excel spreadsheet.

ii.   Immediately take steps to ensure that the results on the server and those being inputted on the Excel spreadsheet are reconciled.

We demand your written assurance that this shall be done, and such assurance must be given by 17:00 PM.

We wish to indicate that this letter is not on letterhead because the military has barricaded and access to the MDC Headquarters where such letterheads are otherwise kept.

Kindly do the right thing as you are mandated by the constitution in the interests of transparency, credibility and verifiability of our election.

Yours faithfully

Morgen Komichi
Chairperson

Jameson Timba
Chief Election Agent

It is notable that ZEC did not respond to this letter because it did not want to commit itself in writing and put itself on the record. The failure of ZEC to respond in writing not only proved that something was fundamentally amiss but was also a blatant and outrageous violation of its constitutional responsibility and duty to act transparently. Why would a constitutional electoral body not respond to a letter from a key stakeholder?

Confirmation that ZEC operated a server, with the result of the presidential election, was given by none other than Emmerson Mnangagwa himself in his sworn opposing affidavit to the founding affidavit filed by Chamisa in the Constitutional Court challenge to ZEC's declaration and announcement of Mnangagwa as the winner of the 2018 presidential election. Mnangagwa makes the confirmation from paragraphs 116 to paragraphs 118.8 of his opposing affidavit produced verbatim below:

116. Paragraph 5.1

I observe that the Applicant confirms that his agents were allowed to freely view what was happening within the 23rd Respondent's command centre, belying any suggestion that there was something to hide. The short sentence: 'for close to two days that process continued' is important: Applicant's representatives had an unlimited time within which to observe what was going on. And it is crucial to bear in mind that the people they were watching were '… in excess of twenty'.

117. *The suggestion that an organisation with a nefarious plan to steal an election as Applicant suggests would have 'in excess of twenty' people working independently of each other under the full glare of election agents but still manage to run a coordinated and systematic conspiracy to defraud one candidate is just not credible. How is it being suggested that they relayed messages to each other as to how many votes needed to be 'massaged'? Excel as far as I am aware is not a messaging service, so how is it being suggested that these 'in excess of twenty people' received instructions from 23rd Respondent to steal the election in front of Messrs Komichi and Timba?*

118. Paragraph 5.2

*The Applicant says here: "**I was also aware that twenty third respondent [ZEC] had received, as it should do, results from all polling stations in real time and stored them into its server".** I think at this point it is necessary to pause and reflect on the following very important issues:*

118.1 *This is not an ordinary matter that the Court has to decide, but one which determines, for good or ill, the person that gets to be head of state of our country for the next five years. It is a solemn matter.*

118.2 *23rd Respondent is trusted with the solemn duty of superintending over one of our democracy's most important moments: national elections.*

118.3 *In order to carry out this solemn duty 23rd Respondent is trusted with very sensitive information on each of our citizens old enough to vote. Names, addresses, ID numbers, sex, fingerprints and photographs.*

118.4   *The Applicant confirms in his papers, and the affidavits of his surrogates, that he was refused access to the 23rd Respondent's server.*

118.5   *We know from 23rd Respondent that sensitive information on our citizens had been hacked, and people have been able to access said information and even amend it.*

118.6   *But, again, we know that Applicant's representatives were denied access to what they called a server.*

118.7   *So, one must ask, exactly how did applicant know that results from all polling stations were being received in that putative server in real time? The only inference that can be drawn is that the applicant or those working with him were responsible for the hacking, accessing of data on 23rd Respondent's server.*

118.8   *It is known that one of the websites utilising information obtained from 23rd Respondents website through hacking has published graphs and statistics that are eerily similar to those that were simultaneously being filed with this S93 application.*

It is notable that under paragraph 118.4 of his opposing affidavit, Mnangagwa made a startling confirmation of the existence of the ZEC server:

> **The Applicant [meaning Nelson Chamisa] confirms in his papers and affidavits of his surrogates that he was refused access to the 23rd Respondent's Server.**

Yes, refused. One cannot be refused something that is not there.

Mnangagwa further averred, under oath, that Chamisa **confirms**, not **alleges**, but *confirms*, that he was denied access to the ZEC server.

What this means is that Mnangagwa, not only as a presidential candidate, but, more importantly, as President of Zimbabwe, acknowledged that there was indeed a ZEC server and stated, under oath, without any argument or disputation whatsoever that Chamisa was denied access to that server by ZEC.

Even more startling is that Mnangagwa asserted under paragraph 118 of his opposing affidavit that:

> **We know from the 23rd Respondent [ZEC] that sensitive information on our citizens [voters] had been hacked and people have been able to access information and even amend it.**

This is mind-boggling. It is beyond belief that a legal mind of Chief Justice Malaba's standing and experience, who has declared himself to be averse to numbers, allegedly in favour of facts, was not drawn to these manifestly scandalous facts about the existence of the ZEC server, admitted by Mnangagwa under oath.

Although it is unnecessary and is certainly of no major consequence given Mnangagwa's effective confirmation of the existence of the server, it is instructive to examine ZEC's position on the matter.

What is clear is that ZDF and ZEC realised on the night of 30 July 2018 that Mnangagwa had lost the presidential election by a landslide, and that it would be more than a tall order to fiddle with the results in the ZEC server; or to process the result of the presidential election in the prescribed manner. Thus, a plot was hatched to alter the results of the presidential election by abandoning the ZEC server and inventing a different route and different destination for the collation, compilation and transmission of the result of the presidential election. This was "Plan B", whose alternative to the server was an Excel spreadsheet. As part of the execution of its "Plan B", ZEC played fast and loose with V11s at the national command centre, where V11s not are collated or compiled at all. This was **EXCELGATE** in motion.

Apart from the senior securocrat who contacted me in the wee hours on 30 July 2018, impeccable sources inside ZEC, some technical staff and two commissioners, confirmed in the strictest of confidence that according to the presidential results in the ZEC server, Chamisa got 66% of the vote and Mnangagwa 33%.

The information from the confidential ZEC sources is important not for purposes of confirming that there was a ZEC server, but for disclosing its content.

This is because the existence of the server ended up as common cause. In fact, ZEC had multiple servers. One such server was confirmed on Twitter by ZEC Commissioner N Mushonga, on 8 July 2017. Another was donated by the UNDP. Even more importantly, ZEC had the IPSIDY server that was confirmed by the Administrative Court on 20 February 2018. Indeed, the existence of the ZEC main server was confirmed also by none other than Mnangagwa himself, in his opposing affidavit in the ConCourt case.

Regarding the content of the ZEC server, it is notable that the ZEC figures generated from its Excel spreadsheet were by all accounts, untraceable, unverifiable, unreliable and therefore inherently unusable.

On paragraph 31 of their affidavit opposing Chamisa's founding affidavit in the ConCourt Court challenge to ZEC's declaration and announcement of Mnangagwa as the winner of the 2018 presidential election, Priscilla Chigumba and ZEC made this averment:

> Despite the applicant's averments under paragraph 4.5.32 and 4.5.33 of his founding affidavit to the effect that his election agents were not notified of the date and place of verification and were not given an opportunity to make notes of the contents of the constituency returns, applicant under paragraph 5.1 of his founding affidavit makes the opposite averment. He admits that his election agents were called for a verification process, he admits that they heeded this call and came to the 23rd respondent's national command centre where the verification was taking place, he admits that his agents were present when the verification process was underway, he admits that the verification process went on for two days with his election agents in attendance. This coupled with the affidavits by Mrs. Pamela Mapondera and Mrs. Mavis Mudiwakure attached and already referenced, shows that not only were his agents in attendance, they participated in the verification process. As part of the verification process, the applicant's election agents, election agents for other presidential candidates as well as election observers had full access to the original V11s and V23s with respect to the presidential election from which they could make notes as they required.

The submissions by Chigumba and ZEC, under oath, are significant in two important respects:

First, they clearly confirm that, at the national command centre, the verification of presidential election results is supposed to verify constituency returns, and these are V23B Forms. In other words, unlike the polling stations and the ward collation stations that verify V11 Forms, the national command centre **only** verifies the V23B Forms forwarded from the country's 210 constituencies.

Second, Chigumba and ZEC confirm that *what they describe as* the verification exercise took two days. But what was being verified?

Although Chigumba and ZEC started by submitting that the national command centre was verifying constituency returns (that is V23B Forms from 210 constituencies), they, perhaps inadvertently, revealed that the verification at the national command centre also included polling stations returns, namely V11s.

There is no need for a rocket scientist to understand or realise that it is impossible to verify V23B Forms from 210 constituencies and V11s from 10,985 polling stations and V23As from 1,958 wards across the country in **two days**. But, anyway, what V11 Forms were these? Were the V11 Forms being verified at the national command centre over two days from the all the country's 10,985 polling stations in all the 1,958 wards? How traceable were these V11s? How were they transmitted from source to the national command centre?

The untraceability of these V11s, whose data was input into the Excel spreadsheet was poignantly raised by the EU Observation Mission:

> … ZEC provided stakeholders with a free CD-ROM copy of presidential results, in a protected Excel format. Local council election results and details on postal ballots remain outstanding. The results provide a breakdown per polling station, apparently based on original V11s. As these results are not in the official V11 form, they do not provide the full traceability which the EU EOM had called for in its preliminary statement.

On paragraph 32.2 of their opposing affidavit, Chigumba and ZEC made the following submission under oath:

> His [Chamisa's] suggestion is also curious as it comes immediately after he avers that for close to two days the Electoral Commission's staff were busy manually entering data from original V11 Forms onto an Excel spreadsheet.

Effectively Chigumba and ZEC admitted that their officers, whose unchallenged number is given as around 20 and who included security operatives, spent two days "**busy manually entering data from original V11 Forms onto an Excel spreadsheet**".

This is scandalous.

Seemingly unaware of the scandalous implications of their submissions under oath, Chigumba and ZEC asserted, with amazing irony, on paragraph 32.3 of their opposing affidavit that:

---

[84] EU EOM, *Zimbabwe Harmonised Elections 2018: Final Report*, October 2018, page 37.

> As he [Chamisa] has alleged the existence of a server, it is incumbent upon the applicant to prove his allegation.

The assertion that it was incumbent on Chamisa to prove the existence of the server on account of "his allegation", is at the heart not only of what is wrong with ZEC, as a Chapter 12 constitutional commission, but also what is wrong with the judiciary in Zimbabwe, against the backdrop of Zimbabwe's new Constitution.

In the first place, as a Chapter 12 constitutional commission, ZEC must not play hide-and-seek with contestants in elections, asking them to prove ZEC violations and irregularities in bad faith, opaquely or unconstitutionally. As a Chapter 12 constitutional commission, ZEC has the following duties arising from its constitutional objectives as set out under section 233 of the Constitution:

> The independent Commissions [of which ZEC is such] have the following general objectives in addition to those given to them individually –
>
> (a) to support and entrench human rights and democracy;
> (b) to protect the sovereignty and interests of the people;
> (c) to promote constitutionalism;
> (d) to promote transparency and accountability in public institutions;
> (e) to secure the observance of democratic values and principles by the State and all institutions and agencies of government, and government-controlled entities; and
> (f) to ensure that injustices are remedied".

More specifically, section 239(a) of the Constitution gives the following key functions to ZEC:

> (a) to prepare for, conduct and supervise –
>
> (i) elections to the office of President and to Parliament;
> (ii) elections to provincial and metropolitan councils and the governing bodies of local authorities;
> (iii) elections of members of the National Council of Chiefs established by section 285; and
> (iv) referendums;
> (v) and to ensure that those elections and referendums are conducted efficiently, freely, fairly, transparently and in accordance with the law;

Therefore, in general, regarding the question of its server, ZEC dismally failed to discharge its constitutional duty to be transparent, as it is required to be under section 239(a) of the Constitution.

ZEC's position that Chamisa needed to prove that it had a server belies the evidence provided by none other than Mnangagwa, whose submissions under oath in his opposing affidavit left absolutely no doubt that there was indeed a ZEC server. Attempts by ZEC to either hide or run away from this fact are not only unconstitutional, but are also a telling manifestation of a disposition of rigging aforethought.

Chapter 7

HARARE MASSACRE

ON 15 November 2017, the Zimbabwe Defence Forces (ZDF), led by General Constantino Chiwenga, now one of Zimbabwe's two Vice-Presidents, staged a military coup, dubbed "Operation Restore Legacy", that toppled Robert Mugabe and his government. The military coup was daring and unprecedented. Although the ZDF presented its intervention as a "coup that was not a coup", and alternatively as a "military assisted transition" that had taken Zimbabwe to "another level", there is now no doubt that the military action was a coup. Mugabe, who was alleged to have voluntarily and freely resigned, even by Chief Justice Malaba sitting alone in his chambers without hearing evidence and without a case before him, put these claims to shame by coming out in public to state categorically that he was forced to resign by coupists whom he described as his "tormentors".

Officially, as declared by ZDF, the coup lasted from 15 November to 18 December 2017, when the post-coup ZDF Commander, General Philip Valerio Sibanda, declared "Operation Restore Legacy" officially over. By this time of the coup, the following situation obtained in the country:

- Zimbabwe was under *de facto* military rule.

- Over 2,000 soldiers had been deployed and embedded in every rural community across the country.

- The rule of law in Zimbabwe had effectively been overthrown in blatant violation of sections 213 and 214 of the Constitution of Zimbabwe under a scandalous interpretation of section 212 which was controversially endorsed by the Judge President of the High Court of Zimbabwe, Justice George Chiweshe, on 24 November 2017, the day Emmerson Mnangagwa was inaugurated – in fact, imposed as a coup President.

- The military had embedded itself in key institutions of the state and in ZANU PF, with General Chiwenga, Air Marshal Perence Shiri and General Sibusiso B Moyo, who had announced the military takeover on 15 November 2017, having become Cabinet ministers, and General Engelbert Rugeje having been deployed to ZANU PF headquarters to run the party's all-too-important commissariat department, as national political commissar.

- Other institutions that the military had targeted for takeover included the National Prosecuting Authority (NPA), the judiciary, state media, local authorities, especially in rural areas, traditional leaders, and the Zimbabwe Election Commission (ZEC), to which additional military officers were seconded, with the electoral body coming under the direct control of Defence House.

- Notably, "Operation Restore Legacy" was officially declared by the military to be over only six months before Zimbabwe was to hold its constitutionally due general harmonised elections. The military ousted Mugabe seven months before the expiry of his five-year term, which had started on 22 August 2013.

Against this backdrop, Zimbabwe went to the polls on 30 July 2018 with the following political situation on the country ground:

- The country had a constitution without constitutionalism. Ironically, the overthrown constitution had been fully adopted only on 22 August 2013 with entrenched security-sector reforms that went up in smoke on 15 November 2017.

- The judiciary had become jittery and acquiescent, with its leadership functioning as an extension of the Junta.

- The media, civil society and opposition political parties that had supported the coup and participated in the "Mugabe Must Go" march on 18 November 2017, and which had taken Mugabe's departure as a change of the system, had come to understand, rather too late and with a lost opportunity and lots of regret, that Zimbabwe had effectively become a *de facto* military state.

- Anxiety and palpable fear were gripping the public, who were failing to come to terms with the unprecedented military engagement in civilian affairs, having initially embraced the military coup on 15 November 2017 under the "Mugabe Must Go" mantra.

- The rural community was literally under military occupation and had become intimidated, cowed, fearful and immobilised.

The implication of the military coup on the 2018 general election was highlighted and dramatised by the following statements made key official figures:

- On 18 January 2018, General Engelbert Rugeje threatened that the army, which had staged the military coup two months earlier, would **repeat** the widely condemned atrocities it had committed in the June 2008 presidential run-off election campaign, during which some 200 people had been killed and many others tortured or displaced as internal or external refugees.

- On 21 May 2018, Deputy Finance Minister, Terrence Mukupe, announced at a ZANU PF election campaign rally in Harare East that the military would not allow the MDC leader, Nelson Chamisa, to rule if he won the 2018 general election.

- On 22 May 2018 Josiah Hungwe, Minister of State for Provincial Affairs for Masvingo Province, told a public meeting where he commissioned a clinic in Chiredzi that if Mnangagwa could shoot his way into power in November 2017, then there was nothing to stop him from doing the same thing to keep himself in office.

- On 18 June 2018, General Chiwenga, as Vice-President and Minister of Defence, whose office headed the Defence House operation that directed and controlled ZEC before, during and after the election, told a ZANU PF election campaign rally in Tafara (Mabvuku) in Harare that the military's "Operation Restore Legacy" which reached its tipping point on 18 November 2017 would end with the election of Mnangagwa on 30 July 2018. This was the most ominous statement whose unmistaken message was that the military operation that had started on 15 November 2017 was still underway and would end only with the election of Mnangagwa on 30 July 2018.

- The biased election messaging prompted the Commonwealth Observer Group to make this damning finding:

... the acute bias of the state media in favour of the governing party, persistent allegations of intimidation reported to the Group, and the unfair use of incumbency privileges, tilted the playing field in favour of the governing party. The post-election violence, which resulted in fatalities, and the behaviour of security forces, marred this phase of the elections. For these reasons, we are unable to endorse all aspects of the process as credible, inclusive and peaceful.[79]

- Unlike any other election since 1980, the 2018 general election was unique in that it was the first to be run directly and openly by the ZDF as a military operation. The constant and unmistakable subliminal, but occasionally explicit, campaign message at ZANU PF rallies and in state media reports was that the army had not ousted Mugabe on 15 November 2017 in order to let go of the power it had grabbed through the barrel of the gun via the ballot box on 30 July 2018. The claim by a host of election observers that the election campaign period was free and fair could not have been further from the truth. The proposition that an election in a military state after a military coup could be free and fair was an oxymoron.

So it is that, against this background, on 1 August 2018, while twenty or so ZEC officers, who included ZDF officers and CIO operatives, were manually inputting data from V11s and V23s into an Excel spreadsheet at ZEC's national command centre in Harare, soldiers and the police were letting blood in the city centre, leaving at least six civilians dead, shot in cold blood, and at least 35 others with serious gunshot wounds.

The carnage was confirmed by the Kgalema Motlanthe Commission, which found that:

> It is undisputed that six (6) people died as a result of gunshot wounds and according to the evidence from the two major hospitals twenty-three (23) people were injured as a result of gunshots and one (1) person of assault. As noted above, in addition to these persons there were eleven (11) persons who did not attend these hospitals, who were injured as a result of actions of the Military and the Police. The total number of persons injured is therefore thirty-five (35).[80]

While there were attempts by the ZDF, ZANU PF, government and the State media to place the blame for the dead and the wounded on the MDC-Alliance and civil society, the Motlanthe Commission was clear and specific on whose actions were behind the deaths and injuries:

> The Commission's finding on a balance of probabilities from all the evidence received is that the deaths of these six (6) people and the injuries sustained by thirty-five (35) others arose from the actions of the Military and the Police.[81]

It was no coincidence that the 1 August 2018 Harare Massacre was committed as a motley crew of twenty or so coupists were manually inputting fresh data from unverified, and in

---

[79] Commonwealth Observer Group, "Letter of Transmittal: Zimbabwe Harmonised Elections", Zimbabwe Harmonised Elections, July 2018, page iv.
[80] Zimbabwe. *Report of the Commission of Inquiry into the 1st of August 2018 Post-Election Violence*, Harare, page 47.
[81] Ibid., page 48.

fact unverifiable, V11s and V23s into an Excel spreadsheet, after ZEC had commandeered the result for the presidential election from all ward centres by inventing a different route and different destination for the collation, compilation and transmission of the result. The simultaneous occurrence of the Harare Massacre and the Excel spreadsheet event at ZEC's national command centre was no coincidence, given the bahaviour of the ZDF and ZRP forces who committed atrocities in Harare on 1 August 2018.

It is revealing that, according to the Motlanthe Commission, the ZDF and ZRP anticipated the 1 August 2018 "public disorder" in Harare and on 29 July 2018, had pre-planned how to deal with it, even before the 30 July 2018 elections. This is contained in a letter to the Officer Commanding Harare Province written by Chief Superintendent A. Ncube, Officer Commanding Police in Harare Central District, who prefaced his letter thus:

> I refer to my letter dated 29 July 2018 on anticipated public disorder in my district. There are approximately four thousand protesters on the streets of the Central Business District (CBD) of Harare protesting against alleged rigging of the just ended elections.[82]

On the same day, 1 August 2018, the Commissioner-General of Police, T G Matanga wrote to Obert Mpofu, Minister of Home and Cultural Affairs:

> I write to request, in terms of Section 213(2) of the Constitution of Zimbabwe, as read with Section 37(1) of the Public Order and Security Act (Chapter 11:17), for the immediate assistance of the Zimbabwe Defence Forces to suppress the violent disturbance of peace and security in Harare Central Police District, and other districts around Harare Metropolitan Province.[83]

The chain of letters then scaled up, with Obert Mpofu writing to General Chiwenga:

> As per our telephone conversation in the morning in connection with the above matter [request for immediate assistance to by the Zimbabwe Defence Forces maintain public order in Harare Central Police District], please find attached self-explanatory letters from the Commissioner-General of Police dated 29th July and 1st August 2018 respectively.[84]

Further to Obert Mpofu's letter, Chiwenga then upped the ante by writing to Mnangagwa:

> Your Excellency, pursuant to Section 213(2)(b) of the Constitution of Zimbabwe as read with Section 37(1) of the Public Order and Security Act (Chapter 11:17), the Minister of Home Affairs and Cultural Heritage is requesting for the immediate assistance of the Defence Forces for the purpose of suppressing violent disturbances in Harare Central Police District and other areas in Harare Metropolitan Province.[85]

---

82 Ibid., page 93.
83 Ibid., page 95.
84 Ibid., page 97.
85 Ibid., page 98.

To complete the not-so-subtly choreographed plot, punctuated by a series of premediated letters designed to create a paper trail of false legality to cover the operation hatched on 29 July 2018, Chiwenga wrote to the ZDF Commander, General Philip Valerio Sibanda:

> **General, pursuant to Section 213(2)(b) of the Constitution of Zimbabwe as read with Section 37(2) of the Public Order and Security Act, the President as Commander-in-Chief of Defence forces has authorised the deployment of the Defence Forces, in support of the Police Service in the maintenance of Public Order.**[86]

The chain of letters is revealing in the following ways:

- The letters motivating the deployment of ZDF soldiers reference 29 July 2018 correspondence that had **anticipated public disorder** in Harare. The letter from Obert Mpofu to Chiwenga was a ploy to deploy soldiers in Harare on 1 August 2018 as a pre-planned operation: Mpofu reminds Chiwenga that he is writing to him, **"As per our telephone conversation of this morning** in connection with the [request for immediate assistance to the Zimbabwe Defence Forces to maintain public order in Harare Central Police District]".

- The conversation between Mpofu and Chiwenga was purportedly in the morning of 1 August 2018, before any situation in Harare warranted deploying the police, let alone soldiers. This, along with the 29 July 2018 correspondence, gives away the pre-planned plot to deploy ZDF soldiers on the same day that 20 or so ZEC/ZDF/CIO people were manually inputting V11 and V23 data into an Excel spreadsheet to alter the presidential election result from what was in the ZEC server.

What was the purpose of unleashing ZDF soldiers in Harare on 1 August 2018?

Aware that rigging was under way at the ZEC national command centre in Harare, the main strategy behind the Harare Massacre was to send an ominous message to the public in general, and especially to Harare residents, that any protests after the rigged result for the presidential election was announced would be a life-threatening proposition.

The deployment of ZDF soldiers on 1 August 2018 had nothing to do with what was obtaining on the ground in Harare on that day but was informed by the objectives of the plot hatched on 29 July 2018 in "anticipation of public disorder" in the capital city.

By 29 July 2018, all survey polls by each of the security organs (MID, CIO and PISI) that make up the Joint Operations Command (JOC), to predict the outcome of the 30 July 2018 presidential election, were showing Mnangagwa badly trailing Nelson Chamisa, and getting no better than 33% of the vote.

In fact, it is curious that, on 19 July 2018, hardly a week before the revealing 29 July 2018 correspondence that **anticipated public disorder** in Harare to occur on 1 August 2018, ZEC alleged that its server had been hacked. The media reported that:

---

[86] Ibid., page 99.

> Underfire Zimbabwe Electoral Commission (Zec) chairperson Justice Priscilla Chigumba had sensationally claimed that suspected hackers recently broke into the electoral management body's database and stole crucial information on the biometric voters' roll, escalating fears of electoral manipulation ahead of the polls.[87]

The claim was sensational and suspicious, not least because Chigumba made it in response to allegations that ZEC had leaked personal phone numbers of registered voters to ZANU PF from the ZEC server. Given the pre-election survey polls by security agencies that showed Mnangagwa losing to Chamisa, the link between claims that the ZEC server had been hacked and the 29 July security correspondence is unmistakable.

Chigumba's claim on 19 July 2018 that the ZEC database had been hacked was significant in two respects. First, it contradicted an earlier ZEC assertion made in September 2017 and reported by a local daily newspaper that:

> The Zimbabwe Electoral Commission (Zec) has said data collected during electronic voter registration will be stored in tamper-proof flash drives before the information is fed into a central data base which is hack-proof.[88]

What happened to the supposedly tamper-proof flash drives and the hack-proof central data base that ZEC claimed to have in September 2017? Was the hacking of the ZEC database that Chigumba alleged on 19 July 2018 a true incident or was it a fake narrative to justify a sinister agenda related to the rigging of the presidential election, which was under way?

There is a second and more worrying issue about Chigumba's claim that the ZEC database, meaning the server, had been hacked. Some 15 days later, ZEC used an Excel spreadsheet, not a server, to determine and announce the results of the 2018 presidential election; and 12 days later, on 15 August 2018, Chigumba signed an opposing affidavit to Nelson Chamisa's Constitutional Court application in which she swore that ZEC had no server and challenged Chamisa to prove the existence of one.

What had happened to the ZEC server, within a short 27 days after Chigumba had alleged on 19 July 2018 that the server had been hacked?

It is important to take as a fact that ZEC indeed had a server which stored voting information that included the results of the 2018 presidential election.

The security pre-election survey polls, prepared by the CIO's Data Recovery Centre, raised concerns about Mnangagwa's non-electability and fed into impeachment chatter in ZANU PF ranks against Mnangagwa. On 30 May 2018, South Africa's *Independent Online* reported that Mnangagwa had said that he had unearthed a plot to impeach him soon after the elections by legislators from his own ZANU PF party.[89]

---

[87] Blessed Mhlanga, "Security breach at Zec, database hacked", *NewsDay,* 19 July 2018, Harare.
[88] Farayi Machamire, "BVR computer system tamper-proof: Zec," *Daily News,* Harare, 27 September 2017.
[89] "Zimbabwe's Mnangagwa says Zanu PF legislators plotting to impeach him", *IOL*, 30 May 2018.

Given the security survey polls that showed Mnangagwa being humiliated by Chamisa on 30 July 2018, the 29 July plot was threefold:

> First, hijack and literally steal the result for the presidential election by inventing and using a different route and different destination for the collation, compilation and transmission of the result from all the 1,958 ward centres to the national command centre in Harare, via all the 63 district officers, in violation of s37C(4) of the Electoral Act which prescribes one route and one destination for the processing of the all the results in the harmonised elections.

> Second, come up with a "Plan B" of collating and compiling the results of the presidential election hijacked from all the ward centres at ZEC's national command centre by mixing the V11s and V23As hijacked from wards with fresh V11s completed days after the election on 30 July 2019 in places such as Makoni North, confirmed by EU observers, and input the data from the new mixture of V11s and V23As into an Excel spreadsheet to generate a new result of the presidential election different from the result that was in the V11s and V23As hijacked from all of the country's 1,958 ward centres.

> Third, show and use massive lethal force in the City of Harare by deploying dangerously armed ZDF soldiers ahead of the ZEC declaration and announcement of the new result of the presidential election based on the Excel spreadsheet to intimidate the public, Harare residents, ZEC and the judiciary in order to get everyone to accept the rigged result on the Excel spreadsheet.

When ZDF soldiers were deployed in Harare with lethal ammunition, their mission was not to restore any public order, because there was no public disorder in Harare at the time, but was to show what lethal force the army was prepared to use against fleeing and defenceless civilians. It is in this context that ZDF soldiers used disproportionate lethal force. In this regard, the Motlanthe Commission made the following observation about the disproportionate force used by the army on 1 August 2018 in Harare:

> The Commission has considered the proportionality of the Army's actions in relation to the available evidence of the threat to public safety that had to be addressed. There was evidence received of life and property being under direct threat as noted above. In these limited circumstances, the use of warning shots could be considered proportionate. However, where there is evidence of civilians being directly fired on (as summarised below), the equation clearly changes. The evidence provides no justification for the use of live ammunition directly against protestors.[90]

Again, the purpose of the lethal force used by the ZDF is to be found not in what was happening in the streets of Harare but in what was happening at the ZEC national command centre, where data from some dubious V11s and V23s, such as the set from Makoni North completed by ZEC officers alone two days after the election, was being mixed with V11s and

---

[90] *Report of the Commission of Inquiry into the 1st of August 2018 Post-Election Violence*, pages 39–40.

V23As hijacked from ward centres and input into a ZEC Excel spreadsheet to generate a rigged result.

It is notable that the V11s and V23s that were input into the ZEC Excel spreadsheet and the result of the presidential election that was declared and announced by Priscilla Chigumba on 3 August 2018 were done against the backdrop of the bloodbath of ZDF atrocities committed in Harare on 1 August 2018.

There is an umbilical nexus between the ZDF atrocities of 1 August 2018 and the ZEC manipulation, in fact theft, of the 2018 presidential election. The essence was the hijacking of the result of the presidential election from all ward centres and the use of a different route with a different destination to collate, compile and transmit that result at ZEC's national command centre in Harare, where it was changed by being contaminated with other untraceable and unverifiable V11s and V23As that were input into an Excel spreadsheet.

It is apparent that the ZDF and ZEC became aware on the night of 30 July 2018 that Mnangagwa had been dramatically defeated by Chamisa, based on the results that had been entered into the ZEC server.

The makings of **EXCELGATE** became all too apparent on 2 August 2018, the day after the Harare Massacre, with reports that the ZEC website had been hacked. A Bulawayo-based daily reported that:

> The Zimbabwe Electoral Commission (Zec) website was yesterday [2 August 2018] temporarily shut down after unknown hackers posted images of the MDC-Alliance fuelled mayhem in Harare on it to replace official communication from the electoral body. The hackers allegedly tampered with the official 2018 Harmonised Election results which were on the website and posted controversial updates.[91]

The alleged hacking was confirmed by a ZEC Commissioner, Qhubani Moyo, who told the media that the ZEC website that had been set up to publish the 2018 election results had been hacked and suspended. A picture acknowledging the 1 August 2018 protests was placed by the alleged hackers front and centre where the Commission used to host its own content.[92] This curious incident was used to justify abandoning the ZEC server in favour of an Excel spreadsheet.

---

[91] Thandeka Moyo, "ZEC website hacked", *The Chronicle*, 3 August 2018.
[92] "ZEC Website hacked, suspended", Zimtechreview.co.zw/index-id-News-story-.293html, 2 August 2018.

Chapter 8

POISONED CHALICE

ALTHOUGH Zimbabweans believe that election rigging in Zimbabwe is widespread, their belief is not matched by the necessary vigilance to checkmate the rigging. One of the major reasons for this is because there is little regard in the body politic for the dictum that an election is a rule-bound political process which is a legal event.

ZEC's brazen rigging of the 2018 presidential election by collating, compiling and transmitting the result of the presidential election using a different route and a different destination from what is prescribed in s37C(4) of the Electoral Act went undetected in real time because there is little appreciation of an election as a rule-bound political process which is a legal event. By and large, Zimbabweans view an election as "just politics".

In the case of the 2018 presidential election, not only did ZEC blatantly violate s37C(4) regarding the collation, compilation and transmission of the result for the presidential election but it also audaciously violated s110(3)(d) with respect to the verification and determination of the result for the presidential election. Instead of using the constituency return, the V23B, ZEC turned its national command centre in Harare into a giant polling station and ward centre to collate and compile the results of the presidential election it had commandeered from all the 1,958 ward collation centres in the country, the V11s and V23As, in gross violation of the Electoral Act. ZEC was able to do this with no resistance or intervention from political parties, civil society or election observers.

The law that governs the verification of the presidential election result is section 110, as read with sections 65(2)(b), 65A(2)(b) and 65B(2)(b), of the Electoral Act [*Chapter 2:13*].

Section 65(2)(b) provides that:

> **At the time notified in terms of subsection (1) and in the presence of such candidates, election agents and observers as are present, the ward elections officer shall verify each polling-station return [V11] by ensuring that it purports to be duly certified by the presiding officer of the polling station concerned.**

And s655A(2)(b) provides that:

> **At the time notified in terms of subsection (1) and in the presence of such candidates, election agents and observers as are present, the constituency elections officer shall verify each ward return by ensuring that it purports to be duly certified by the ward elections officer concerned.**

While s65B(2)(b) provides that:

> **At the time notified in terms of subsection (1) and in the presence of such candidates, election agents and observers as are present, the provincial elections officer shall verify each constituency return by ensuring that it purports to be duly certified by the constituency elections officer concerned.**

(1)   Where only one candidate for President is validly nominated at the close of the day on which a nomination court sits in terms of section 38(1)(a), the Chairperson of the Commission (or, in his or her absence, the Deputy Chairperson or, in his or her absence, a Commissioner designated by the Chairperson) shall declare such candidate to be duly elected as President without the necessity of a poll.

[Subsection amended by s. 39 of Act No. 6 of 2014]

(2)   Where two or more candidates for President are validly nominated, a poll shall be taken in each constituency for the election of a President.

(3)   Subject to this Part, Part XIII shall apply, with any changes that may be necessary, to an election to the office of President (any references to a constituency centre or a constituency elections officer being construed as references to a presidential constituency centre or a presidential constituency elections officer respectively), other than sections 66, 67 and 68, for which the following provisions are substituted –

(a)   after the number of votes received by each candidate as shown in each polling-station return has been added together in terms of section 65(3)(i) and the resulting figure added to the number of postal votes and special votes received by each candidate, the constituency elections officer shall forthwith –

(i)   record on the constituency return the votes obtained by each candidate and the number of rejected ballot papers in such a manner that the results of the count for each polling station are shown on the return; and

(ii)   display the completed constituency return to those present and afford each candidate or his or her election agent the opportunity to subscribe their signatures thereto; and

(iii)   transmit to the Chief Elections Officer by hand through a messenger the constituency return or a copy thereof certified by the constituency elections officer to be correct;

(b)   immediately after arranging for the constituency return to be transmitted in terms of paragraph (a)(iii), the constituency elections officer shall affix a copy of the constituency return on the outside the constituency centre so that it is visible to the public;

(c)   immediately after receiving all the constituency returns transmitted in terms of paragraph (a)(iii), the Chief Elections Officer shall verify them, having given reasonable notice to each candidate or to his or her chief election agent of the time and place at which the returns are to be verified;

(d)   at the time and place notified for the verification of the constituency returns referred to in paragraph (c) and in the presence of such candidates, their chief election agents and observers as are present, the Chief Elections Officer shall display each constituency return to those present and shall, on request, allow a candidate or chief election agent of a candidate to make notes of the contents of each constituency return;

(e)   when the Chief Elections Officer has completed the verification of the constituency returns under paragraph (d) the Chief Elections Officer shall, in the presence of such persons referred to in paragraph (d) as are present, add together the number of votes received by each candidate as shown in each constituency return;

(f) subject to paragraph (h), after the number of votes received by each candidate as shown in each constituency return has been added together in terms of paragraph (e), the Chairperson of the Commission (or, in his or her absence, the Deputy Chairperson or, in his or her absence, a Commissioner designated by the Chairperson) shall –

    (i) where there are two candidates, forthwith declare the candidate who has received the greater number of votes to be duly elected as President of the Republic of Zimbabwe with effect from the day of such declaration; or

    (ii) where there are more than two candidates, forthwith declare the candidate who has received more than half the number of votes to be duly elected as President of the Republic of Zimbabwe with effect from the day of such declaration; or

    (iii) where there are more than two candidates, and no candidate has received more than half the number of votes, forthwith declare that a runoff presidential election shall be held on the date fixed by the President in terms of section 38(1)(a)(iii) (that is to say, a fixed date not less than twenty-eight and not more than forty-two days after the polling day or last polling day, the case may be, of the original election):

Provided that the Electoral Court, on the application of the Commission, may for good cause extend the period;

[Paragraph amended by s. 39 of Act No. 6 of 2014]

(g) subject to this section, if a runoff presidential election is required to be held –

    (i) only the two candidates who received the highest and next highest numbers of valid votes cast at the previous election shall be eligible to contest the election; and

    (ii) the election shall be held in accordance with this Act or, in case any situation arises that may be peculiar to such election, in the manner prescribed;

    (iii) after the number of votes received by each candidate at a presidential runoff election as shown in each constituency return has been added together in terms of paragraph (e), the Chairperson of the Commission (or, in his or her absence, the Deputy Chairperson or, in his or her absence, a Commissioner designated by the Chairperson) shall forthwith declare the candidate who has received the greater number of votes to be duly elected as President of the Republic of Zimbabwe with effect from the day of such declaration:

Provided that if the two candidates receive an equal number of votes, Parliament shall, as soon as practicable after the declaration of the result of that election, meet as an electoral college and elect one of the two candidates as President by secret ballot and without prior debate;

[Subparagraph amended by s. 39 of Act No. 6 of 2014]

(h) a declaration by the Chairperson of the Commission (or, in his or her absence, the Deputy Chairperson or, in his or her absence, a Commissioner designated by the Chairperson) under paragraph

(f) or (g)(iii) shall be made not later than –

    (i) five days after the polling day or last polling day, as the case may be, in the presidential election or runoff presidential election concerned; or

(ii) where a recount has been ordered in terms of section 67A, five days after the completion of the recount:

Provided that the Electoral Court may, on application by the Commission, for good cause extend the ten-day period;

[Paragraph amended by s. 39 of Act No. 6 of 2014]

(i) a declaration by the Chairperson of the Commission (or, in his or her absence, the Deputy Chairperson or, in his or her absence, a Commissioner designated by the Chairperson) under paragraph (h) [shall] be final, subject to reversal on petition to the Electoral Court that such declaration be set aside or to the proceedings relating to that election being declared void;

[Paragraph amended by s. 39 of Act No. 6 of 2014]

(j) the Chairperson of the Commission (or, in his or her absence, the Deputy Chairperson or, in his or her absence, a Commissioner designated by the Chairperson) shall as soon as possible after he or she has declared the result of an election to the office of President in terms of paragraph (i), publish such result by notice in the *Gazette* and in such other manner as he or she considers necessary to give sufficient publicity to the result, which notice shall also, in the event that the candidate in question has obtained more than half of the votes at the election, give the full name of the person duly elected as President of the Republic of Zimbabwe and the day with effect from which he or she was so elected.

[Paragraph amended by s. 39 of Act No. 6 of 2014]

(4) Subject to this Part, Parts XIV, XIVA and XV, shall apply, with any changes that may be necessary, to an election to the office of President, any references to a constituency centre or a constituency elections officer being construed as references to a presidential constituency centre or a presidential constituency elections officer respectively.

(5) In accordance with section 94 of the Constitution, a person elected as President assumes office when he or she takes, before the Chief Justice or the next most senior judge available, the oath of President in the form set out in the Third Schedule to the Constitution.

[Subsection substituted by Part VI of Schedule to Act No. 3 of 2016]

[Section substituted by s. 29 of Act No. 3 of 2012]

Given the foregoing, it is instructive to look again at what ZEC and Chigumba said under oath in their opposing affidavit about how they handled the verification process.

At the bottom of paragraph 31 of the opposing affidavit, ZEC and Chigumba say the following:

> **As part of the verification process, the applicant's election agents, election agents for other presidential candidates as well as election observers had full access to the *original V11s* and V23s with respect to the presidential election from which they could make notes as they required.**

This claim is fundamentally wrong on two fronts. In the first place, ZEC's hands were already dirty prior to any verification process after it used a different route with a different destination to collate, compile and transmit the result of the presidential election. This illegality was more than enough to invalidate the election. Second, the verification process that ZEC purported to do was based on verifying V11s and V23As that it had illegally commandeered from the ward centres following an illegal route with an illegal destination. The election return that is verified to determine the presidential election is the constituency return, the V23B Forms from the 210 constituency centres and 10 V23C Forms from 10 provincial command centres.

Under paragraph 32.2 of their opposing affidavit Chigumba and ZEC say:

> **His [Chamisa's] suggestion is also curious as it comes immediately after he avers that for close to two days the Electoral Commission's staff were busy manually entering data from original V11 forms onto an Excel spreadsheet.**

ZEC and Chigumba confirm on this paragraph, by approvingly quoting Chamisa, that the V11s it had commandeered from ward centres were used to extract data which was manually entered into an Excel spreadsheet. In terms of the law, the only data that ZEC could have extracted to input into the Excel spreadsheet for purposes of determining the presidential election result was from V23B forms, the constituency returns.

Any doubt about what ZEC was up to with V11s at the national command centre is removed by paragraph 34.2 of ZEC's and Chigumba's opposing affidavit where they make this startling admission:

> **The verification process itself consisted of election agents verifying the V11s and V23s that the Electoral Commission had and was using to compile the full result of the presidential election.**

There are two things that standout from ZEC's and Chigumba's paragraph 34.2.

ZEC and Chigumba say that election agents at the national command centre were "verifying V11s and V23s". Which election agents were verifying V11s at the national command centre and in terms of what law? There were 10,985 polling stations that produced V11s: did all the election agents from these come to the national command centre to verify their V11s? And were these 10,985 V11s manually processed over two days to enter their data into an Excel spreadsheet at the ZEC national command centre?

However, ZEC and Chigumba are correct that they, with the 20 or so officers who included military officers, did indeed manually compile their own result using an Excel spreadsheet over a period of two days. This result compiled by ZEC was based on unverifiable and un-traceable data, after the V11s and V23As containing the result of the presidential election hijacked from all the ward centres were mixed with bogus V11s that were completed well after the election, as exemplified by the case of Makoni North where EU observers reported that:

> The EU EOM observed ZEC officers in Makoni North completing V11 Forms two days after Election Day, even though polling staff and party agents were not present. They claimed this was due to the earlier lack of V11 forms.[93]

There is no telling how many V11 forms these two officers – who were in ZEC regalia, but who may very well have been army officers – completed. There is also no telling how many other such incidents occurred elsewhere.

Under paragraph 34.3 of the opposing affidavit, Chigumba made this startling submission:

> I have already averred, over the two day period, the applicant's election agents had unlimited access to all the original V11 and V23 forms relating to the presidential election and had the opportunity, at their discretion, to make notes from those V11 and V23 forms or to raise any queries with the Electoral Commission officials where they had problems with the information that was on the V11s and V23s being used by the Electoral Commission versus what they had through their own election agents from various polling stations.

The submission by Chigumba that Chamisa's election agents had **"unlimited access"** "to all the **original** V11 forms" that ZEC used at the national command centre over two days is strange. It is telling that Chigumba referred to V11s **"from various polling stations"**. What does "various" mean? What number of polling stations is equal to "various polling stations"? Is it all or some polling stations? Besides, it is common cause that the legal process of verifying the presidential election uses presidential constituency returns, the V23 B forms, not polling station returns, the V11s.

Under paragraph 34.6 of their opposing affidavit, Chigumba and ZEC make a factually and legally misleading averment regarding the presence of V11s during the verification of the result of the presidential election at the national command centre where they noted that:

> In terms of s110(3)(d) of the Electoral Act, the subject of a verification process are the actual returns from the various constituencies across the country. These returns consist of the V11 and V23 Forms. The addition of the figures specified on the V11 and V23 forms on an Excel spreadsheet is not the verification described in s110(3)(d).

While it is true that s110(3)(d) provides for the verification of the result of the presidential election, it is important to note that the specific return referred to in s110(3)(d) is the con-stituency return, the V23B. Section 110(3)(d) of the Electoral Act provides as follows:

---

[93] EU EOM, *Zimbabwe Harmonised Elections 2018: Final Report*, October 2018, page 35.

> At the time and place notified for the verification of the *constituency returns* referred to in paragraph (c) and in the presence of such candidates, their chief election agents and observers as are present, the Chief Elections Officer shall display each constituency return to those present and shall, on request, allow a candidate or chief election agent of a candidate to make notes of the contents of each *constituency return*.

The constituency return, the V23B, cannot also be referred to as the V11, the polling station return or V23A, the ward return. As already established, there are five returns that are used at various election centres in the collation and recording of the result of the presidential election and these are:

> Polling Station Return, the V11.
> Ward Return, V23A
> Constituency Return, V23B
> Provincial Return, V23C
> National command centre form, V23D

Section 110(3)(d) only mentions the constituency return, which is the V23B form, and no other return. The construction of this statute is unambiguous. Consequently, its interpretation should also be unambiguous. It is an established presumption of statutory interpretation that *expressio unius est exclusio alterius*: the explicit mention of one thing (constituency returns or V23s) is the exclusion of another thing (polling station returns or V11s).

Section 65A(3)(b) provides that the constituency election officer must:

> Ensure that a copy of the constituency return is displayed prominently outside the constituency centre so that all members of the public who wish to do so may inspect it and record its contents

This provision cannot possibly mean that the V11s are also displayed outside the constituency centre. V11s are displayed only outside polling stations and nowhere else. They certainly cannot legally be displayed at the national command centre in Harare.

In the circumstances, it is patently preposterous, in fact corrupt and criminal, that by its own admission ZEC had 20 or so officers, who included military officers, manually inputting data from V11s at its national command centre into an Excel spreadsheet over a period of two days, after which ZEC declared and announced Emmerson Mnangagwa as the winner of the presidential election.

It is no wonder that the EU Observation Mission highlighted this problem:

> Presidential results announced by ZEC were based on figures from the provincial level. ZEC also provided a CD-ROM with polling station figures set out in Excel format. As this was not a presentation of the actual V11 forms from each polling station, the CD-ROM did not provide the level of transparency, traceability and verifiability which was hoped for and which could have been achieved. Further, the figures presented by ZEC in the CD-ROM contained a large number of errors and inaccuracies.[94]

---

[94] Ibid., page 2.

Besides the question of what business ZEC had, handling V11s at the national command centre, picking and choosing V11s, and having 20 or so officers inputting the selected V11s into an Excel spreadsheet, there are other troubling questions whose inescapable answers point to the rigging of the election.

Why did ZEC have two different results for Mnangagwa: one announced on 3 August 2018 and another published on its website, a few days later?

The indisputable fact that ZEC officials were able to fill up V11s forms two days after the election, and when they were all by themselves, means that the source of the V11s that became available at the national command centre was necessarily suspicious. This may also explain why there were strange V11s there, including one that improbably had zero votes for Nelson Chamisa.

Another explanation of why ZEC had two conflicting results, with neither being reliable, has to do with how the ZEC results from the Excel spreadsheet included the counting of invalid votes cast. The EU Observer Mission report captured this aptly:

> **Intriguingly, the figure of 50.8% of votes initially announced for the winning candidate, which is the most widely-reported, appears not to have been a percentage of the total number of valid votes cast (if it is so, it should be 51.5%), but it is the respective percentage of the total number of votes cast** (*including invalid votes*). **All-in-all the CD-ROM provided by ZEC attests to a lack of quality control in its work and such errors and lack of transparency opened the process to legal jeopardy.**[95]

Invalid votes were counted and input into the Excel spreadsheet once Excelgate was in full swing in the hands of dark forces beyond ZEC.

In the final analysis, the ZEC figures, which Chief Justice Malaba ran away from, claiming to prefer facts over numbers, were a festival of inaccuracies about which the EU Observer Mission had this to say:

> **The figures presented by ZEC contain many anomalies and inaccuracies … Examples of inaccuracies include inaccurate totals for constituencies and/or provinces, inaccurate sums for the two main candidates in two provincial level cases, double entry of some polling stations, and, in some cases, more voters apparently having voted than are on the voter roll. ZEC later corrected some errors and amended the election result, meaning that ED Mnangagwa was attributed with 50.67% rather than 50.8%. These errors were highlighted in the court case brought by Chamisa …**[96]

The use of Excel in this manner took the process away from ZEC. I was told by the senior CIO securocrat who first gave the result of the presidential election in the early hours of 31 July 2018 that three ZEC commissioners threatened to resign as they waited for the results of Mashonaland Central and Mashonaland West provinces. The waiting was too long, and ZEC commissioners did not know what the results were because they were being calculated outside and beyond ZEC by an army technical team under the command of Defence House. The

---

[95] Ibid., page 37
[96] Ibid.

EU Observation Mission made this telling observation about the confusion that enveloped the results from the provinces of Mashonaland Central and Mashonaland West, as well as Harare and Zaka West constituency in Masvingo:

> The Provinces of Mashonaland Central and West show major discrepancies in vote totals for candidates in comparison with the ZEC summation (Mnangagwa received more than 6,000 extra votes and Chamisa received over 1,000 votes too few). In four polling stations in Zaka West Constituency, wards 22 and 23 have exactly the same result, which is close to impossible to achieve under normal circumstances. A polling station in Harare was entered twice with complete information. And, seven polling stations recorded a turnout above 100%, and many polling stations close to 100%.[97]

From the foregoing, it is quite clear that ZEC's use of a different route with a different destination to collate, compile and transmit the result of the presidential election from ward centres to the national command centre, was done to create a rigging opportunity through which the V11s and V23As containing the result of the election commandeered from all the 1,958 wards were mixed with fake V11s, such as the ones that the EU observers found ZEC officials completing by themselves in Makoni North, two days after the 30 July 2018 election.

The outcome was a poisoned chalice. But even without being mixed with Makoni North-type V11s, about which there is no reasonable doubt that they existed, having the result of the presidential election that ZEC hijacked from all ward centres transmitted through a route with a destination different from the one prescribed in s37C(4) of the Electoral Act, and which was collated and compiled at ZEC's national command centre, necessarily produced the poisoned chalice shown on **Diagram 16** below:

---

[97] Ibid.

DIAGRAM 16:
ZEC'S CONTAMINATION OF RESULT OF PRESIDENTIAL ELECTION

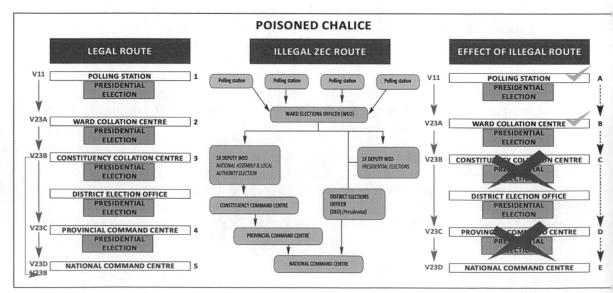

From the foregoing, the gravamen of Chamisa's ConCourt is that ZEC's server accurately captured the correct result of the presidential election as having been won by Chamisa with 66% of the vote against Mnangagwa who got 33%, but, at the behest of Defence House, the server was abandoned to facilitate the rigging of the result in favour of Mnangagwa. ZEC facilitated the rigging by inventing a route and destination for the collation, compilation and transmission of the result of the presidential election which was different from the route and destination used for the collation, compilation and transmission of the results of the national assembly election.

In his single-minded determination to dismiss Chamisa's application, as per his stance taken at Pretoria Sheraton hotel, even before seeing the full application and hearing the arguments, Chief Justice Malaba, and indeed the rest of the ConCourt judges, did not put their minds to why the server was at the core of Chamisa's case. They were assisted in this by Chamisa's lawyers who did not insist on having the issue addressed, save for a passing mention in their heads of argument.

To Malaba, the critical primary evidence was the residue in the sealed ballot boxes. At page 97 of his "fully dressed" judgment, Malaba opines that:

> It has already been established that the duty lay on the applicant to prove the factual allegations that he made regarding the authenticity of the Presidential election result that was declared in favour of the first respondent. He had the *onus* of providing evidence that would best facilitate the central task of accurately resolving the disputed presidential election result. The applicant ought to have gone to the used ballot papers in terms of s 67A of the Act and sought the truth of the matter. The truth sought lay in the determination of the question whether or not the votes as declared by the twenty-fourth respondent tallied with what was contained in the ballot boxes.

> Section 67A of the Act was enacted upon the realisation that it is only the used ballot papers themselves that are clear, sufficient, direct and credible evidence of what actually transpired when the electorate made their choices in a Presidential election. The counterfoils from which the ballot papers are torn are the evidence of residue. They remain sealed in separate packets at the end of the poll. They are the evidence of residue of what actually transpired as to the number of persons that participated during the vote.

> The purpose of the remedies provided for under ss 67A and 70(4) of the Act is to ensure that a decision to embark on unnecessary litigation challenging the validity of a Presidential election is not made. The remedies also ensure that a litigant who embarks on litigation has the necessary evidence with which to establish his or her case. In that way, any doubt as to whether or not the presidential election itself was properly conducted, and whether the true expression of the will of the voters was announced, would have been addressed by the parties before the court application was lodged.[98]

Malaba went to town, pontificating about the "remedies" for an aggrieved "losing" election candidate that are in sections 67A and 70(4) of the Electoral Act fully aware that the courts in Zimbabwe have been hostile to these provisions and have invariably viewed applicants who seek to apply the provisions as having no case and thus being on fishing expeditions in the hope of finding evidence to build an otherwise non-existent case.

---

[98] Judgment No. CCZ 21/19, pages 97–8.

At pages 98 and 99 of his judgment, Malaba purported to be generous to Chamisa by advising:

> **When the Presidential election result was declared in the early hours of 3 August 2018 the applicant knew he was an aggrieved candidate.** *He may not have known the exact or precise reason why he was aggrieved,* **but the law-makers in their wisdom created an avenue for the applicant to ensure that he had all the evidence necessary to prove his case if he wished to exercise his right to challenge the result. Time was on his side to obtain such evidence from the Presidential election residue.**

It was cunning for Malaba to suggest that, even if Chamisa "may not have known the exact or precise reason why he was aggrieved", he could have sought a recount under s67A of the Act or sought to have the sealed ballot boxes opened to inspect the election residue under s70(4). In this connection, Malaba gleefully noted at page 99 of his judgment that:

> **The applicant did not exercise his right in terms of s 70(4) of the Act as an aggrieved candidate in the Presidential election. His main reason for not resorting to s70(4) of the Act was that** *'he could not drink from a poisoned chalice'.* **One wonders how he knew that the chalice was poisoned without establishing if indeed it was poisoned.** *It was the Court that needed to be satisfied from real evidence that the sealed ballot boxes and the sealed packets were indeed 'poisoned chalices'.*

If it was "the Court that needed to be satisfied from real evidence that the sealed boxes and sealed packets were indeed 'poisoned chalices', then the Court had the power to make an appropriate order in that regard. Otherwise the sealed boxes and sealed packets referred to by Malaba were not the primary evidence upon which Chamisa's case was based. The crucial evidence was the server and Chamisa did the needful to have produced through a subpoena, which was blocked by Malaba.

It is clear that Malaba's claim that Chamisa should have relied on sections 67A and 70(4) of the Act to either seek a recount or the inspection of sealed ballot boxes and sealed packets was nothing but political grandstanding to cover up the relevant and best evidence that Malaba knew was in the server.

As I pointed out in Chapter 2, Malaba's "fully dressed judgment" failed to take judicial notice of ZEC's Report on the 2018 harmonised elections. Had he done so, as would be expected of a competent Chief Justice with a competent Constitutional Court, he would have realised, as he ought to have done, that ZEC admits to having breached the capturing, collation and transmission of the results of the presidential election prescribed in s37C(4) of the Act. In particular, Malaba would have been shocked by this admission by ZEC:

> **The results [of the presidential election in the form of V11s and V23As] were taken [from all ward collation centres] to the national command/collation centre physically by the District Elections Officers** *where they were captured and collated on a results collation template at the National Collation Centre* [emphasis added].[99]

---

[99] ZEC, *Zimbabwe 2018 Harmonised Elections Report*, pages 67–8.

This is shocking. What it means is that ZEC deharmonised the election by delinking the collation, compilation and transmission of the results for the presidential and national assembly elections from ward centres in order to have the results, that is the V11s and V23As, for the former captured and collated at ZEC's national command centre in Harare. The staggering implication that does not require rocket science to figure out is that the sealed ballot boxes and sealed packets of this result were irrelevant because their content was void *ab initio*, as they contained results whose route and destination for capturing, collation and transmission were manifestly illegal. The results in the sealed ballot boxes and sealed packets were by definition poisoned chalices.

Chapter 9

THE SUBPOENA

THE evidence of the existence of a ZEC server and its contents, which showed that Chamisa had received 66% of the vote and Mnangagwa 33%, was key to Chamisa's ConCourt case. The results in the server triggered the rigging operation.

When Chigumba and ZEC refused to discharge their constitutional duty in terms of being transparent about the server and its contents, Nelson Chamisa turned to Chief Justice Malaba, ahead of the hearing of the presidential election constitutional challenge.

Upon lodging his Constitutional Court application to ZEC's declaration of Emmerson Mnangagwa as the winner of the presidential election, and given ZEC's refusal to discharge its constitutional duty to be transparent about its election server and contents thereof, Chamisa procedurally served a *Subpoena Duces Tecum* on Chigumba, ZEC and ZEC's Chief Elections Officer, as well as on the rest of the respondents, including Mnangagwa. The wording of the subpoena was as follows:

IN THE CONSTITUTIONAL COURT OF ZIMBABWE   CASE No. CCZ 42/18

HELD IN HARARE

In the matter between:

NELSON CHAMISA	APPLICANT
EMMERSON DAMBUDZO MNANGAGWA	1st RESPONDENT
JOSEPH BUSHA	2nd RESPONDENT
MELBAH DZAPASI	3rd RESPONDENT
NKOSANA DONALD MOYO	4th RESPONDENT
NOAH NGONI MANYIKA	5th RESPONDENT
PETER HARRY WILSON	6th RESPONDENT
BRYN TAURAI MTEKI	7th RESPONDENT
THOKOZANI KHUPE	8th RESPONDENT
DIVINE MHAMBI-HOVE	9th RESPONDENT
LOVEMORE MADHUKU	10th RESPONDENT
TENDAI PETER MUNYANDURI	11th RESPONDENT
AMBROSE MUTINHIRI	12th RESPONDENT
TIMOTHY JOHANNESS TONDERAI MAPFUMO CHIGUVARE	13th RESPONDENT
JOICE TEURAI ROPA MUJURU	14th RESPONDENT
KWANELE HLABANGANA	15th RESPONDENT
EVARISTO WASHINGTON CHIKANGA	16th RESPONDENT
DANIEL KUZOVIRAVA SHUMBA	17th RESPONDENT
VIOLET MARIYACHA	18th RESPONDENT
BLESSING KASIYAMHURU	19th RESPONDENT
ELTON STEERS MANGOMA	20th RESPONDENT
PETER MAPFUMO GAVA	21st RESPONDENT
WILLIAM TAWONEZVI MUGADZA	22nd RESPONDENT
ZIMBABWE ELECTORAL COMMISSION	23rd RESPONDENT
THE CHAIRPERSON OF THE ELECTORAL COMMISSION	24th RESPONDENT
THE CHIEF ELECTIONS OFFICER	25th RESPONDENT

SUBPOENA DUCES TECUM

To: Daniel John Chigaru

of   The Zimbabwe Electoral Commission .

      HARARE

You are required and directed to attend before the **CONSTITUTIONAL COURT** of Zimbabwe, at Harare on Wednesday, the 22ᵈ August 2018, at the hour of 10 o'clock in the forenoon, and so from day to day until the above case is tried, to give evidence on behalf of the Plaintiff, and also to bring with you and produce at the time and place aforesaid:

1. All details of the ZEC server and in particular as it shows the results which were inputed into the ZEC server from the 30th of July 2018 to the 3rd of August 2018.

Witness: The Honourable Mr Justice Luke Malaba, Chief Justice of Zimbabwe at Harare this

day of August 2018.

_____
Registrar of the Constitutional Court

Applicant's Legal Practitioners:
ATHERSTONE & COOK
Praetor House
119 J. Chinamano Avenue
Cnr. 4th Str/ J. Chinamano Avenue
HARARE (Mr. Chagonda)

We, Atherstone & Cook, legal practitioners for the Applicant hereby accept responsibility for the payment of all expenses found by the taxing officer to be due to the witness abovenamed.

_____
Mr. Chagonda
ATHERSTONE & COOK
Praetor House
119 J. Chinamano
Avenue
Cnr. 4th Str/ J. Chinamano Avenue
HARARE

On 20 August 2018, the ConCourt Registrar responded to the subpoena with the following directive from Chief Justice Luke Malaba:

Your Reference:
My Reference:
Telephone : 798634/ 5

ZIMBABWE

CONSTITUTION COURT OF ZIMBABWE
P O Box CY 870
Causeway, Zimbabwe

20 August 2018

Atherstone and Cook
Applicant's Legal Practitioner
Praetor House
119 J Chinamano Avenue
Cnr 4th St / J Chinamano Avenue
HARARE

RE: **SUBPOENA DUCES TECUM**

The above matter refers.

Kindly take note that we are unable to accept the subpoena duces tecum in question since there is no provision for its issuance in the Pre-Trial Conference order issued by the Honourable Chief Justice on 16 August 2018.

....
for REGISTRAR
wpc

REGISTRAR
CONSTITUTIONAL COURT
2 0 AUG 2018
PO. BOX 870, CAUSEWAY
ZIMBABWE Tel: 01 798634/5

Using a baseless technicality, given the importance of the matter, Malaba singularly, and without reference to any law, blocked Chamisa's subpoena for the ZEC server or the contents thereof, in relation to the 30 July 2018 presidential election, to be brought to the ConCourt for legal scrutiny. This is the same Malaba who went to town about the legal remedies available to election contestants who have cause to challenge ZEC for one reason or another. It is also the same Malaba who went beyond himself during the ConCourt with the rather misplaced refrain that "he who alleges must prove". How does a litigant in an election petition prove anything when and where a Chief Justice endorses the opaque and unconstitutional conduct of an election body?

By blocking the subpoena on the flimsiest of technical excuses, while sitting alone in his chambers, Malaba acted ultra vires, given ZEC's constitutional duty under section 239 of the Constitution.

Malaba has no power to prevent a Chapter 12 constitutional commission from being transparent in the discharge of its constitutional functions. In any event, it was disingenuous for Malaba to refer to the 16 August 2018 Case Management Meeting as a Pre-Trial Conference.

Given the stalemate, on 20 August 2018, Chamisa's lawyers wrote to Malaba requesting an audience with him:

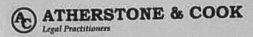

ATHERSTONE & COOK
Legal Practitioners

Attorneys • Notaries and Conveyancers • Executors and
Administrators of Estates • Patent and Trade Mark Agents

Praetor House
119 J. Chinamano Avenue

P.O.Box CY 1254, Causeway
Harare, Zimbabwe

Telephone: 263 8677 044999
              263 04 794994
              263 04 704244
Fax: 263 04 705180
Email: ic@praetor.co.zw
Website: www.atherstoneandcook.com

Our ref:

Your ref: CM/IC

REGISTRAR
CONSTITUTIONAL COURT

2 0 AUG 2018

P.O. BOX 8 ... CAUSEWAY
ZIMBABWE TEL. 04 70...

20 August 2018.

The Chief Registrar
Constitutional Court of Zimbabwe
HARARE

Dear Sir,

NELSON CHAMISA v EMMERSON DAMBUDZO MNANGAGWA AND 24 OTHERS: CCZ 42/18

We have seen the letter by the Chief Registrar concerning the subpoena we issued.
Pursuant to our previous correspondence we contend that it is still an issue to be
dealt with by the Chief Justice and we kindly request audience with him.

Yours faithfully

ATHERSTONE & COOK

Partners: L.H Cook   B.Comm. LL.B;   S.G.J Bull B.L, LL.B;   G.M Crossland B.A, LL.B;   L.A Cook B.Proc;
            I. Chagonda B.L, LL.B;   C.C Chihiyo B.L, LL.B;   C Mhike LL.B (Hons);   T. Nyamanika LL.B (Hons)
            M. F Khumalo B.S.S, LL.B;   T.I Gumbo LL.B (Hons)
Assisted by: T. Chagodumbie LL.B (Hons);   A.N Manuel LL.B (Hons);   T. M Chagonda LL.B.

On 21 August 2018, Malaba responded by advising that he was no longer meeting any lawyers:

Your Reference:
Our Reference:
Telephone: 798634/5

Fax: 700907

ZIMBABWE

CONSTITUTIONAL COURT OF ZIMBABWE
P.O. Box 870
Causeway, Zimbabwe

REGISTRAR
CONSTITUTIONAL COURT

21 AUG 2018

P.O. BOX 870, CAUSEWAY
ZIMBABWE

21 August 2018

Atherstone and Cook
Applicant's Legal Practitioners
Praetor House
119 J Chinamano Avenue
Cnr 4th St/J Chinamano Avenue
Harare

RE: **NELSON CHAMISA VS EMMERSON DAMBUDZO MNANGAGWA CASE NUMBER
CCZ 42/18**

The above matter and your letter dated 20 August 2018 wherein you requested audience with the Honourable Chief Justice refer.

We placed the letter before the Honourable Chief Justice who advised that he is no longer meeting any lawyers and that if there are any issues they should be raised in court.

A. Tshuma
REGISTRAR CONSTITUTIONAL COURT
/cm

When the lawyers pressed on with their request, Malaba responded by shutting the door:

Your Reference:
Our Reference:
Telephone:798634/5

Fax: 700907

ZIMBABWE

CONSTITUTIONAL COURT OF ZIMBABWE
P.O. Box 870
Causeway, Zimbabwe

21 August 2018

Atherstone and Cook
Applicant's Legal Practitioners
Praetor House
119 J Chinamano Avenue
Cnr 4ᵗʰ St/J Chinamano Avenue
Harare

RE: SUBPOENA DUCES TECUM

The above matter refers.

Kindly take note that we placed your letter dated 20 August 2018 before the Honourable Chief Justice who gave the following directive:

> "The decision whether or not the subpoena is to be issued is for the full court to decide after weighing the issue of relevance of the proposed evidence."

A. Tshuma
REGISTRAR CONSTITUTIONAL COURT
/cm

Chief Justice Malaba was now raising the issue of the evidentiary relevance of the server. Is it possible that a server with the results of the presidential election could be irrelevant? Malaba had changed goal posts in less than 24 hours. The previous day, he had said the matter was not among the issues included in his Pre-Trial Conference Order of 16 August 2018. Next, he sought to kill the matter by saying he was no longer meeting any lawyers; now the issue had changed to the admissibility of the subpoena, regarding its relevance from an evidentiary point of view.

Malaba's shifting stance was of great concern given that the subpoena had been pursued in accordance with the rules of the High Court to unravel ZEC's plot to shield from the court key evidence that was at the heart of the rigging of the poll. The issue was that ZEC had had the result of the presidential election in its server from the early hours on 31 July 2018, but did not want to share that result with the court because ZEC had abandoned the result in the server and scandalously invented a different route and different destination for the collation, compilation and transmission of the result for the presidential election. ZEC later adopted an Excel spreadsheet for purposes of altering and rigging the result that was in the server.

In the circumstances, ZEC denied the existence of the server in which it received, stored and processed voter information with election results. Consequently, ZEC did not cooperate with Chamisa's request to access the server, as it maintained that it had no such server.

In terms of the rules of the High Court, a subpoena is an appropriate remedy where a litigant does not cooperate with a reasonable request to supply information in their knowledge. In this connection, Rule 430(3) provides that:

> **Where in proceedings on motion a person has refused to make an affidavit of facts within his knowledge, the party desiring such person's evidence may sue out a *subpoena* compelling such person to appear on the day of the hearing to give evidence *viva voce*.**

The Rule impels the subpoenaed official to appear before the Court and to give evidence on the issue in question as a matter of law. It is against this legal backdrop that Chamisa sought to subpoena ZEC on the issue of the server.

But Malaba would have none of it. He radically changed the goal posts overnight. Raising the matter before the full bench during the hearing had become a pie in the sky and therefore out of the question. Time had run out. Malaba had succeeded in keeping the ZEC server outside the hearing and thus off the case. This was repugnant to justice and a travesty of the Constitution. Rigging was in full swing. Malaba had become a cog in the operation to rig the election. His unilateral decision to block the subpoena, without hearing the parties, killed Chamisa's Constitutional Court application well before it was heard. Malaba's decision was a pivotal plank in the rigging of the 2018 presidential election.

Besides the use, and more accurately the abuse, of office on the back of the *de facto* military coup that had been in force since 15 November 2017, the rigging invented a different route and different destination for the collation, compilation and transmission of the result for the presidential election in order to facilitate the use of a potpourri of authentic and fake V11s and V23As – no V23Bs were used – and to input fresh data from the fake returns into an insecure Excel spreadsheet to produce a rigged result.

As to the question whether the ZEC server existed or not, Mnangagwa's response under paragraph 118 of his opposing affidavit is unambiguously in the affirmative. A more telling confirmation of the existence of the ZEC server is found in the position taken by Malaba on Chamisa's subpoena for the server. Malaba literally used subterfuge to block the subpoena. In the first place, he invoked an unconvincing, and in fact a disingenuous, administrative excuse to block the subpoena by holding that the matter had not been included in his order after "the Pre-Trial Conference" of the 16 August 2018. But there was no Pre-Trial Conference. Instead there was a Case Management Meeting which dealt with process issues, especially timelines for service of court process. Nothing was said nor could be said about legal issues or even matters of fact because the focus was only on the timeline for service of court process.

At the last minute, on 21 August 2018, Chamisa's lawyers indicated that they disagreed with Malaba's view that the subpoena had fallen away because he did not include it in his "Pre-Trial Conference order", on 16 August 2018, and requested an audience with him over the subpoena. Realising that the subpoena issue was not going away but was escalating, Malaba sprang an untested legal reason for excluding the subpoena. He directed through the ConCourt Registrar that he did not see the **relevance** of the ZEC server in Chamisa's Constitutional Court challenge to ZEC's declaration of Emmerson Mnangagwa as the winner of the 2018 presidential election.

Chief Justice Malaba was now raising the issue of the admissibility of the ZEC server. He was making this ruling, while seeming to suggest that the matter could be decided by the full bench, at the eleventh hour, yet he was fully aware that it would have been futile to take the matter to a full bench, given the constitutional timelines for determining the case.

It is trite to mention that all relevant evidence in a case is admissible. It is only irrelevant evidence that is inadmissible. Was the ZEC server irrelevant evidence in Chamisa's Constitutional Court challenge to ZEC's declaration of Emmerson Mnangagwa as the winner of the 2018 presidential election? There's no need for a lawyer to answer this question. The ZEC server was at the core of the Constitutional Court challenge. It was the most relevant and best evidence in the case. Why then did Malaba question the relevance of the ZEC server as evidence? It is because he was determined to block the subpoena – and, *ipso facto*, block the production of the ZEC server in court – in order to assist Mnangagwa's case by harming Chamisa's plea. Malaba had read Mnangagwa's opposing affidavit which confirmed the existence of the ZEC server, and he was clear that its production in court would be like a nuclear bomb on ZEC and its Excel spreadsheet shenanigans.

Chief Justice Malaba's question was not whether the ZEC server existed or not, in the same way he asked about the existence of V11s to support Chamisa's case, but he asked whether the server was **relevant** evidence that was admissible or not.

This means that even Malaba was clear that the ZEC server existed. The existence of the server, whose production Malaba was blocking, confirmed the existence of a rigging plot. While the confirmation raises fundamental criminal questions about the scandal, one unavoidable conclusion is that the 2018 presidential election was stolen when ZEC was stolen. This resulted in ZEC using an insecure and unreliable Excel spreadsheet into which falsified data, some of it based on fake V11s and V23As, was manually input over two days at the ZEC national command centre by twenty or so ZEC officers, who included ZDF personnel. This electoral theft led to ZEC's declaration and announcement of Mnangagwa as the duly elected President of Zimbabwe. In effect, this was a coup against the sovereignty of the people.

Against this backdrop, it was astonishing that the subpoena features quite extensively in Malaba's 137-page "fully dressed" judgment released on 7 November 2019. At page 44 of his judgment, Malaba incorrectly recalls that:

> On 20 August 2018 the applicant's legal practitioners sent copies of a *subpoena duces tecum* to the Registrar, with an accompanying written request that it be issued. The *subpoena* sought to compel the Commission to produce its server at the hearing of the court application. The request that the *subpoena* be issued by the Registrar was placed before the Chief Justice. He gave the following direction:
>
> 'The decision whether or not the *subpoena* is to be issued is for the full Court to make after weighing the issue of relevance of the evidence to be produced.'
>
> The decision was communicated to the applicant's legal practitioners by the Registrar by an accompanying letter on 21 August 2018 and received on the same day at 11:05 am.[100]

Malaba's recollection quoted above from his judgment is not only in incorrect but also grossly misleading, because it gives the false impression that what he quotes was his only communication on the matter. The fact is that, through the Registrar of the Constitutional Court, Malaba gave Chamisa's lawyers three different directives regarding the subpoena on the ZEC server.

The first directive was on 20 August 2018, in which the ConCourt Registrar said on Malaba's behalf:

> Kindly take note that we are unable to accept the *subpoena duces tecum* in question since there is no provision for its issuance in the Pre-Trial Conference order issued by the Honourable Chief Justice on 16 August 2018.

Malaba was clearly and unequivocally rejecting the subpoena on the grounds that it was not part of his Pre-Trial Conference order. He wanted, and certainly hoped, that the matter would end with his directive, but it did not end there because Chamisa's lawyers persisted by requesting an audience with Malaba in a letter dated 20 August 2018 in which they pleaded that:

> We have seen the letter by the Chief Registrar concerning the *subpoena* we issued. Pursuant to our previous correspondence, we contend that it is still an issue to be dealt with by the Chief Justice and we kindly request audience with him.

---

[100] Judgment No. CCZ 21/19, page 44.

On the next day, 21 August 2018, Malaba issued a second directive through the ConCourt Registrar:

> **The above matter and your letter dated 20 August 2018 wherein you requested audience with Honourable Chief Justice refer.**
>
> **We placed the letter before the Honourable Chief Justice who advised that he is no longer meeting any lawyers and that if there are any issues they should be raised in court.**

Again, through the ConCourt Registrar, the lawyers pressed on with their request for an audience with Malaba. In a letter from the Registrar dated 21 August 2018, on the eve of the ConCourt hearing, Malaba made his third intervention in which the Registrar wrote:

> **Kindly take note that we placed your letter dated 20 August 2018 before the Honourable Chief Justice who gave the following directive:**
>
> > **'The decision whether or not the subpoena is to be issued is for the full court to decide after weighing the issue of relevance of the proposed evidence.'**

This is the only directive that Malaba recalls in his "fully dressed" judgment, to the exclusion of the first two; and this directive was given the day before the ConCourt hearing commenced on 22 August 2018.

Against this backdrop, it was surprising that in his "fully dressed" judgment Malaba wrote:

> **It is necessary to deal with the issue of the *subpoena duces tecum* the applicant sought from a Judge in Chambers.**

But Malaba did not establish or explain the necessity that prompted him "to deal with the issue of the *subpoena*". The fact of the matter is that the subpoena was never raised in chambers with any judge because Malaba refused to hear it in chambers, nor was it placed before the court, because the lawyers had no time to place it. In this connection, Malaba observed at page 46 of his judgment that:

> *The question of legitimacy of the subpoena sought was never determined by the Court. It remains unanswered, as no application for the subpoena was made to the Court to determine the matter,* **despite the applicant having been notified that this was required** [emphasis added].[101]

While Malaba states in his "fully dressed" judgment that no application for the subpoena was made for the court to determine the matter, meaning that the matter was not before the court, he nevertheless found "it necessary to deal with the issue of the *subpoena duces tecum*".

Furthermore, considering that there was no application for the subpoena, Malaba notes at page 46 of his judgment that:

---

[101] Judgment No. CCZ 21/19, pages 45–6.

No-one knows what, in the circumstances, the decision of the Court would have been had the application been made for the *subpoena duces tecum* to be issued compelling the Commission to produce its server at the hearing of the application. No-one knows what the responses of the respondents would have been to such an application had it been made, considering the requirements of ss 93(1) and 93(3) of the Constitution.

What is surprising and not in the interest of justice is that, despite the fact that there was no application, and while he said that no one would know what the application would have contained had it been made, what the responses of the respondents would have been, or what the decision of the Court would have been, Malaba proceeded to make extensive *obiter dicta* that exposed his bias against the applicant and showed favour for the respondents. In effect, Malaba opined that he blocked the issuance of the subpoena because he thought "it was a fishing expedition".

It is mind-boggling that Chief Justice Malaba found it proper to make findings on the subpoena, including citing case law authorities, when he did not hear arguments on the matter, not even in chambers, because he refused to have it heard by blocking the subpoena and making the filing of an application impossible. This was an extension and example of the extensive rigging of the 2018 presidential election. Because he was part of the rigging conspiracy, Malaba was playing it to the detriment not only of the rule of law and constitutionalism but also, which is even more damaging, to the standing, integrity and credibility of the Consitutional Court.

Chapter 10

REBUTTING CHIGUMBA

IN their opposing papers to Nelson Chamisa's founding affidavit in his Constitutional Court challenge, Chigumba and ZEC made some specific submissions on whether there was a server with presidential election results, and on the legal requirements for the determination and verification of result. These submissions are important to highlight, unpack and critique because they are factually unsustainable, and are so irrational and shocking that they establish, quite clearly, that the 2018 presidential election was brazenly and massively rigged against Chamisa in favour of Mnangagwa.

Accordingly, based on their opposing affidavit in Chamisa's Constitutional Court challenge, seven key submissions and sub-submissions by Chigumba and ZEC on the verification and determination of the result of the presidential election are presented below. These are critically analysed to expose their deceit and rigging effect, against the backdrop of Chamisa's founding averments to which the submissions respond. The founding averments are delineated under "Chamisa", the responses under "Chigumba" and each of the responses is followed by my analytical exposé of its rigging deception.

Rebuttal One

Chamisa: 5.1. On the 1st of August 2018 twenty third respondent [ZEC] started what it called a verification process and which it asked Messrs Komichi and Timba to witness. The process involved a group of people, in excess of twenty, punching in what was identified as V11 data into an Excel spreadsheet. For close to two days that process continued. I defer to the affidavits of the two gentlemen which explain the manner in which that process was being conducted.

Chigumba: 31. Ad Para 5.1 Despite the applicant's averments under paragraph 4.5.32 and 4.5.33 of his founding affidavit to the effect that his election agents were not notified of the date and place of verification and were not given an opportunity to make notes of the contents of constituency returns, the applicant under paragraph 5.1 of his founding affidavit makes the opposite averment. He admits that his election agents were called for a verification process, he admits that they heeded this call and came to the 23rd respondent's national command centre where the verification was taking place, he admits that his agents were present when the verification process was underway, he admits that the verification process went on for two days with his election agents in attendance. This coupled with the affidavits by Mrs. Pamela Mapondera and Mrs. Mavis Mudiwakure attached and already referenced, shows that not only were his agents in attendance, they participated in the verification process. As part of the verification process, the applicant's election agents, election agents for other presidential candidates as well as election observers had full access to the original V11s and V23s with respect to the presidential election from which they could make notes as they required.

Here we should note that the ZEC/Chigumba response creates the false impression that the issue at stake here is whether Chamisa's election agents were notified about "the verification" and whether they participated in that "verification". In so doing, ZEC/Chigumba divert attention away from three crucial issues in paragraph 5.1 of Chamisa's averment, which the response does not address, and these are the following:

- First, on 1 August 2018 the 23rd Respondent (ZEC) "started *what it called a verification process*", which it asked Messrs Komichi and Timba (Chamisa's election agents) to participate in. There is a world of difference between "what ZEC called the verification" process and the "determination and verification" of the result of the presidential election provided under the Electoral Act. Chamisa's election agents, Komichi and Timba, expected to witness the determination and verification of the result of the presidential election in terms of the Electoral Act, the Electoral Regulations and established ZEC policy and administrative procedures. What they in fact witnessed was an entirely different process, which ZEC called "a verification process". As has been shown in this book, and will be further elaborated below, there was no legal, factual and rational determination and verification of the result of the presidential election in terms of the Electoral Act.

- Second, the process that Komichi and Timba witnessed on 1 August 2018 "*involved a group of people, in excess of twenty*". Chigumba did not challenge or deny this and therefore confirmed it. But who was in this group of people in excess of twenty and where did "what was identified as V11 data", that these people were punching into an Excel spreadsheet, come from? Section 110(3)(d) of the Electoral Act requires the verification of the (presidential) constituency returns, and that is V23B Forms. What was the group of people in excess of 20 doing with V11 forms, which are polling station returns? And Chigumba refers to **original** V11s and V23s. Where did these originals come from and where were they stored? How did the group of people access these purportedly original V11s and V23s? It is clear that this capturing of V11 and V23A data and punching it into an Excel spreadsheet was a direct result of ZEC's illegal use of two different routes with two different destinations for the capturing, collation and transmission of the results for the presidential and national assembly elections. The capturing and collation of presidential elections at ZEC by a group of people in excess of 20 was an illegal exercise in daylight rigging.

- Third, given the critical importance of transparency, reliability and accountability in the management of elections, what was an Excel spreadsheet doing at the ZEC national command centre? As has been presented above, and as will be further elaborated below, the use of an Excel spreadsheet by ZEC was illegal and scandalous, and specifically used to facilitate the rigging of the election. This is because, in terms of electoral law, the only election return that is captured and collated at ZEC's national command centre is the V23D, which captures and collates V23Cs, or provincial returns. Polling station returns, V11s, and ward centre returns, V23As, are not captured or collated at the national command centre. In terms of s110(s)(d), the result of the presidential election is determined by capturing and collating constituency returns, V23Bs; not V11s or V23As. When ZEC invented a different route with a different destination from ward centres for capturing and collation at the national command centre, it only got or hijacked V11s and V23As, which by law cannot be captured or collated in Harare.

Rebuttal Two

Chamisa: 5.2. I was also aware that twenty-third respondent [ZEC] had received, as it should do, results from all the polling stations in real time and stored them into its server.

Chigumba: 32. Ad Para 5.2. This is denied.

As I show in greater detail below, Chigumba's bare denial has no basis in fact, the Electoral Act, the Electoral Regulations, or the ZEC 2018 *Manual for Electoral Officers*.

Chigumba: 32.1. Transmission of results from polling stations, wards and constituencies is done manually. This is consistent with the provisions of s64(2) of the Electoral Act. The Electoral Commission had no server set up at the national command centre or anywhere else, on which results were sent and stored in real time as the applicant suggests.

In the first place, it is not correct for Chigumba to just declare that "transmission of results from polling stations, wards and constituencies is done manually". Transmission of results in the Electoral Act includes "notification" thereof. For example, s67 of the Act provides that:

> **As soon as the constituency elections officer has declared a candidate to be duly elected, he or she shall, without delay,** *notify the Chief Elections Officer, by telegram, telefacsimile, electronic mail* **or such other means as may be prescribed, of the names of the person declared duly elected, the day with effect from which he or she was declared elected, the number of votes received by the respective candidates and the number of rejected ballot papers** [emphasis added].

Quite clearly, the law does provide for the notification of the result of elections electronically. It stands to reason that a result notified electronically is also stored electronically; and that the appropriate storage for such data is a server.

Section 64(2) of the Electoral Act provides that "immediately after affixing a polling station return on the outside of the polling station in terms of subsection (1)(e), **the presiding officer shall personally transmit** to the ward elections officer for the ward in which the polling station is situated …". This is indeed the case with respect to the **original polling station return (the V11)**. The polling station return is sent to the ward centre where all V11s in the ward are collated and verified for their results to be recorded on V23A Form, the ward return. This position is clearly set out in s37(4)(b)(i) & (ii) which stipulates that:

(b)   with respect to –
   (i)   presidential elections, polling-station returns gathered from every polling station within a ward shall be transmitted to the appropriate ward centre for collation at that centre, the results of which collation shall be embodied in a return ("presidential election ward return") distinctly indicating the results obtained in each polling station relating to that election; and

   (ii)   national assembly elections, polling-station returns gathered from every polling station within a ward shall be transmitted to the appropriate ward centre for collation at that centre, the results of which collation shall be embodied in a return ("national assembly election ward return") distinctly indicating the results obtained in each polling station relating to those elections:

   Provided that duplicate copies of the polling-station returns gathered from every polling station within a ward for the purposes of subparagraph (i) and (ii) shall also be transmitted through the appropriate ward centre directly to the national command centre.

The proviso of s37(4)(b) subparagraphs (i) & (ii) of the Electoral Act disproves the claim by Chigumba that the transmission of results from polling stations, wards and constituencies is done only manually in terms of the provisions of s64(2) of the Electoral Act. Section 64(2) applies only to the **movement of original results returns** from a polling station to a ward centre. from a ward centre to a constituency centre, from a constituency centre to a provincial command centre, and from a provincial command centre to the national command centre. The section does not apply to the **movement of copies of results returns** from a ward centre or a constituency centre or a provincial command centre to the national command centre. **Copies** of results returns are sent directly to the national command centre from polling stations, ward centres, constituency centres and provincial centres; and this is done by Election Officers on their own, in the absence of election agents and election observers. That is the import of the proviso of s37 (4)(b)(i) & (ii) of the Electoral Act.

The factual and legal position is that the transmission of results from polling stations, referred to in s64(2) of the Electoral Act, is not the only way of transmitting results in terms of the law. Statutory Instrument 21 of 2005 (Electoral Regulations), provides that, after polling station returns (the V11s) have been completed at a polling station, they must be distributed as follows:[102]

Presidential election: Affix original copy outside of polling station; Provide original copy to each candidate, or to his or her election agent if present, and to each observer present at polling station; Seal original copy in ballot box; Send original return to ward collation centre and duplicate copies to presidential constituency centre, provincial command centre and national command centre.

Quite clearly, the law provides for **copies** of polling station returns (V11s) to be sent to the constituency centre, provincial command centre and the national command centre **immediately** after an original copy has been affixed outside the polling station and before the original has reached the ward collation centre. There is no law that says these copies must be sent personally or manually. Only the original copy of the V11 that is sent to the ward collation centre, must be sent personally, physically or manually. The reason the original V11 (polling station return) is personally delivered from the polling station to the ward collation centre is because it must be accompanied by election agents and election observers as well as the police who are involved in its transmission, unsealing and collation at the ward centre by law. The same applies to the transmission of ward returns to constituency centres, constituency returns to provincial command centres, and provincial returns to the national command centre.

Otherwise it is important to underscore once again, that Electoral Regulations provide for the transmission of results to the national command centre by electronic and other means besides personal or physical or manual delivery. Regarding the result of a presidential election, the Form for doing that is a V18.

Chigumba: 32.2. His suggestion is also curious as it comes immediately after he avers that for close to two days the Electoral Commission's staff were busy manually entering data from original V11 Forms onto an Excel spreadsheet.

---

[102] Statutory Instrument 21 of 2005 (Electoral Regulations), pages 14 and 15. The same distribution procedure is provided by ZEC in its *Electoral Officers Manual*, pages 14 and 15.

Chamisa's averment, which Chigumba did not deny, that for close to two days the Electoral Commission's staff were busy manually entering data from **original** V11 forms into an Excel spreadsheet, is crucial as it proves that ZEC hijacked original V11s and V23As from ward centres; and used an illegal route with an illegal destination to transmit the result of only the presidential election for illegal capturing and collation at the national command centre using an Excel spreadsheet. The capturing and collation of original V11s and V23As in Harare is how the result of the 2018 presidential election was rigged.

Chigumba: 32.3. As he has alleged the existence of a server, it is incumbent upon the applicant to prove his allegation. Again, he places no evidence before the court in respect of this issue.

Chapter 12 constitutional bodies such as, and especially, ZEC have a constitutional duty to be transparent. The common law doctrine that he who alleges must prove is a wrong standard to apply to such constitutional institutions that have specific constitutional duties or obligations, such as to be transparent. Where an allegation is made against constitutional bodies regarding a failure to perform a constitutional duty transparently, they have an obligation to be transparent, because they must not have anything to hide. But it has been shown earlier in this book that ZEC treats its servers as national security facilities to which political parties and election candidates must not have access. Military and intelligence staff are seconded to or embedded in ZEC structures under conditions of unacceptable secrecy and opaqueness. Added to this is the fact that ZEC operates like a secret society and its staff are forced to sign an oath of secrecy under Form V19 (Declaration of Secrecy) in terms of sections 86 and 87 of the Electoral Regulations. It is absurd to even suggest that a modern electoral body in a modern country, which is a constitutional democracy, can organize and run a harmonised election, bringing together and managing local authority elections, parliamentary elections and presidential elections, without a server for receiving, storing and processing voting information and data.

Rebuttal Three

Chamisa: 5.5. In the meantime the punching in of the V11 data at the national command centre ended. This was at or around 21:00 P:M on the 2nd of August 2018. It is at that stage that the verification process was supposed to start. We were to verify:

a.   *The details of the constituency returns, V23b forms and see how they compared to the details on the Excel spreadsheet.*

b.   *What had been punched into Excel and see how it compared to the V11 forms that we all had.*

c.   *The tally yielded by the process which ZEC had preferred and how that total compared to what we had.*

d.   *What was on the server was to be compared and if need be contrasted with what was on the V23b forms, the V11 forms and what had been punched into Excel.*

Chigumba: 34. Ad Para 5.5. This is denied.

34.1. Verification of presidential election results was done over the two-day period that the applicant acknowledges his election agents were present and participating at the national command centre.

Significantly, Chigumba admitted to two different processes having taken place simultaneously: one was "the punching of V11 data" into the Excel spreadsheet and the other was "verifying the V11s and V23s".

ZEC did not challenge or deny Chamisa's key averment, under paragraph 5.1 of his founding affidavit, about the situation that obtained at the ZEC collation room at the national command centre, as witnessed by his election agents and attested to in their supporting affidavits, namely that:

> On the 1st of August 2018 twenty third respondent started what it called a verification process and which it asked Messrs Komichi and Timba to witness. The process involved a group of people, in excess of twenty, punching in what was identified as V11 data into an Excel spreadsheet. For close to two days that process continued.

The "verification process" involving "a group of people, in excess of twenty, punching in what was identified as V11 data into an Excel spreadsheet", which ZEC did not deny, was patently illegal and constituted a substantial violation of electoral law. As already pointed out, it was illegal for ZEC to re-route the capturing and collation of the result for the presidential election, and to capture and collate V11s and V23As at ZEC's national command centre in Harare. Also, the verification and determination of the result of the presidential election is based on V23Bs and not V11s or V23As.

Section 110(3)(d) of the Electoral Act, which deals with the determination and verification of the result of the presidential election provides that:

> At the time and place notified for the verification of the constituency returns referred to in paragraph (c) and in the presence of such candidates, their chief election agents and observers as are present, the Chief Elections Officer shall display each constituency return to those present and shall, on request, allow a candidate or chief election agent of a candidate to make notes of the contents of each constituency return.

The import of s110(3)(d) is that the determination of the final result of the presidential election begins with the verification of the constituency returns. These must be displayed one at a time at a place notified in advance to allow candidates or their election agents to verify the returns to confirm or raise queries about them. During this process, there can be no "group of people, in excess of twenty, punching in what was identified as V11 data into an Excel spreadsheet" going on for close to two days, as happened at the ZEC national command centre from 1 to 2 August 2018.

Regarding the procedure for the addition of the votes in the constituency returns to get the final result of the presidential election, s110(3)(e) of the Electoral Act provides as follows:

> … when the Chief Elections Officer has completed the verification of the constituency returns under paragraph (d) the Chief Elections Officer shall, in the presence of such persons referred to in paragraph (d) as are present, add together the number of votes received by each candidate as shown in each constituency return.

What this means is that the verification of constituency returns at the national command centre cannot legally or rationally start or run concurrently with the punching of V11 data into an Excel spreadsheet. More specifically, the addition of votes cannot be done before verification has been completed. The verification and addition of votes in the presidential constituency returns are sequential and not simultaneous processes.

Chigumba: 34.2. The verification process itself consisted of election agents verifying the V11s and V23s that the Electoral Commission had and was using to compile the full result of the presidential election.

The agreed facts are that over the two-day period in question, a group of people in excess of twenty were punching data from what ZEC alleged were original V11s and V23s into an Excel spreadsheet. That was not a verification of anything. Rather, it was origination of new and unverified data into an illegal return, an Excel spreadsheet. In other words, this was rigging. Factually and legally, **the data on V11s is collated and verified at ward centres.**

By assembling a group of people in excess of twenty at the national command centre to punch data into an Excel spreadsheet from original V11s and V23As, ZEC was illegally, irrationally and incredibly setting its national command centre as one giant polling station. Again, the point must be repeated with greater emphasis that V11s are collated and verified at ward centres. The collation of V11s at the national command centre was irregular and illegal, and constituted substantial non-compliance with electoral law.

In terms of the law, data from V11s is punched into V23As, not an Excel spreadsheet but V23As at the 1,958 ward centres and nowhere else. The V23A is the only authoritative return with data from V11s. An Excel spreadsheet has no legal standing whatsoever in the collation and verification of election results. Whereas a V23A with polling station data can be verified, an Excel spreadsheet simply cannot be verified.

There are three source documents that define the forms or returns that must be verified: these are the Electoral Act (Chapter 2:13), Statutory Instruments (Electoral Regulations), as amended, and ZEC's 2018 *Electoral Officers Manual*. None of these key source documents refers to an Excel spreadsheet as an election return. None whatsoever. Indeed, the effective use of an Excel spreadsheet as an election return was a brazen and scandalous rigging venture of untold proportions. This is because all the source documents, of which an Excel spreadsheet is not, are agreed that the following are the presidential election returns for collation and verification, leading to the final result of a presidential election:

- **Form V11**: generated at a polling station under s64(1)(c) of the Electoral Act; **collated and verified** at the ward centre in terms of s65(2) of the Act.
- **Form V23A**: generated at a ward centre under s37C(4)(a) of the Electoral Act; **collated and verified** at a constituency centre in terms of 65A(2) of the Act.
- **Form V23B**: generated at a constituency centre under s37(C)(4)(b)(i) of the Electoral Act; collated and verified at the provincial command centre and national command centre, respectively.

First, **Form V23B**, the key presidential constituency return, is **collated and verified** at the provincial command centre in terms of s65B(2) of the Electoral Act.

Second, and critically important, **Form V23B**, the presidential constituency return, is **collated and verified** at the national command centre in terms of s110(3)(d) of the Electoral Act.

Form V23C is generated at a provincial centre under 37(C)(4)(b)(i) of the Electoral Act, as the provincial return. The V23C forms are **collated and verified** at the national command centre in terms of s65(3), (4) & (5) of the Electoral Act, and entered on to the V23D form, which has the initial national result of the presidential election.

It is notable that, in ZEC's deceptive catch-all reference to V23s, it is impossible to know that there is an election return called a V23C, and that this provincial return is critically important because it is a key component of the preliminary or initial result of the presidential election. This fact is borne out by s37C(4)(f), which stipulates that:

(f) *after the collation of the results of the presidential election at each provincial command centre, provincial returns for the presidential election gathered from every provincial command centre shall be transmitted to the national command centre, where –*

    (i) *the provincial returns shall be collated to obtain the initial results of the presidential election; and*

    (ii) *the final result of the presidential election shall, after **reconciling the provincial returns with the polling station returns and presidential constituency returns referred to in the provisos to paragraphs (b) and (d) respectively,** be reflected in a return that distinctly reflects number of votes cast for each presidential candidate at every polling station, ward centre, presidential constituency centre and provincial command centre.*

Section 37C(4)(f) of the Electoral Act is crucially important in so far as it makes clear ZEC has a legal obligation to transparently produce two distinct results of the presidential poll. These are an ***initial*** result based on the collation and verification of Form V23Cs (the presidential provincial return), and a ***final*** result, based on the collation and verification of V23Bs dealing with the presidential constituency return.

The initial or preliminary result of the presidential election is collated and verified at the national command centre as stipulated in s37C(4)(f), as captured above, and is contained in Form V23D, a national command centre return in line with s110(3)(d) of the Act.

Form V23D is described in Statutory Instrument 21 of 2005 (Electoral Regulations). Save for its Report on the 2018 harmonised elections, nowhere in its opposing papers in the Constitutional Court challenge did ZEC refer to the V23D, a critical return with the preliminary result of the presidential election in terms of s37C(4)(f) of the Electoral Act. Subparagraph (ii) of that section provides that:

    (ii) *the final result of the presidential election shall, after **reconciling the provincial returns with the polling station returns and presidential constituency returns referred to in the provisos to paragraphs (b) and (d) respectively,** be reflected in a return that distinctly reflects number of votes cast for each presidential candidate at every polling station, ward centre, presidential constituency centre and provincial command centre.*

For the avoidance of doubt, because this is important, paragraphs (b) and (d) and their provisos, that are referred to above, state as follows:

(b) *with respect to –*

    (i) *presidential elections, polling-station returns gathered from every polling station within a ward shall be transmitted to the appropriate ward centre for collation at that centre, the results of which collation shall be embodied in a return ("presidential election ward return") distinctly indicating the results obtained in each polling station relating to that election; and*

(ii) *National Assembly elections, polling-station returns gathered from every polling station within a ward shall be transmitted to the appropriate ward centre for collation at that centre, the results of which collation shall be embodied in a return ("national assembly election ward return") distinctly indicating the results obtained in each polling station relating to those elections:*

Provided that duplicate copies of the polling-station returns gathered from every polling station within a ward for the purposes of subparagraph (i) and (ii) shall also be transmitted through the appropriate ward centre directly to the national command centre.

(d) *after collation of the results of the presidential election at each presidential constituency centre, presidential constituency returns gathered from every presidential constituency centre shall be transmitted to the provincial command centre for collation at that centre, the results of which collation shall be embodied in a return ("provincial return for the presidential election") distinctly indicating the results obtained in each constituency relating to those elections.*

Provided that duplicate copies of the presidential constituency returns gathered from every presidential constituency centre shall also be transmitted directly from the provincial command centre concerned to the National Command Centre.

Against this backdrop, s37C(4)(f) requires that there be a reconciliation of these results generated from copies with the results generated from original V11s from polling stations and V23As from ward centres attached to the original presidential constituency returns (V23Bs) that are physically sent to the national command centre and are verified in terms of s110(3)(d) of the Electoral Act. ZEC did not verify V23Bs as required by the law. Instead, ZEC announced a tainted presidential election result based on a tainted V23D, which had provincial returns (V23Cs) that ended up giving Mnangagwa two different results, initially 50.8% of the vote later reduced to 50.67%.

Chigumba: 34.3. As I have already averred, over the two day period, the applicant's election agents had unlimited access to all the original V11 and V23 Forms relating to the presidential election and had the opportunity, at their discretion, to make notes from those V11 and V23 forms or to raise any queries with the Electoral Commission officials where they had problems with the information that was on the V11s and V23s being used by the Electoral Commission versus what they had through their own election agents from various polling stations.

It is common cause that the two-day period had, from the beginning to the end, two processes. One involved "a group of people, in excess of twenty, punching in what was identified as V11 data into an Excel spreadsheet"; and the other involving what ZEC called a verification exercise in which Chamisa's *"election agents had unlimited access to all the original V11 and V23 Forms relating to the presidential election and had the opportunity, at their discretion, to make notes from those V11 and V23"*.

Having the two processes active at the same time was in violation of s110(3)(d) read with s110(3)(e). The two processes are sequential, not simultaneous. The submission by ZEC that election agents had "the opportunity at their discretion to make notes from the V11 and V23 forms being used by the Electoral Commission" was deliberately opaque in order to deceive and cover up brazen rigging.

In the first place, s110 (3)(d) is clear that the form to be verified in order to determine the result of the presidential election is the presidential constituency return, which is Form V23B, and not V11. In the second place, ZEC's reference to V23 lacks the necessary legal specificity, given that there are four distinct presidential election returns, all which are V23 forms: V23A, the ward return; V23B, the constituency return; V23C, the provincial command return; and V23D, the national command centre return. So, which of these are included or meant by ZEC's catch-all reference to V23s? All or some of them? The law is clear – s110(3)(d) refers to only one of the V forms: V23B. Chigumba and ZEC did not refer to V23Bs in their opposing papers, save, for instance, where the reference was not an election return.

By constantly referring to V23s, in a catch-all manner, ZEC was lost in the forest of V23 forms without finding the legally necessary tree, called a V23B form. This was either due to ignorance of the law or a constructive intent to rig, neither of which is defendable or acceptable.

Chigumba: 34.4. As already averred, Mr. Jameson Timba during this process, had occasion to request V11 and V23 forms for several constituencies, he examined those forms and made whatever notes he wished to make, he did not raise any queries with respect to those V11s or V23s.

Indeed, Jameson Timba had occasion to request the forms that ZEC was ostensibly using to verify the result of the 2018 presidential election. On paragraphs 13 and 14 of his supporting affidavit, Mr Timba made the following fundamental submission that settles the issue about the identity of the V23 Form that ZEC used:

*13. On the 1ˢᵗ of August 2018, I was invited by ZEC to verify **constituency returns** for the presidential election. On arrival at National Results Centre where ZEC was collating results for the presidential election on the basis of data from all ward returns, that is **Form V23a** accompanied by **polling station returns (i.e. Form V11)**, these forms were laid before me by Mr. Murenje, the ZEC Director of Elections and Training.*

*14. "**Mr. Murenje did not present to me the constituency return (that is Form V23b)**.*

The submission by Timba was not rebutted by Chigumba or ZEC in their opposing papers, nor did Mr Murenje, the ZEC Director of Elections, submit an affidavit to rebut Timba's averment. **ZEC used the V23A Form when it was required by law to use the V23B Form.** Therefore, it is an undisputed fact that the process that ZEC put in place to determine and verify the result of the presidential election was grossly contrary to s110(3)(d) of the Electoral Act. It involved verifying polling station and ward centre returns, V11s and V23As, which had been hijacked from ward centres and whose origin could not be verified or traced.

Chigumba: 34.5. Further, as I have already averred, there was no server kept by the Electoral Commission on which election results were transmitted from polling stations and stored.

If this submission by Chigumba is to be believed, where were the copies of polling station returns, ward returns, constituency returns, and provincial command returns kept and how was the data on them extracted? Since ZEC said it did not use the Excel spreadsheet as a data-storage and data-processing system but only as an addition tool, where and how was the massive amount of election-result data stored? And, results aside, without a server with voting information, how did ZEC transmit, store and process the data on voter turnout that Chigumba announced at intervals throughout voting day on 30 July 2018? Did ZEC use an Excel spreadsheet to collect and compile that data?

The submission by Chigumba that "there was no server kept by the Electoral Commission on which election results were transmitted" is contradicted by a public statement made through two public interventions by ZEC, one after and another before the election.

In the afternoon of 31 July 2018, a ZEC Commissioner responsible for media liaison, Qhubani Moyo, virtually confirmed that ZEC had already by then received the result of the presidential election when he said:

> **In the morning we were seeing certain trends that were trending on social media regarding how the elections have, you know, been progressing and who has won. But the actual results that we have received so far indicate a different trend altogether.**[103]

Moyo had let the cat out of the bag. By 31 July 2018, ZEC had received "the actual results" of the presidential elections. But how had ZEC received the results and been able to know who had won or who had not won? Again, Moyo provided the answer:

> **We are not allowed to declare results on the basis of soft copies or anything that has been sent by scan.**

There can be no clearer confirmation than this public statement by Moyo, whose message content is that there was a server kept by ZEC on which election results were transmitted from polling stations and ward centres; and not only stored but also processed. To think or believe otherwise, in the face of such evidence, would be infantile and irrational.

What Moyo revealed about the existence of a server with poll results, after the election on 31 July 2018, was consistent with the disclosure made by Justice Rita Makarau, that ZEC would have a server for poll results, well before the election on 3 October 2017, as the then ZEC Chairperson, when the ZBC reported that:

> **The Zimbabwe Electoral Commission (ZEC) says it will guard jealously information on the voters roll and results to enable credible elections.**[104]

---

[103] Interview with Zimbabwe Election Commission (ZEC) Commissioner, Qhubani Moyo, South African Broadcasting Corporation Digital News, 31 July 2018. https://www.youtube.com/watch?v=sNIo_pGGbmo
[104] "Parties not allowed to access servers: ZEC", @zbcnewsonline, 3 October, 2017.

It is beyond the thinkable, in fact an absurdity, to imagine that in July 2018 there was a better or more secure way to "guard jealously information on the *voters roll* and *results* to enable credible elections" without keeping, securing and processing that information on a server.

Justice Makarau made it clear that she was talking about jealously guarding 'the voters roll and **results**' on a server. In this connection she said that:

> **Access to the server containing information on the voting process will be restricted to selected ZEC employees. "The server is a security area and all political parties will no be allowed to access it."**

This ZEC position was not retracted or modified before or during the 2018 presidential election until Chigumba's affidavit opposing Chamisa's Constitutional Court application. It would therefore require more than a leap of faith to believe that the ZEC server that Justice Makarau had been open about had suddenly disappeared as a direct consequence of Chamisa's Constitutional Court challenge.

Chigumba: 34.6. In terms of s110(3)(d) of the Electoral Act, the subject of a verification process are the actual returns from the various constituencies across the country. These returns consist of the V11 and V23 forms. The addition of the figures specified on the V11 and V23 forms on an Excel spreadsheet is not the verification described in s110(3)(d).

Of course, it is a no brainer that the Excel spreadsheet is not the verification described in s110(3)(d). A verification in terms of s11(3)(d) can only be a verification of V23Bs and nothing else. Based on the unrebutted submission in Jameson Timba's affidavit on the verification forms he was given and not given by ZEC, it is common cause that ZEC presented for verification V23A forms, presidential ward returns with V11s attached to them, and not V23B forms, presidential constituency returns (with original V11s and V23As attached on the back) as specified in s110(3)(d) of the Electoral Act. V23A forms are not "the actual returns from the various constituencies across the country", as claimed by Chigumba. It is also strange, and without the necessary legal specificity, that in their opposing affidavit Chigumba and ZEC referred to "various constituencies across the country". The country does not have "various constituencies", it has 210 constituencies. Factual specificity is critical in such instances, not hyperbolic statements.

Regarding the Excel spreadsheet, ZEC says it used it to collate some results, but those results had no legal basis whatsoever because V11s and V23As are not captured and collated at ZEC's national command centre. It is also not known, and there is no way of telling, what figures from V11s, and from which polling stations were obtained by "a group of people, in excess of twenty, punching in what was identified as V11 data into an Excel spreadsheet" over a two-day period. The validity and traceability of V11s and V23As used by this group were major issues that left the result of the presidential election declared and announced by Chigumba bereft of credibility.

For example, EU EOM observers reported that they had found ZEC officers in Makoni North completing V11 forms two days after election day, without polling staff and party agents who had long left. The ZEC officers told the EU observers that they were doing this due to the earlier lack of V11 Forms".[111] This is but just one telling example of the brazen and scandalous daylight election theft that characterised Zimbabwe's 2018 presidential election. It would be irrational not to link this illegal and scandalous conduct by ZEC with the population of V11s that "a group of people, in excess of twenty, punching in what was identified as V11 data into an Excel spreadsheet" over a two-day period produced.

EU observers also reported that the results were not posted at polling stations, as required by electoral law, in 10 of the 52 polling stations they observed. This is 20%, a figure that reflects the pattern EU observers reported where the results were not posted at the polling station, as required by law.

The incidents of ZEC officers completing V11 forms all by themselves, two days after the election, when ZEC's bogus verification exercise had commenced, explains why the V11s published by ZEC were neither traceable nor verifiable, as they had been contaminated by ZEC.

As the V11s became unreliable and untraceable, floodgates opened to alter the 2018 presidential election result. In this regard, it is important to underscore that, on the back of the rerouted transmission and collation of the result of the presidential election from ward centres, **the contamination of V11s,** exemplified by ZEC officials who were found by EU observers in Makoni North completing V11 forms all by themselves two days after election day, is consistent with the unimpeached submission by Timba, Chamisa's election agent, that the election returns that ZEC presented to him did not include V23Bs, the presidential constituency returns.

ZEC's preoccupation with V11s, while disregarding V23Bs in violation of s110(3)(d) of the Electoral Act, for purposes of rigging the presidential election by altering its result, was evidenced by the unexplained fact that the number of votes cast for the presidential election ended up exceeding the number of votes cast for each parliamentary election. This discrepancy was a result of rigging through the manipulation of V11s, as had happened in Makoni North.

It is trite that the essence of Zimbabwe's harmonised elections is that it brings together the holding of presidential, parliamentary and local government elections that were previously held separately. As a result, in the harmonised election each voter is given three ballot papers. The fact that a voter must place the ballot paper for each of the three elections that are harmonised in its corresponding ballot box means that the number of votes cast for the presidential election must equal the number of votes cast for the parliamentary election. In rare situations, it is possible that a voter may decline a parliamentary election or presidential election ballot paper. In such situations, s56(3a) of the Electoral Act is clear about what must happen and stipulates that:

> If polling in two or more elections is being conducted simultaneously at the polling station and an applicant declines to accept a ballot paper for any one or more of those elections, the presiding officer shall not hand the applicant a ballot paper for that election and shall record in such manner as may be prescribed or directed by the commission that the applicant did not, at his or her request, receive the ballot paper.

In compliance with this clear legal requirement, whose effect would be to ensure that the number of votes cast in the presidential election would be equal to the votes cast in the parliamentary election, the ZEC 2018 *Electoral Officers Manual* has the unequivocal instruction that:

> **If a voter declines to accept a ballot paper for anyone or more of the Elections, this must be brought to the attention of the Presiding Officer. The Presiding Officer shall not hand the applicant a ballot paper for that Election and shall record the details of this person on form PE2005/AA [Electoral Act Section 56(3a)].**

According to data in the court record, and not disputed by ZEC, the total number of votes cast in the parliamentary election was 4,734,161, against 4,774,878 cast in the presidential election. This means some **40,717 more votes** were cast in the presidential election than were cast in the parliamentary election. Again, this figure was not disputed by ZEC.

In clear evidence that V11s were contaminated, as happened in Makoni North where EU observers found ZEC officers completing V11s whose number could have totalled any target amount they wished to achieve, **ZEC did not produce a single PE2005/AA form to show that the 40,717 more votes cast in the presidential election than were cast in the parliamentary election were in fact legitimate votes cast by genuine and not "ghost" voters.**

The reason that ZEC could not produce the required evidence through Form PE2005/AA is because Chigumba conspired with Defence House to deharmonise the harmonised election by delinking the presidential and national assembly elections in order to process the result of the presidential election separately and differently for purposes of rigging it.

There can be no legal or rational explanation for ZEC's failure to comply with s56(3a) of the Electoral Act. The discrepancy is an objective expression of the consequence of the kind of conduct exemplified by the ZEC officers in Makoni North. ZEC's illegal failure to account for the 40,717 more votes that were cast in the presidential election than were cast in the parliamentary election is a major issue, given that, even with ZEC's rigged result, Mnangagwa avoided a run-off by a paltry 31,830 votes.

Parenthetically, while ZEC clearly rigged the result of the presidential election for Mnangagwa against Chamisa, it failed to rig it to match Mnangagwa's performance with that of ZANU PF in the parliamentary elections.

As shown on Diagram 17, Mnangagwa not only lost to Chamisa but also performed badly compared to his parliamentary candidates: ZANU PF's numbers were far better than Mnangagwa's numbers. Put simply, ZANU PF outperformed its leader. Altogether, Mnangagwa won 125 constituencies and ZANU PF won 145 constituencies. On the other hand, Chamisa won 85 constituencies, while the MDC-Alliance won 63.

CONSTITUENCIES WON BY MNANGAGWA & CHAMISA VERSUS THOSE WON BY THEIR PARTIES

Mnangagwa	ZANU PF
125 (59.5%)	145 (69.1%)
Chamisa	MDC-A
85 (40.5%)	63 (30%)

The constituencies that were won by ZANU PF and lost by Mnangagwa were Beitbridge East, Buhera West, Bulawayo South, Chegutu West, Chiredzi West, Gokwe Central, Goromonzi West, Gwanda North, Harare South, Lupane West, Makoni West, Magunje, Mhondoro Mubaira, Musikavanhu, Marondera West, Mutasa North, Nyanga South, Seke, Zvimba East, Zvimba West and Zvishavane Ngezi.

Chigumba: 34.7. The process prescribed by law is what was happening over the two day period confirmed by the applicant where full and unlimited access was granted to all presidential candidates and their agents to the various original returns from the constituencies allowing them, if they believed any data recorded thereon was incorrect, to question such data and have the query so raised related to and dealt with by the Electoral Commission.

First, and most important, there's no law that gives ZEC the power and authority to vary and reroute the transmission of the results for the presidential election to enable the capturing and collation of V11s and V23As at the national command centre in Harare.

Second, in terms of s110(3)(d) of the Electoral Act, the determination and verification of the result of the presidential election is about verifying each of the 210 presidential constituency returns – that is, V23Bs which have attached on the back original V11s and V23A forms. The undisputed fact, based on the court papers, is that ZEC transformed its collation room into an illegal polling station in which, right from the start of the alleged verification process on 1 August 2018, it violated s110(3) of the Electoral Act by having **"a group of people, in excess of twenty, punching in what was identified as V11 data into an Excel spreadsheet. For close to two days that process continued"**.

Rebuttal Four

Chamisa: 5.6. My agents demanded that the verification process take place. It had to take place by operation of law at any rate. It had to take place for all the issues set out above to be dealt with. The ZEC CEO Mr Salaigwana accepted that position and assured my agents that the results would not be announced without that process taking place and to that end, Mr Komichi was going to be called in for the verification process. Indeed, in terms of that process, Messrs Komichi and Timba had to sign off on the results before they were announced.

5.7. *An indication had previously been given that there was to be an announcement of the presidential results at 22:00hrs. As at 21:55hrs Mr Komichi had received no call from the CEO, no verification had taken place and no signing of the papers to signify the fact that there had been a verification had also taken place. He accordingly visited the CEO's office who told him that he was still going to contact him as he was still working on some processes. On his part, Mr Komichi was to patiently wait for that call.*

5.8. *As Mr Komichi was still waiting for the call, ZEC started announcing the results on live television. Mr Komichi had been sold a ruse. There was something that ZEC wanted to hide. It is those results that are challenged. It is the declaration made by the Chairperson pursuant to that announcement that is in issue and whose validity the court ought to look into.*

Chigumba: 35. *Ad Para 5.6- 5.8. This is denied.*

35.1. *The applicant, with respect, contradicts himself in this paragraph. Having previously averred in paragraph 5.1 of his affidavit that on August 1ˢᵗ his election agents, Mr. Komichi and Mr. Timba, were called for verification of the presidential election results and that that process took two days, his deposition under paragraph 5.6 that no verification took place is at variance with his previous evidence.*

The verification is not determined merely by having a group of people in excess of twenty punching data from V11s and V23As into an Excel spreadsheet but by whether the group were acting within the law in doing what they were observed doing on 1 August 2018. The evidence from Timba, which Chigumba and ZEC did not, and could not, rebut is that he was given V11s and V23As but not a single V23B, which is the presidential constituency return referred to in s110(3)(d) of the Electoral Act. This was illegal. This illegality was compounded by the fact that the V11s and V23As, whose data was punched into an Excel spreadsheet by the group of people in excess of twenty, were hijacked from ward centres using a route and destination not prescribed in any law.

Chigumba: 35.2. *Verification of presidential election results in terms of s110 (3)(d) of the Electoral Act took place.*

Verification of the presidential election results could not legally take place simultaneously with "a group of people, in excess of twenty, punching in what was identified as V11 data into an Excel spreadsheet". This process continued for two days, using V11s and V23As that were hijacked from ward centres and transmitted through an illegal route to an illegal destination. Furthermore, no verification of presidential election results could take place in terms of s110(3)(d) without Form V23Bs, which ZEC did not present to Timba, Chamisa's election agent.

Chigumba: 35.3. *Because the provisions of Part XIII of the Electoral Act are imported, with necessary changes, into s110 of the Electoral Act, (except for sections 66, 67 and 68), it may also be helpful to refer to the provisions that describe and give colour and context to the verification process in Part XIII of the Act, these are s65(2)(b), s65A(2)(b) and s65B(2)(b).*

There was no verification of the presidential constituency return, Form V23B, equivalent to the verification of the presidential polling station return (V11) at the ward collation station as provided by the Electoral Act in s65(2)(b), or to the verification of the presidential ward return (V23B) at the constituency centre in terms of s65A(2)(b), or to the verification of the presidential constituency return (V23B) at the provincial command centre according to s65B(2)(b). The equivalent verification would have been of the presidential constituency return (V23B), delivered by the Constituency Election Officer to the Chief Elections Officer at the National Commander Centre, verified in terms of s110(3)(d) of the Electoral Act.

Chigumba: 35.4. In all three subsections, the process of verification enjoins ensuring that each return purports to be duly certified by the presiding officer of the polling station concerned or the ward elections officer for the ward concerned or constituency elections officer for the constituency concerned respectively. This is why the original returns are used in the verification process and candidates and their election agents, including the applicant's election agents, were given full access to those returns during the verification process as I have averred above.

ZEC used V11s and V23As that were hijacked from ward centres and transmitted through an illegal route to an illegal destination. Voting data on these V11s and V23As was illegally captured and collated at ZEC's national command centre by "a group of people, in excess of twenty, punching in what was identified as V11 data into an Excel spreadsheet. For close to two days". The relevant presidential constituency return, the V23B containing originals, was not presented, in violation of s110(3)(d) of the Electoral Act.

Rebuttal Five

Chamisa: 6.2. I contend that ZEC failed to follow mandatory legal processes and that such failure invalidates its processes which have to do with the announcement of the results and the declaration of a winner. The following are the respects in which ZEC deliberately flouted statutory processes bearing on a credible outcome;

Chigumba: 37. Ad Para 6.2. This is denied. I reiterate my averments made above.

Reiterating a false averment does not make it true.

The mandatory process is twofold. First, the results of the presidential and national assembly elections must be collated and transmitted using one route to one destination at all times throughout the process, in accordance with s37C(4) of the Electoral Act. Second, the result of the presidential election must be verified in terms of s110(3)(d) on the basis of the presidential constituency return, the V23B, which ZEC failed to present to Timba, as per his unrebutted submission in his affidavit. The latter is impossible to do, without the former.

Rebuttal Six

Chamisa: 6.2.1. In terms of the law, a presidential election is constituency based. What is collated and verified at the National Command Centre are the v23b forms which show the constituency totals. Those were never made available to me or my agents prior to the announcement of the so-called results and the purported declaration of a winner. Those were never verified. Indeed the constituency totals were not even announced by ZEC. What ZEC purported to do was to announce provincial results in a manner that sought to and did mask the many mathematical irregularities afflicting the results. The announcement of results by province does not itself have any known statutory parentage. Accurate elections results are those that are declared and announced at the Polling Stations and contained in the Forms V11 and collated in v23a forms. Elections cannot be said to be verifiable if the primary source documents are not delivered and confirmed by the person making the final declaration of results.

Chigumba: 38. *Ad Para 6.2.1. This is denied.*

38.1. *All V11s and V23s for the presidential election were physically delivered by all relevant elections officers to the Electoral Commission's national command centre and formed the basis of collation and verification of the results for the presidential election.*

The delivery of V11s and V23s to the national command centre is prescribed by law. It is mandatory that the results from ward centres, the V23As, must be transmitted for capturing and collation at constituency centres; the results from constituency centres, the V23Bs, must be transmitted for capturing and collation at provincial command centres, (while a copy certified by the Constituency Elections Officer is transmitted to the Chief Elections Officer at the national command centre); the results from provincial command centres, the V23Cs, must be delivered to the national command centre, where, in the case of the presidential election, the V23Cs are captured and collated onto a V23D, which contains the initial result of the presidential election. The final result is verified and determined on the basis of the V23Bs, the constituency returns.

In the first place, ZEC has admitted in its Report on the 2018 harmonised elections that:

> **Results for the presidential and the National Assembly elections were transmitted using different routes from the ward collation centre. While the destination for the National Assembly election results was the constituency centre, the Presidential results were forwarded to the district centre for onward transmission to the national command centre in Harare. Verification was done at each point by checking the accuracy of every collation return and whether it was properly completed If not, corrections would be effected by use of polling station source documents (V11s).**

Having illegally disharmonised the 2018 general election, ZEC has further admitted that:

> **The results were taken to the national command/collation centre physically by the District Elections Officers where they were captured and collated on a results collation template at the National Collation Centre.**

> **The prescribed process is that the capturing, collation and transmission of the presidential results must be from polling station to ward centre; from ward centre to constituency centre; from constituency centre to provincial command centre; and from command centre to the national command centre.[105]**

---

[105] ZEC, *Zimbabwe 2018 Harmonised Elections Report*, pages 67–8.

Chigumba: 38.2. I have, in my depositions thus far, shown that not only were the original V11 and V23 forms used in the collation and verification of presidential election results at the national command centre but also that the applicant's election agents were involved in that process and were given, upon request, access to any of the V11 and V23 forms for purposes of verification.

It was plainly illegal, and in gross violation of the Electoral Act, for ZEC to collate V11s and V23As at the national command centre under the guise of determining and verifying the result of the presidential election. V11s are collated and verified at ward collation centres in terms of s65, while V23As are collated at constituency centres under s65A of the Act. Section 110(3)(d) enjoins ZEC to verify the presidential constituency return, the V23B, which was not presented for verification, as ZEC was preoccupied with collating V11s and presenting V23As, in blatant contravention of the law.

Chigumba: 38.3. The provisions of s110 of the Electoral Act do not oblige the Electoral Commission, in the declaration of a winner in a presidential election, to announce constituency totals. That no constituency totals were announced, therefore, cannot be a basis for a legal challenge to the results of the presidential election. In any event, the averment by the applicant regarding announcement of constituency totals must always be linked to a material change in the election's outcome as to justify the relief that he seeks. He does not make this link in his founding depositions.

The provisions of s110, as read with s65B and s37C(4)(f) of the Electoral Act prohibit ZEC from announcing the result of the presidential election on the basis of provincial subtotals. Specifically, s37C(4)(f) provides that:

> after the collation of the results of the presidential election at each provincial command centre, provincial returns for the presidential election gathered from every provincial command centre shall be transmitted to the national command centre, where –
>
> (i) the provincial returns shall be collated to obtain the initial results of the presidential election; and
>
> (ii) the final result of the presidential election shall, after reconciling the provincial returns with the polling station returns and presidential constituency returns referred to in the provisos to paragraphs (b) and (d) respectively, be reflected in a return that distinctly reflects number of votes cast for each presidential candidate at every polling station, ward centre, presidential constituency centre and provincial command centre.

The provincial returns contained in 10 V23Cs and totalled in Form V23D, forms which ZEC did not present for verification between 1 and 3 August 2018, provide **only the initial result** of the presidential election. By announcing the result on the basis of a V23D, which is the only legal meaning that can be given to what she did, Chigumba was announcing an initial result in breach of the Electoral Act.

Subparagraph (ii) of s37C(4)(f) enjoins ZEC to determine **the final result** of the presidential election in terms of the presidential constituency returns (V23Bs) as provided in s110(3)(d). As such, there are only two legal options for announcing the **final result** of the presidential election and these are either by giving the 210 constituency subtotals as per the 210 V23Bs, the presidential constituency returns, or by giving the total of the 210 subtotals. Anything else has no legal basis.

Rebuttal Seven

*Chamisa: **6.2.3** Any verification process would have entailed the verification of the data on v23, V11 forms and the details punched into the ZEC sever [sic]. That process did not take place. In addition, there was not even any verification of the Excel data and the totals allegedly produced by the figures inputed [sic]. That failure led to some glaring irregularities that will be related to later on. Indeed Excel sheet cannot form a basis for the announcement of results or a declaration. Excel sheet is the most insecure document that can deployed in elections. Its contents can be so easily manipulated and changed by the person making the entries or at a later time once the entries are made. Failure to refer to the V11 Forms and the results posted on the servers would mean the elections are not verifiable. Adopting the use of technology in the elections was in furtherance of constitutional principles of transparency, accountability and verifiability. Sending results in advance to the servers was to protect against tampering with results once a declaration is made at the polling station. If those results cannot be accounted for then the elections fail the test of verifiability and accountability.*

***6.2.4.** I point out that the most important stage of an election is the process of ascertaining the votes cast. The law has evolved certain safeguards that must be followed when a result is being ascertained. The process preferred by ZEC was meant to murky the waters, lacked transparency and credibility and ought to be interfered with.*

*Chigumba: **40.** Ad Para 6.2.3- 6.2.4. This is denied.*

***40.1.** There was no server used by the Electoral Commission for transmission of election results.*

The claim by Chigumba that "there was no server used by the Electoral Commission for transmission of election results" is not supported by the law or facts. Statutory Instrument 21 of 2005 (Electoral Regulations), as amended, and which was published by ZEC on 8 June 2018, clearly provides for the transmission of the notification of the presidential election results by telegram, telefacsimile or electronic mail using V16 Forms. The Statutory Instrument also provides for the transmission of the detailed results of the presidential election by telegram, telefacsimile or electronic mail using V18 Forms.

What is electronic mail and where does it go? As already established, Justice Rita Makarau made it official in December 2017 that ZEC had a server for the voters' roll and election results and that the server was accessible only to a select few staff members of ZEC and not to political parties or candidates. This position was not retracted or refuted before the elections. ZEC staff confirmed to me that there was a server.

In any event, the proposition that ZEC did not have a server for election results is so absurd and irrational that it can only be believed by a fool. If ZEC did not have a server for election results, where did it store and process voting information? If the voting information was not stored in and processed through a server, how secure and reliable was it?

The most direct and clearest impeachment of ZEC's claim that "*there was no server kept by the Electoral Commission on which election results were transmitted from polling stations and stored*" is in the court record of Chamisa's Constitutional challenge and it came from none other than the First Respondent in the case, Emmerson Mnangagwa. In paragraph 118 of his opposing affidavit, Mnangagwa admitted to the existence of the server with the result of the presidential election. He wondered how Chamisa had got to know about the results in the server and alleged that it was because of hacking by associates linked to Chamisa. In this regard Mnangagwa alleged that:

118.6 **But, again, we know that Applicant's representatives were denied access to what they called a server.**

118.7 **So, one must ask, exactly how did applicant know that results from all polling stations were being received in that putative server in real time? The only inference that can be drawn is that the applicant or those working with him were responsible for the hacking, accessing of data on 23rd respondent's server.**

118.8 **It is a known fact that one of the websites utilising information obtained from 23rd Respondent's website through hacking has published graphs and statistics that are eerily similar to those that were simultaneously being filed with this S93 application.**

Mnangagwa did not deny the existence of the ZEC server which had the "results from all polling stations" but he questioned "*exactly how did applicant know that results from all polling stations were being received in that putative server in real time?*" The answer that Mnangagwa provides to his own question shows that the server was not "putative" but was real. This is why he made the startling conclusion that "the only inference that can be drawn [as to how Chamisa got to know about the results in the server] is that the applicant or those working with him were responsible for the hacking of data on 23rd respondent's server". This conclusion by Mnangagwa confirmed, beyond doubt, that ZEC indeed had a server with the results of the 2018 presidential election.

Chigumba: 40.2. Verification was done in terms of the law. The V11 and V23 forms were available and were used in that process.

Repeated and pervasive references to "V11 and V23 forms" or to "V11s and V23s" in Chigumba's opposing affidavit demonstrate an unfortunate commitment to deception, in violation of the requirements of transparency imposed on ZEC by the Constitution. The references give the impression that the verification was about adding V11s to V23s to produce a result equivalent to adding oranges to apples.

It has been established that ZEC illegally hijacked V11s and V23As from ward centres and took them for capturing and collation at its national command centre using an illegal route with an illegal destination in violation of the law. The illegality cannot have any other effect save to void whatever result was produced by the unlawful process.

Chigumba: 40.3. The Excel spreadsheet was a tool for addition of totals. It is not part of the verification in terms of the law. Even when one considers the statutory framework set out in s110 of the Electoral Act, verification is provided for under s110(3)(d) and thereafter addition of the verified totals is provided for under s110(3)(e). The later [sic] does not factor into the former. The verification provided for in s110(3)(d) was done.

Chigumba submitted that "the Excel spreadsheet was a tool for addition of **totals**". Totals of what? And why totals (plural), how many totals were there?

In terms of s37C(4)(f) of the Electoral Act, one total is the initial result contained in Form V23D, based on the addition of subtotals of presidential provincial returns or V23Cs, and the other total is the final result based on the addition of subtotals of presidential constituency returns or V23Bs that are determined and verified in terms of s110(3)(d) which provides that:

> **At the time and place notified for the verification of the *constituency returns [V23Bs]* referred to in paragraph (c) and in the presence of such candidates, their chief election agents and observers as are present, the Chief Elections Officer shall display each *constituency return [V23B]* to those present and shall, on request, allow a candidate or chief election agent of a candidate to make notes of the contents of each *constituency return [V23B]*.** [emphasis added]

ZEC did not determine and verify the result of the presidential election on the basis of V23Cs and could not possibly have a legitimate V23D form, given that it had hijacked the results of the presidential election from ward centres, and used an illegal transmission route that avoided, as destinations, constituency centres and provincial centres. It is also common cause that ZEC did not determine the result by verifying V23Bs, the presidential constituency returns, as required by s110(3)(d). Rather, ZEC misdirected itself and, by its own admission, used V11s and V23s illegally rerouted from ward centres to the national command centre to compile a fraudulent result of the presidential election.

The fraudulent result was produced by "a group of people, in excess of twenty, punching in what was identified as V11 data into an Excel spreadsheet" for close to two days. This is precisely what was witnessed by Chamisa's election agents, Komichi and Timba, whose averments in this regard were not rebutted by Chigumba and ZEC in their opposing papers.

Section 110(3)(e) provides as follows, regarding when the total of the final result of the presidential is determined:

> **When the Chief Elections Officer has completed the verification of the constituency returns [V23Bs] under paragraph (d) the Chief Elections Officer shall, in the presence of such persons referred to in paragraph (d) as are present, add together the number of votes received by each candidate as shown in each constituency return [V23B].**

Against this backdrop, s110(3)(f) provides the following about the declaration of results of the presidential election determined and verified in terms of s110(3)(d) and whose total is arrived at in terms of s110(3)(e):

> **Subject to paragraph (h), after the number of votes received by each candidate as shown in each *constituency return [V23B]* has been added together in terms of paragraph (e), the Chairperson of the Commission (or, in his or her absence, the Deputy Chairperson or, in his or her absence, a Commissioner designated by the Chairperson) shall –**

(i)   where there are two candidates, forthwith declare the candidate who has received the greater number of votes to be duly elected as President of the Republic of Zimbabwe with effect from the day of such declaration; or

(ii)   where there are more than two candidates, forthwith declare the candidate who has received more than half the number of votes to be duly elected as President of the Republic of Zimbabwe with effect from the day of such declaration; or

(iii) where there are more than two candidates, and no candidate has received more than half the number of votes, forthwith declare that a runoff presidential election shall be held on the date fixed by the President in terms of section 38(1)(a)(iii) (that is to say, a fixed date not less than twenty-eight and not more than forty-two days after the polling day or last polling day, as the case may be, of the original election):

Provided that the Electoral Court, on the application of the Commission, may for good cause extend the period.

ZEC put the cart before the horse and started its Excel spreadsheet additions even before its own "verification" had started, let alone ended. ZEC violated s110(3)(d) of the Electoral Act in that it did not verify the presidential constituency return (V23B) but instead purported to verify V11s and V23A forms that it had hijacked from ward centres for illegal capturing and collation at its national command centre in Harare.

Chapter 11

UNIMPEACHED

WITH the uncritical approval of Chief Justice Malaba, Justice Priscilla Chigumba, the ZEC Chairperson, claimed that the Commission had followed s110(3)(d) of the Electoral Act to verify and determine the result for the 2018 presidential election. The claim permeates her opposing papers in the ConCourt application filed by opposition leader Nelson Chamisa to challenge the declaration of Emmerson Mnangagwa as the winner of the presidential election.

Section 110(3)(d) of the Electoral Act provides as follows:

> **At the time and place notified for the Chigumba's verification of** *the constituency returns* **referred to in paragraph (c) and in the presence of such candidates, their chief election agents and observers as are present, the Chief Elections Officer** *shall display each constituency return* **to those present and shall, on request, allow a candidate or chief election agent of a candidate to make notes of the contents of each** *constituency return.*[emphasis added]

From ZEC's Report on the 2018 harmonised elections prepared in fulfilment of its constitutional duty in terms of s241 of the Constitution of Zimbabwe, it is clear that the result for the presidential election was not verified or determined in accordance with s110(3)(d) of the Electoral Act. Rather, ZEC compromised and invalidated the result when it invented a different route and different destination for the collation, compilation and transmission of the result from ward centres to the national command centre in Harare. The prescribed destination of the result from ward centres is constituency centres. ZEC confirmed its alteration of the route and destination in its Report in this manner:

> **Results for the presidential and the national assembly elections were transmitted using different routes from the ward collation centre. While the destination for the National Assembly election results was the constituency centre,** *the Presidential results were forwarded to the district centre for onward transmission to the national command centre in Harare.* [emphasis added]

The plain and staggering fact confirmed in the ZEC Report is that the Commission was used by "the system" through Defence House to hijack the result for the 2018 presidential election by changing its prescribed transmission route from ward centres to constituency to a different route and destination from ward centres to the national command centre in Harare, via ZEC district offices. The change of route and destination was illegal and was done for purposes of rigging the election result.

After commandeering the result for the presidential election on 31 July 2018, as shown in Diagrams 2 and 3 in Chapter 1, ZEC transformed its national command centre into a one giant polling station for purposes of illegally collating and compiling the V11s and V23As it had hijacked from 1,958 ward centres. The illegal collation and compilation of V11s and

V23As at ZEC's national command centre started on 1 August 2018, the day of the Harare Massacre in which ZDF soldiers murdered six fleeing and defenceless civilians and critically injured 35 others in Harare.

The consequence of ZEC's invention of a different route and different destination for the collation, compilation and transmission for the presidential election results was vividly portrayed by Chamisa in paragraph 5.1 of his founding affidavit in his ConCourt case in these words:

> On the 1st of August 2018 twenty third respondent [ZEC] started what it called a verification process and which it asked Messrs Komichi and Timba to witness. The process involved *a group of people, in excess of twenty, punching in what was identified as V11 data into an Excel spreadsheet. For close to two days that process continued.* I defer to the affidavits of the two gentlemen which explain the manner in which that process was being conducted [emphasis added].

To the question, what did ZEC do with the results for the presidential election that it commandeered from the country's 1,958 ward collation centres on 31 July 2018, the answer cannot be clearer: they were taken to the national command centre for collation and compilation as described by Chamisa on paragraph 5.1 of his founding affidavit. Malaba and his fellow ConCourt judges ignored Chamisa's submission in his affidavit. Yet the submission was telling.

Even more telling is that Chamisa's submission was based on eyewitness evidence from Chamisa's election agents, Morgen Komichi and Jameson Timba, who lodged supporting affidavits about what they saw and heard at ZEC's national command centre on 1 August 2018.

Their revealing affidavits follow.

IN THE CONSTITUTIONAL COURT OF ZIMBABWE   CASE NO. CCZ.................../18
HELD IN HARARE

In the matter between:

NELSON CHAMISA	APPLICANT
and	
EMMERSON DAMBUDZO MNANGAGWA	1st RESPONDENT
and	
JOSEPH BUSHA	2nd RESPONDENT
and	
MELBAH DZAPASI	3rd RESPONDENT
and	
NKOSANA DONALD MOYO	4th RESPONDENT
and	
NOAH NGONI MANYIKA	5th RESPONDENT
and	
PETER HARRY WILSON	6th RESPONDENT
and	
BRYN TAURAI MTEKI	7th RESPONDENT
and	
THOKOZANI KHUPE	8th RESPONDENT
and	
DIVINE MHAMBI-HOVE	9th RESPONDENT
and	
LOVEMORE MADHUKU	10th RESPONDENT
and	
TENDAI PETER MUNYANDURI	11th RESPONDENT
and	
AMBROSE MUTINHIRI	12th RESPONDENT
and	
TIMOTHY JOHANNESS TONDERAI MAPFUMO CHIGUVARE	13th RESPONDENT
and	
JOICE TEURAI ROPA MUJURU	14th RESPONDENT

and

KWANELE HLABANGANA 15th RESPONDENT

and

EVARISTO WASHINGTON CHIKANGA 16th RESPONDENT

and

DANIEL KUZOVIRAVA SHUMBA 17th RESPONDENT

and

VIOLET MARIYACHA 18th RESPONDENT

and

BLESSING KASIYAMHURU 19th RESPONDENT

and

ELTON STEERS MANGOMA 20th RESPONDENT

and

PETER MAPFUMO GAVA 21st RESPONDENT

and

WILLIAM TAWONEZVI MUGADZA 22nd RESPONDENT

and

ZIMBABWE ELECTORAL COMMISSION 23rd RESPONDENT

SUPPORTING AFFIDAVIT BY JAMESON TIMBA

I, **JAMESON TIMBA** do hereby take oath and solemnly state that:

1. I was the **Chief Election Agent** for **Nelson Chamisa** (the Applicant in this case) in the 2018 Zimbabwean Harmonised Elections.

2. I have read the Founding Affidavit by **Nelson Chamisa** and Supporting Affidavits by Morgen Komichi and other deponents in this matter, as well as the accompanying annexures thereof.

3. I hereby associate myself fully with the contents of those Affidavits as far as they specifically relate to my involvement in the subject election, as being true and correct.

4. As Chief Election Agent for my party's Presidential Candidate, my role was to, *inter alia* liaise with the 23rd Respondent, that is the Zimbabwe Electoral Commission (ZEC) on all matters pertaining to Applicant's participation in the Presidential Poll.

5. On the 2nd of July 2018 I met with the ZEC Chairperson Justice Priscilla Chigumba at the ZEC Head Office in Harare where:

   5.1 I presented Applicant's concerns regarding ZEC's transparency in the electoral process with reference to the design and printing of ballot papers, their storage and subsequent distribution. With respect to the design of the ballot paper I raised the issue of its lay out which in my view was designed to advantage the 1st Respondent in that ZEC had designed a ballot paper with two columns where fourteen (14) candidates were put in the first column and nine (9) in the other column in a way that placed the 1st Respondent as number one (1) in the second column; and

   5.2 I stated Applicant's intention and request to observe and participate in these processes.

6. The ZEC Chairperson said she was not averse to the request by the Applicant for as long as there was consensus amongst the other candidates in the election on these proposals.

7. I followed up the issues that I raised in the meeting of 2nd of July 2018 with the Chairperson in writing in a letter dated 4th of July 2018 as more fully appears from the **attached** document marked Annexure S

8. On 10th of July 2018, I received a response on the issues from the Acting Chief Elections Officer in which he also confirmed that the concerns of the Applicant would best be addressed after consensus was reached by all participating candidates/ parties through the multiparty liaison committee meetings. A copy of that response is **attached** to this Affidavit as Annexure T

9. On the 13th of July 2018, I responded to the letter from the Acting Chief Elections Officer dated 10th July 2018. A copy of that response is **attached** to this Affidavit as annexure U

10. In addition to raising issues on behalf of the 1st Applicant I also persistently requested the ZEC Chairperson to meet with the 1st Applicant to no avail as shown in the letters that I have cited. There was no desire on the part of the ZEC Chairperson to meet with the first applicant for reasons known only to herself

11. I attended two (2) multiparty liaison committee meetings in which I tabled the concerns of the Applicant and sought consensus amongst the parties attending. Such consensus was reached in the presence of the three (3) Commissioners of ZEC.

12. On the third and last meeting of the multiparty liaison committee which was chaired by ZEC's Commissioner Qubani Moyo, the meeting chairperson (i.e Commissioner Moyo) informed the committee that notwithstanding the consensus that had been reached by the parties, ZEC was not willing to concede to any of the requests made by the Applicant save for one, being keeping the position of the polling booth as it was in the previous election.

13. On the 1st of August 2018, I was invited by ZEC to verify constituency returns for the Presidential Election. On arrival at the National Results Centre where ZEC was collating results for the Presidential Election on the basis of data from all ward returns, that is Form V23a accompanied by polling station returns (i.e Form V11), these forms were laid before me by Mr. Murenje, the ZEC Director of Elections and Training.

14. Mr. Murenje did not present to me the constituency returns (that is Form V23b).

15. I observed that ZEC was entering information from the Polling Station Returns (V11 Forms) onto a formatted Excel spreadsheet in order to generate the constituency return for the Presidential Election which was supposed to be laid before me for inspection and or taking notes. This did not happen.

16. The next I heard from ZEC was when results were being announced on television around 22:00 hours of 2nd of August 2018.

8. I associate myself the Applicant's prayer as laid out in the Draft Order.

97

THUS SWORN TO AT HARARE THIS..........5th.......... DAY OF AUGUST 2018.

SIGNED

_____
JAMESON TIMBA

BEFORE ME

_____
COMMISSIONER OF OATHS
W. MARO......
Commissioner of Oaths, Notary ......
Focal Point, Shop No. 7, Old Mutual Building
Avondale, Harare, Zimbabwe
Cell: 0783 187 171

98

IN THE CONSTITUTIONAL COURT OF ZIMBABWE   CASENO. CCZ.............../18

HELD IN HARARE

In the matter between:

NELSON CHAMISA   APPLICANT

and

EMMERSON DAMBUDZO MNANGAGWA   1st RESPONDENT

and

JOSEPH BUSHA   2nd RESPONDENT

and

MELBAH DZAPASI   3rd RESPONDENT

and

NKOSANA DONALD MOYO   4th RESPONDENT

and

NOAH NGONI MANYIKA   5th RESPONDENT

and

PETER HARRY WILSON   6th RESPONDENT

and

BRYN TAURAI MTEKI   7th RESPONDENT

and

THOKOZANI KHUPE   8th RESPONDENT

and

DIVINE MHAMBI-HOVE   9th RESPONDENT

and

LOVEMORE MADHUKU   10th RESPONDENT

and

TENDAI PETER MUNYANDURI   11th RESPONDENT

and

AMBROSE MUTINHIRI   12th RESPONDENT

and

TIMOTHY JOHANNESS TONDERAI MAPFUMO CHIGUVARE	13th RESPONDENT

and

JOICE TEURAI ROPA MUJURU	14th RESPONDENT

and

KWANELE HLABANGANA	15th RESPONDENT

and

EVARISTO WASHINGTON CHIKANGA	16th RESPONDENT

and

DANIEL KUZOVIRAVA SHUMBA	17th RESPONDENT

and

VIOLET MARIYACHA	18th RESPONDENT

and

BLESSING KASIYAMHURU	19th RESPONDENT

and

ELTON STEERS MANGOMA	20th RESPONDENT

and

PETER MAPFUMO GAVA	21st RESPONDENT

and

WILLIAM TAWONEZVI MUGADZA	22nd RESPONDENT

and

ZIMBABWE ELECTORAL COMMISSION	23rd RESPONDENT

SUPPORTING AFFIDAVIT BY MORGEN KOMICHI

I, **MORGEN KOMICHI** do hereby take oath and solemnly state that:

1. I was the Chief Election Agent for the MDC - Alliance party in the 2018 Zimbabwean Harmonised Elections.

2. I have read the Founding Affidavit by **Nelson Chamisa** and I hereby associate myself fully with the contents therein. I also confirm the contents of that Affidavit as far as they specifically relate to me, as being true and correct.

3. In the morning of the 2nd of August 2018, I met with Mr. Utoile Silaigwana, the Acting Chief Elections Officer (C.E.O) for the 23rd Respondent and requested copies of the Presidential Elections constituency returns for verification before the announcement of results for the Presidential election by the Chairperson of ZEC.

4. Mr. Silaigwana promised to comply with our request, and at 21:58 hours on 2 August 2018 I reminded the ZEC C.E.O about the agreed procedure that we had set out earlier on in the day regarding the V11 Forms.

5. The ZEC C.E.O assured me that the Presidential Results would not be announced before the above-mentioned verification process. However, in violation of our agreement and contrary to the procedure laid out at law, the ZEC Chairperson went to announce the results without affording me or any representative of MDC Alliance party to verify the result that was announced.

6. I felt strongly that the Zimbabwe Electoral Commission had misled me, to the prejudice of the MDC Alliance party generally, and the party's candidate specifically.

7. I associate myself the Applicant's prayer as laid out in the Draft Order.

THUS SWORN TO AT HARARE THIS........................ DAY OF AUGUST 2018.

SIGNED:

MORGEN KOMICHI

BEFORE ME:

COMMISSIONER OF OATHS

The affidavits by Timba and Komichi are instructive. On paragraphs 13, 14 and 15 Timba makes the following key averments:

13. On the 1st of August 2018, I was invited by ZEC to verify *constituency returns for the presidential election. On arrival at National Results Centre where ZEC was collating results for the presidential election on the basis of data from all ward returns, that is Form V23a accompanied by polling station returns (i.e. Form V11)*, these forms were laid before me by Mr. Murenje, the ZEC Director of Elections and Training.

14. *Mr. Murenje did not present to me the constituency return (that is Form V23B).*

15. *I observed that ZEC was entering information from polling station Returns (V11 Forms) onto a formatted Excel spreadsheet in order to generate the constituency return for the presidential election* which was supposed to be laid before me for inspection and taking notes. This did not happen.

The critical issue that arises from Timba's averments, especially the parts that are not rebutted by ZEC and Chigumba in their opposing affidavits on record, is that the one and only presidential polling return that is required by law to be verified, the constituency return or form V23B, was totally ignored not only by ZEC but also by the Constitutional Court in the rush to be preoccupied with V11s.

The verification of the result for presidential election is governed by section 110 as read with sections 65(2)(b), 65A(2)(b) and 65B(2)(b) of the Electoral Act [*Chapter 2:13*]. Section 110(3)(d) specifically and only mentions the constituency return, which is the V23B form, as the return to be verified. On paragraph 14 of his affidavit Timba avers, without being contradicted by ZEC or Chigumba, that Mr Murenje, the ZEC Director of Elections and Training who was in charge of the "verification" process, did not present to him the constituency return, namely, Form V23B.

In paragraph 3 of his affidavit Komichi avers that:

> **In the morning of the 2nd of August 2018, I met with Mr. Utoile Siliagwana, the Acting Chief Elections Officer (C.E.O.) for the 23rd Respondent [ZEC] and requested copies of the Presidential Elections constituency returns for verification before announcement of the results for the Presidential election by the Chairperson of ZEC.**

Komichi's averments on paragraphs 3 and 4 of his affidavits are crucial in that they place on record the fact that ZEC was specifically requested by Chamisa's election agents to present constituency returns, that is Form V23Bs, for the verification of the result for the presidential election in accordance with section 110(3)(d) of the Electoral Act but ZEC failed to do so.

Instead, ZEC illegally insisted on using the ward returns, namely, the V23A forms, to which were attached untraceable and unverifiable V11 forms that some 20 ZEC and army officials had manually input onto an Excel spreadsheet over two days.

The damning evidence in the supporting affidavits of Komichi and Timba on how V11s and V23As were manually input onto an Excel spreadsheet by 20 or so ZEC officers over two days from 1 August 2018 is unimpeachable. As already shown, Mnangagwa, Chigumba, and ZEC's Chief Election Officer corroborate that unimpeachable evidence. Yet Malaba and his fellow ConCourt judges ignored the unimpeached affidavits.

But why did ZEC display only V11s and V23As for the verification exercise it undertook at its national command centre on 1 August 2018?

The reason is straightforward, given the fact that, by its own admission, ZEC intercepted the results for the presidential election from all ward centres and redirected their transmission, away from constituency centres where it sent the results for the national assembly election, directly to Harare via its 63 district offices. The redirected results, using a different route and different destination, were V11s from the polling stations and V23As from ward collation centres.

Once at the national command centre, the results were collated and compiled by ZEC as if the national command centre was a giant polling station, a giant ward collation centre, a giant constituency centre and a giant provincial command centre, all rolled into one. The critical evidence of this travesty is the unimpeached affidavits supplied by Komichi and Timba.

In this connection, it is important to recall Timba's unimpeached evidence on what he saw at the collation facility at ZEC's national command centre in Harare:

On the 1st of August 2018, I was invited by ZEC to verify constituency returns for the presidential election. On arrival at National Results Centre where ZEC was collating results for the presidential election on the basis of data from all ward returns, that is Form V23a accompanied by polling station returns (i.e. Form V11).

The collation was done "on the basis of all ward returns, that is Form V23A, accompanied by polling station returns (i.e. Form V11)".

Furthermore, Timba submitted:

I observed that ZEC was entering information from polling station Returns (V11 Forms) onto a formatted Excel spreadsheet in order to generate the constituency return for the presidential election which was supposed to be laid before me for inspection and taking notes.

Against this backdrop, it is not surprising that ZEC ended up producing the wrong return for the final result for the presidential election. In its Report on the 2018 harmonised elections, ZEC notes that:

The Chief Elections Officer who was the Returning Officer for the election completed the V23D Form which is a record of results as collated at national level.[106]

Yet the result for the presidential election cannot be legally declared and announced on the basis of Form V23D, which contains the initial result. According to s37C(4)(f)(ii) of the Electoral Act, the final result for the presidential election is determined on the basis of constituency returns, the V23Bs, and that is done under s110 of the Electoral Act. The unrebutted evidence in the unimpeached affidavits of Komichi and Timba is that ZEC failed to display the V23Bs for the verification and determination of the result for the presidential election. The failure was due to the fact that ZEC had only V11s from polling stations and V23As from ward centres which it had obtained illegally by inventing a different route and different destination for collating, compiling and transmitting results prescribed under s37C(4) of the Electoral Act.

---

[106] ZEC, *Zimbabwe 2018 Harmonised Elections Report*, page 72.

Chapter 12

RECLAIMING THE VOTE

ZIMBABWE'S 2018 presidential election was audaciously rigged. It is important to recall how ZEC, in its own words, captured and collated the results of the presidential election using two different transmission routes, each with its own destination, in a way that was in substantial and gross breach of the prescribed manner. There were two different but related aspects of the breach whose consequence was to void the election. The first aspect relates to the routes and destinations that ZEC used to transmit the results for the 2018 presidential and the national assembly elections about which ZEC confirmed that:

> **Results for the presidential and the national assembly elections were transmitted using different routes from the ward collation centre. While the destination for the national assembly election results was the constituency centre, the Presidential results were forwarded to the district centre for onward transmission to the national command centre in Harare.** [emphasis added]

It is important to underscore that the reference is to "results" for the two elections. This means that prior to using two different routes with different destinations, both results for the presidential and the national assembly elections were available at ward centres in the form of 10,985 V11s from polling stations and 1,958 V23As from ward centres. In terms of the law, V11s and V23As that have been processed at ward centres must be transmitted to constituency centres for collation and compilation onto V23Bs, the constituency returns. The only destination of results for the presidential and national assembly elections from ward centres is the constituency centre, and nowhere else.

The law does not give ZEC any discretion, power or authority to come up with any procedure to vary the transmission route and destination. ZEC violated the peremptory provisions of s37C(4) of the Electoral Act by varying the transmission route for the results for the presidential election from ward centres to constituency centres as prescribed by law. The varied transmission route and destination used by ZEC was from ward centres to district centres for direct onward transmission to the national command centre in Harare. This route and destination invented by ZEC also violated s38 of the Act by separating the presidential and national assembly elections, with the consequence of disharmonising the harmonised elections. ZEC's breach of sections 37C(4) and 38 of the Electoral Act was egregious and, from thereon, necessarily voided any subsequent result for the presidential election.

In addition to violating sections 37C(4) and 38 of the Act by varying the route and destination for the transmission of the results for the presidential election and disharmonising the harmonised elections, ZEC confirmed that:

> *The results were taken to the national command/collation centre physically* by the District Elections Officers where they were *captured and collated on a results collation template at the National Collation Centre.* [emphasis added].

What this means is that the V11s and V23As with the results for the presidential election that were separated from the national assembly election, were rerouted from the ward centres and taken to Harare, via ZEC's district election centres, where they were "captured and collated on a results collation template at the National Collation Centre". This was not only in violation of s37C(4), regarding the transmission of election results, and s38 regarding the harmonisation of the conduct of elections, but also in violation of sections 65, 65A and 65B regarding the procedures to be followed on receipt of election returns at ward centres, constituency centres and provincial command centres, as well as the breach of s110 on the verification and determination of the final result of the presidential election.

The fact that the results for the presidential election were taken from all the ward centres by district election officers directly to the national command centres was not just a breach of the prescribed transmission process but was also a premeditated crime.

It is notable that the confirmation by ZEC in its Report on the 2018 harmonised elections of the use of different routes with different destinations for the collation and transmission of the results for the presidential and national assembly elections was signed off, and thus sanctioned, by all of the electoral body's commissioners as shown below:

Signed:.. Date:..8.|.22.|.19...

Hon. Mrs Justice Priscilla Makanyara Chigumba - Chairperson

Signed:.. Date:..8./.2./.19.

Mr Emmanuel Magade - Deputy Chairperson

Signed:.. Date:..08:..02..2019

Daniel John Chigaru - Commissioner

Signed:.. Date:..08/02/2019

Mrs Joyce Laetitia Kazembe - Commissioner

Signed:.. Date:..11/02/19.

Dr Ngoni Kundidzora - Commissioner

Signed:.. Date:..08 |02 |19

Dr Qhubani Moyo - Commissioner

Signed:.. Date:..08. 02. 19

Ms Netsai Mushonga - Commissioner

Signed:.. Date:..08 |02|2019.

Ms Sibongile Ndlovu - Commissioner

ZEC's commandeering of the result for the presidential election from ward centres to the national command centre while sidestepping constituency centres was audacious rigging. This audacity was possible only because it was done on the back of the November 2017 military coup that had toppled Robert Mugabe and effectively established a military state in Zimbabwe. Despite claims by the Junta which imposed Emmerson Mnangagwa as President on 24 November 2017 that it had ushered in a new democratic dispensation with a mantra that Zimbabwe was "open for business", the reality on the ground was that the army had taken over not just state power but also the ruling ZANU PF party: and it was not going to give up through the ballot box what it had won through the barrel of a gun.

Yet expectations were high that the new dispensation, which had grabbed power with the mantra that "the voice of the people is the voice of God", would turn the page and organise free-and-fair elections for the first time in Zimbabwe since 1980. The proposition that a Junta would organise free-and-fair elections seven months after a coup was untenable right from the beginning. In what was a self-fulfilling prophecy, the regime claimed that the pre-election campaign for the 2018 harmonised elections was the freest ever. It is shocking that this remains the regime's propaganda line. On 17 November 2019, Mnangagwa published a widely circulated article to mark the second anniversary of the 15 November 2017 military coup in which he claimed that:

> **On July 30th 2018, eight months after coming to office, *we held the freest and fairest elections in the country's history*. While no electoral process is perfect, all international monitors noted the new and free environment of the campaigns, and the vast improvement in the electoral process** [emphasis added].[107]

This is a baseless claim.

The alleged freeness and fairness of the campaign period was nowhere near as open and free as the 2008 campaign period for Zimbabwe's first harmonised general election, held on 29 March 2008. In that election, the opposition MDC formations, one led by Morgan Tsvangirai and the other led by Arthur Mutambara, won 110 parliamentary seats out of 210. In that election, Tsvangirai won the presidential election but, controversially, fell short of the threshold of 50% plus one vote, thereby triggering a presidential election run-off, in a hotly disputed outcome. Unlike the open and free campaign period ahead of the 29 March 2008 harmonised general election, the run-up to the run-off was a farce characterised by unprecedented military-led violence in which over 200 opposition supporters were killed, including some from a ZANU PF faction then linked to Joice Mujuru, and many more were tortured, with tens of thousands internally and externally displaced.

The political environment of the run-up to the 2018 general election was no different from the one that had characterised the 2008 run-off election. Both were military grounded environments, the gun dictating politics. Unlike the circumstances surrounding the 2008 presidential run-off, the November 2017 coup, and especially the fact that the military had toppled Mugabe and his government, put the fear of God among traditional leaders and their communities across rural Zimbabwe. The fact that the army had deployed over 2,000 soldiers

---

[107] Emmerson Mnangagwa, "This is how Zimbabwe has changed since I became president", *CNBC Africa*, November 17, 2019, https://www.cnbcafrica.com/zdnl-mc/2019/11/17/op-ed-this-is-how-zimbabwe-has-changed-since-i-became-president-emmerson-mnangagwa/

and embedded them in all rural areas ahead of the military coup put these communities virtually under siege in the run-up to the 30 July 2018 elections, especially because the number of embedded soldiers was bloated to 5,000 by the time of the election on 30 July 2018.

The situation that prevailed in the rural areas ahead of the 2018 general election was particularly conducive for rigging in ways never before seen. This is what was historic about the 2018 elections, not their alleged freeness and fairness. The embedded soldiers were not only out there in the open as ZANU PF political commissars mobilising votes, with the threat of force and violence as their election manifesto, but some were also visible at polling stations on election day, as polling officers. What made this situation worse was that the MDC-Alliance did not have polling agents in some 518 polling stations in rural areas considered to be ZANU PF strongholds; especially in the Mashonaland provinces.

These 518 polling stations were used to contaminate and manipulate V11s and V23As that were commandeered from ward centres between 31 July 2018 and 3 August 2018, when ZEC undertook a controversial exercise that it said was for the verification and determination of the result of the presidential election. The case of the ZEC officers who were found by EU observers to be completing V11s, all by themselves two days after the election, exemplified a rampant act in the 518 polling stations where the MDC-Alliance failed to field election agents. As in Makoni North, the completion of V11s at these centres was done by military and CIO operatives under the cover of ZEC, after the 30 July 2018 election.

Parenthetically, the MDC-A's failure to field candidates in 518 polling stations was bad. However, what was worse was the party's failure to put in place an alternative arrangement to ensure that it captured the full results for the presidential election before they were hijacked from ward centres.

Besides the ZEC main server, there are six ways of knowing and comparing the full result for the presidential election using minimum numbers of election agents deployed at five electoral centres, depending on the capacity of the contesting parties or candidates to deploy election agents. These six different ways are shown in Diagram 18, indicating the minimum number of election agents required at each of the five electoral centres involved:

First, the full result for the presidential election can be captured by a political party or candidate by deploying at least 21,970 election agents – in the case of the 2018 elections – at 10,985 polling stations. The MDC-A failed to do this, as it did not have election agents in

DIAGRAM 18:
SIX WAYS OF KNOWING & COMPARING FULL RESULTS FOR THE PRESIDENTIAL ELECTION USING MINIMUM NUMBERS OF ELECTION AGENTS

	SIX SOURCES OF THE NATIONAL RESULT FOR THE PRESIDENTIAL ELECTION				
	Electoral Centre	Election Return	V Forms	Number of Polling Agents	Source of National Result
1	Polling Station	Polling Station Return	10,985 V11s	21,970	10,985
2	Ward Centre	Ward Return	1,958 V23As	1,958	1,958
3	Constituency Centre	Constituency Return	210 V23Bs	210	210
4	Provincial Command Centre	Provincial Return	10 V23Cs	10	10
5	National Command Centre	Initial Result	1 V23D	2	1
6	National Command Centre	Final Result	210 V23Bs	2	1

some 518 polling stations. In the Zimbabwean context, when a political party or candidate fails to deploy election agents, a risk and real possibility for election rigging, including through ballot-stuffing, is created. In fact, a standard rigging practice in presidential elections used by "the system" over the years, especially before the harmonised elections introduced in 2008, is to scan polling stations to determine those without election agents for opposition parties and candidates in order to use them for stuffing ballot boxes, should that become necessary.

Since it started contesting presidential elections in 2002, the MDC has never been able to deploy election agents at all polling stations. Apart from ever-present capacity issues, a further challenge has been due to the fact that "the system" typically creates phantom polling stations. This used to be rampant before the advent of harmonised elections, and this rigging method was particularly employed in 2002 when the military created and manned a number of tented polling stations specifically meant for ballot-stuffing. The failure to deploy election agents at any polling station in a presidential election can be the difference between winning and losing the election.

Second, and critically important, all the 10,985 polling stations report their results to 1,958 ward collation centres in the country. A political party or presidential candidate can thus obtain the full result for the presidential election from these wards by deploying 1,958 agents. This should be possible to do in a systematic way without much ado, because 1,958 is a manageable number. In fact, a serious political party can double this number just in case something goes wrong with a single agent.

It is inexcusable for a political party to fail to deploy election agents at ward collation centres. These centres are the first and most critical electoral centre for knowing the full results for all the three harmonised elections. These are: the local authority election (council winners are declared at these centres); the national assembly election (a party or candidate can determine the winner by adding the totals of all ward centres in the constituency in advance of the counting at the constituency centre); and the presidential election (by adding the totals of the 1,958 ward centres or 1,958 V23As). The centrality of the result for the presidential election of 1,958 ward collation centres captured in 1,958 V23A forms explains why "the system" used ZEC to hijack the 2018 results for the presidential election from these centres, using a route and destination different from the prescribed manner for their transmission, capture and collation.

Third, the 1,958 ward centres report their results to 210 constituency centres. The results delivered at constituency centres must contain the original 10,985 V11s and 1,958 V23As which are captured and collated onto 210 constituency returns, V23Bs, that are critical for the verification and determination of the final result of the presidential election. An organised political party or presidential candidate ought to get the national result for the presidential election by having competent and vigilant election agents in 210 constituencies, without fail.

It is always a big surprise and a major let down that opposition political parties or presidential candidates fail to ensure that they get the full result for presidential election from just 210 constituencies by ensuring that 210 election agents are deployed for that purpose. The constituency returns, or V23Bs, are the key source materials that are used under s110(3)(d) of the Electoral Act to verify and determine the final result of the presidential election. As such, it stands to reason that, when election agents go to verify the result at the national command centre, they must necessarily carry with them certified copies of the results from 210 constituencies.

Fourth, the full result for the presidential election is obtainable from 10 provincial command centres which receive the 210 constituency returns, the V23Bs, and collate them onto 10 provincial returns, the V23Cs, that in fact make up the initial national result for the presidential election that is captured and collated into form V23D at ZEC's national command centre in Harare.

It is unthinkable to imagine a political party or presidential candidate failing to deploy a minimum of 10 election agents, one per province, to get 10 provincial returns or V23Cs whose total is the initial national result for the presidential election. The election agents who go for the verification and determination of the initial result captured in form V23D and the final result captured in 210 V23Bs must go to the national command centre carrying 10 V23Cs. This ought to be mandatory for the chief election agent of any political party or candidate. That this has not been so, boggles the mind.

Fifth, the full and initial (national) result for the presidential election is obtainable from the national command centre when the Chief Elections Officer captures the results on the provincial command returns, the V23Cs, and collates them onto form V23D. This process is different from the one provided in s110(3) of the Electoral Act meant to verify, determine, declare and announce the final result of the presidential election. All that is required by a political party or presidential candidate is to deploy at the national command centre the chief election agent plus another who go armed with 10 V23Cs from each of the 10 provincial command centres. In the 2018 presidential election, ZEC was not transparent about this. In fact, ZEC violated the law by purporting that form V23D had the final result of the presidential election. It is staggering that in its Report on the 2018 harmonised elections, ZEC confirms that it announced the result for the presidential election on the basis of form V23D.

Sixth, a political party or presidential candidate gets the full and final result for the presidential election by deploying their chief election agent plus another at the national command centre where they go armed with their certified copies of 210 constituency returns, the V23Bs. This final process is defined in s110(3) of the Electoral Act. A chief election agent who goes to the national command centre for the verification and determination of the final result of the presidential election without 10 copies of V23Cs, a copy of the V23D and, most critically, 210 certified copies of constituency returns or V23Bs simply has no business of being at the national command centre.

With these six ways of knowing the full result at five different election centres from polling stations through to the national command centre, it is difficult to understand why political parties and presidential candidates fail to come up with a plan that ensures that they have the full result for the presidential election before its declaration and announcement by ZEC at the national command centre. The six ways are complementary and are intended to ensure the integrity of the aggregation of the result, which must remain the same in each of the six steps outlined above. Any discrepancy must trigger alarm bells.

While ZEC has a constitutional duty and obligation to conduct elections effectively, efficiently and transparently to ensure that they are free and fair, political parties and candidates have an equal duty to play their part. It does not make sense to find political parties and candidates ignorant of the result after the elections, just like the rest of society, anxiously waiting for ZEC to announce the results as if the elections were conducted in secrecy. Much of the rigging culture that has taken root in Zimbabwean elections is a direct result of the incompetence and incapacity of opposition political parties and candidates who have failed to appreciate or understand that elections are not just a political process but are also a legal event. Given the concept advanced in this book that an election is a political process which is a legal event, it is essential that every election is approached both politically and legally from the start.

The six ways of knowing the full result for the presidential election through the five prescribed electoral centres were disrupted and subverted when "the system" got ZEC to hijack the results from ward centres to the national command centre where the data on the V11s and the V23As was captured and collated. This happened after Defence House realised that Chamisa had won the presidential election by 66% of the vote, with Mnangagwa getting 33%. The hijacked results were input by a curious **"group of people, in excess of twenty, punching in what was identified as V11 data into an Excel spreadsheet"** for a period of two days.

This culminated in the massive rigging of the result of the 2018 presidential election. In essence, the capturing, collation and transmission of the results for the presidential election from ward centres using an illegal route and destination, and the verification and determination of the same result were so fundamentally flawed, and fraudulently conducted in breach of s110(3)(d) of the Electoral Act, with the consequence of materially compromising and voiding the result of the presidential election.

The particularity at the core of the rigging was ZEC's premeditated, calculated and deliberate disregard of 210 presidential constituency returns, namely the V23Bs, that are the only returns that must be used to verify and determine the result of the presidential election in terms of s110(3)(d) of the Electoral Act. To obtain the necessary V23Bs, it was not necessary for ZEC to invent a different route and different destination for capturing, collating and transmitting the results for the presidential election from ward centres. The route and destination of the results from ward centres should have been constituency centres.

The unimpeached evidence that ZEC disregarded the presidential constituency returns, the V23Bs, the only legal returns for verifying and determining the result of the presidential election, was given by Jameson Timba, Chamisa's chief election agent. This was not rebutted by ZEC or by Priscilla Chigumba in their opposing papers or heads of argument in Chamisa's ConCourt challenge. The unimpeached, and critically important averment by Jameson Timba was that:

> On the 1st of August 2018, I was invited by ZEC to verify constituency returns for the presidential election. On arrival at National Results Centre where ZEC was collating results for the presidential election on the basis of data from all ward returns, that is Form V23a accompanied by polling station returns (i.e. Form V11), these forms were laid before me by Mr. Murenje, the ZEC Director of Elections and Training.
>
> Mr. Murenje did not present to me the constituency return (that is Form V23B).

It is telling that Mr Murenje, the ZEC Director of Elections, did not file any affidavit to dispute Timba's evidence. And nowhere in their opposing papers or heads of argument did ZEC or Chigumba specifically mention V23Bs as the presidential constituency returns that are referred to in s110(3)(d) of the Electoral Act. Throughout their papers, they kept referring to V23s without acknowledging that in fact there are various V23s. ZEC did not want to distinguish and identify the various V23 forms, as that would have established the particularity of the V23B form as the presidential constituency return. Throughout their court papers, ZEC and Chigumba systematically gave, and maintained, the false and fraudulent impression that V23s are one document or election return, yet the truth is that there are four very different V23s that are election returns.

This misrepresentation and deception over V23s was not an innocent mistake, carelessness or referencing convenience on ZEC's part. It was premediated deception to camouflage the fraud that ZEC had hijacked and rerouted the transmission and destination of the results for the presidential election from ward centres to the national command centre.

The ZEC misrepresentation of V23s to camouflage the particularity of V23Bs with respect to s110(3)(d) of the Electoral Act, and ZEC's deceitful narrative about and around V23s, was greatly assisted by Chief Justice Malaba in ways that risk causing irreparable damage to the judiciary. Malaba sensationalised V11s, treating them in isolation as standalone returns, without assessing them in the context of a specific V23B, or presidential constituency return.

When it comes to verifying and determining the result of the presidential election, V11s and V23As are relevant only as attachments to V23Bs and not as single and isolated returns not connected to any V23B. During the collation of V23B forms at constituency centres, it is mandatory that original V11s and V23As are attached to the back of the V23B from the constituency in order for that V23B to be valid. Any V23B without original V11s and V23As attached to it is invalid; and, conversely, any V11 or V23A not attached to a V23B is invalid for purposes of verifying and determining the result for the presidential election in terms of s110(3)(d) of the Electoral Act.

Regarding the ZEC server that contained the results for the presidential election prior to their being hijacked and rerouted from ward centres to the national command centre in Harare where they were altered, Malaba mishandled the subpoena by blocking it, which would have exposed the manipulation of the results and rigging of the presidential election. What Malaba did in this connection amounted to a corrupt and scandalous judicial cover up of election rigging.

Even worse is how Malaba dealt with the hearing of Chamisa's ConCourt challenge. Most egregiously, Malaba took the position that ZEC did not have to do anything because, in his judgment, it was "incumbent on the applicant [Chamisa] to discharge the *onus* [of proof] which was on him". Wrongly likening ZEC to an accused person in criminal proceedings, where the prosecution must prove its case beyond reasonable doubt, Malaba said, "the accused person does not have to his or her innocence".

Likening ZEC to an accused person in a criminal case was absurd because, unlike in that situation, ZEC is a Chapter 12 constitutional body, with a constitutional duty to be transparent and to discharge and prove its transparency, whenever challenged.

On V11s, Malaba made a mountain out of a molehill, and in the process, gave a hostage to fortune, as far as ZEC's delinquency was concerned. In a startling remark in his judgment Malaba asserted that:

> **The Commission proved through the V11 Forms produced that the allegations that some forms had been signed and not populated was false. … Without access to the sealed ballot boxes residue, this allegation simply remained as refuted.**

While Malaba delivered this remark bombastically to the excitement of the gallery, it was in fact much ado about nothing. Both the allegation and its rebuttal were of no material consequence because there was absolutely no need to be preoccupied or even to be interested in any V11 not attached to a particular V23B, the constituency return, which is the only relevant return for the determination of the result of the presidential election in terms of s110(3)(d).

Seemingly determined to shield ZEC's disputed and conflicting results, one which gave Mnangagwa 50.8% of the vote and another which put him at 50.67%, Malaba opined that:

> **An election result is the declaration of a winner having reached the 50% plus one vote, and no other thing.**

This is not true. In terms of the Electoral Act, an election result is the outcome of an election contest based on the votes obtained by each of the contestants, depending on whether the election is presidential, parliamentary or local authority. The presidential election has three, not one, possible outcomes, which are provided in s110(f) of the Act.

It was disgraceful and an unfortunate erosion of public trust that, after giving a poorly con-structed and badly reasoned preliminary judgment littered with political sentiments devoid of legal reasoning and without a factual basis, Malaba took more than a year to avail his "fully dressed judgment". The inexplicable and unreasonable delay was not in the interest of justice. Interested parties that wanted to take the judgment up with the African Commission on Human and People's Rights were paralysed by Malaba's delayed judgment because they could not seek available regional or continental remedies without it.

In the final analysis, what is most unfortunate is the that Constitutional Court failed to hold ZEC to its constitutional duty as a Chapter 12 institution. ZEC ran the 2018 presidential election in ways that were no different from the way in which the office of the Registrar-General, under Tobaiwa Mudede, used to do, and, in some instances, ZEC was worse as it flatly refused and failed to meet its transparency requirements in terms of s233(d) and s239(a)(iv) of the Constitution.

On balance, and given the conduct of Chief Justice Malaba regarding the server, along with the misrepresentations and deceit of ZEC documented in the preceding chapters, the positions of Malaba as Chief Justice, Chigumba as ZEC Chairperson and Silaigwana as ZEC Chief Elections Officer are untenable. They are irredeemably compromised. Each and all of them have jointly and severally lost all credibility as they arrogantly and shamelessly did not live up to their fiduciary duties to the public. If they continue in their roles, Zimbabwe's capacity to hold free, fair and credible elections will be irreparably damaged. The trio is exactly where Tobaiwa Mudede ended when it became impossible for Zimbabwe to have free, fair and credible elections with him in charge.

For all the dust that Malaba kicked up, it is shocking that he ignored the best evidence submitted by Chamisa which showed that ZEC violated a statutory provision prescribing the procedure for verifying and determining the result for the presidential election. Chamisa's chief election agent, Jameson Timba, lodged a supporting affidavit with the unimpeached evidence that ZEC did not display the presidential constituency returns, the V23Bs, as required under s110(3)(d) of the Electoral Act. ZEC did not dispute or rebut Timba's specific submission that the requisite V23Bs were not displayed. When a fundamental statement of fact by a key witness, such as a chief election agent, is not refuted, then it must stand as an undisputed fact.

It is a travesty of justice that Malaba, and indeed the entire ConCourt bench, that heard Chamisa's application, ignored Timba's averment and its implications in so far as it pointed to the rigging of the 2018 presidential election. The reason that ZEC did not display the presidential constituency returns (the V23Bs) for verification is directly linked to ZEC's illegal decision to invent a different route with a different destination for the collation, compilation and transmission of the result of the 2018 presidential election. Instead of going from ward centre to the constituency centre, the different route and destination used by ZEC was from ward centres to the national command centre via district election officers. The result for the presidential election sent in this illegal manner was in the form V11s (polling station returns) and V23As (ward returns). Timba's affidavit confirms that ZEC did indeed display an assortment of V11s and V23As but did not display the mandatory V23Bs because it did not have them; it did not have them because it could not have them, and it could not have them because the invented route and destination it used for capturing, collating and transmitting the results for the 2018 presidential election was contrary to the prescribed manner.

The fact that ZEC did not have or did not use the V23Bs is amplified in its Report on the 2018 harmonised elections in which the electoral body confirms that it declared and announced the result of the 2018 presidential election on the basis of form V23D, which is a national command centre return that gives the total votes in 10 provincial returns, namely the V23Cs.

In the Report, ZEC confirms that:

> **The Chief Elections Officer who was the Returning Officer for the election completed the V23D Form which is a record of results as collated at national level. The results were subsequently announced by the Chairperson of the Zimbabwe Electoral Commission on that same day in accordance with the provisions of the law.[108]**

In terms of s37C(4)(f)(i) of the Electoral Act, the result of the presidential election captured in form V23D (based on 10 provincial returns known as V23Cs) is only an initial result that is not for declaration or announcement. This is done on the basis of the final result referred to in s37C(4)(f)(ii) of the Act, which result is verified and determined on the basis of 210 presidential constituency returns or V23Bs in accordance with s110(3)(d), (e) and (f). ZEC could not verify and determine the final result in the prescribed manner as a direct consequence of having used an illegal route with an illegal destination to capture, collate and transmit the result for the presidential election from ward centres to the national command centre.

---

[108] ZEC, *Zimbabwe 2018 Harmonised Elections Report*, page 72.

The different route with a different destination led to a result based on form V23D. But the V23D was not based on the legal process because the route and destination invented by ZEC excluded the constituency centres that must produce V23Bs and the provincial centres that must produce V23Cs which are the basis for the legal V23D.

This clearly means that ZEC came up with its own manipulated V23Cs, which it used to compile an unlawful form V23D. The different route with a different destination, along with the use of an illegal V23D, not based on lawfully captured, collated and transmitted V23Cs, were specific and unavoidable outcomes of the rigging system. The unimpeachable evidence for this is in ZEC's Report on the 2018 harmonised elections. In an ill-conceived effort to cover up the evidence by giving the false impression that ZEC had the power and authority to vary the prescribed route and destination for the transmission of election results, the Ministry of Justice, Legal and Parliamentary Affairs planted a story in the state media which claimed that:

> **A report from the inter-ministerial taskforce seen by *The Sunday Mail* details plans to "conduct a study in other jurisdictions" to assess the feasibility of adopting a system that allows for the electronic transmission of results to the National Results Centre.**
>
> **"The recommendation for the expeditious transmission of results to the Command Centre (National Results Centre)** *is already being implemented; for instance, in the 2018 harmonised elections, the Zimbabwe Electoral Commission used a faster procedure that led to the result forms being transmitted directly from District Command Centres to the National Results Centre,"* **the Report says.**
>
> *Previously, the results went through the ward, constituency, district and provincial command centres before being transmitted to the National Results Centre* [emphasis added][109]

Three revealing issues standout in the leak from the Justice Ministry, which oversees ZEC policy and administrative matters affecting ZEC.

First, the reference to a plan by an inter-ministerial taskforce "to assess the feasibility of adopting a system that allows for the electronic transmission of results to the national results centre", clearly shows that "the system" has been shaken by the spotlight on the abuse of the server to cover up the rigging of the 2018 presidential election. As pointed out throughout this book, the Electoral Act and Electoral Regulations do in fact allow for the electronic transmission, or notification, of results from polling stations, ward centres and constituency centres to the national command centre.

Second, the claim by the Justice Ministry that "the Zimbabwe Electoral Commission used a faster procedure that led to the result forms being transmitted directly from district election centres to the National Results Centre", confirms an illegality, albeit in a grossly misleading way, which nevertheless shows that the Ministry was in the loop about the massive and audacious rigging of the 2018 presidential election. The Justice Ministry ought to know that

---

[109] "Govt unveils broad electoral reforms", *The Sunday Mail*, 21 November 2019, Harare.

there is no legal provision under which ZEC can use "a faster procedure" to transmit results forms directly from district command centres to the national command centre, skipping the constituency centres and provincial command centres.

The fact that the Justice Ministry confirms that such an illegal transmission occurred, is an admission of unlawful conduct, whose consequence is to invalidate the result of the presidential election declared and announced by Priscilla Chigumba on 3 August 2018. It is notable that, in order to cover up the illegality, the Ministry of Justice gives the false impression that all harmonised election result forms in the 2018 elections were transmitted through the purported "faster procedure" used by ZEC. The truth is that only the results for the presidential election were subjected to the so-called faster procedure; the national assembly election results were not. The application of the illegal procedure disharmonised the harmonised elections by separating the processing of the results of the presidential and national assembly elections in order to facilitate the rigging of the presidential election.

Third, the claim by the Justice Ministry that "previously, the results went through the ward, constituency, district and provincial command centres before being transmitted to the National Results Centre", gives the false impression that the purportedly "faster procedure" used by ZEC to transmit the results for the 2018 presidential election through a route and to a destination different from the prescribed manner is a new legal position that has replaced the old system used "previously". Nothing could be further from the truth. What the Justice Ministry describes as the previous position is in fact the current legal position, as confirmed by Chief Justice Malaba in his "fully dressed" judgment in Chamisa's ConCourt case, where he summarises the present lawful position as follows:

> The ward elections officer is then enjoined to provide a copy of the completed ward return to every candidate, election agent and observer who requests one. He or she must also ensure that a copy of the ward return is displayed prominently outside the ward centre, so that all members of the public who wish to do so may inspect it and record its contents. Immediately after causing a copy of the ward return to be displayed outside the ward centre, *the ward elections officer must cause the return, certified by himself or herself to be correct, to be transmitted to the constituency centre for the constituency in which the ward is situated.*
>
> Any reference to a constituency centre or a constituency elections officer shall be construed in respect of the Presidential election as reference to a Presidential constituency centre or a Presidential constituency elections officer.
>
> In relation to the Presidential election, the number of votes received by each candidate as shown in each polling station return is added together and the resultant figure added to the number of postal votes received by each candidate. The constituency elections officer shall forthwith record on the constituency return the votes obtained by each candidate and the number of rejected ballot papers in such a manner that the results of the count for each polling station are shown on the return. He or she is required to display the completed constituency return to those present and afford each candidate

or his or her election agent the opportunity to subscribe their signatures thereto. *He or she must then transmit to the Chief Elections Officer by hand through a messenger the constituency return or a copy thereof, certified by the constituency elections officer to be correct* [emphasis added][110]

Malaba is emphatic in peremptory terms that:

> The ward elections officer *must* cause the return, certified by himself or herself to be correct, to *be transmitted to the constituency centre for the constituency in which the ward is situated.*

Yet ZEC has confirmed in its Report on the 2018 harmonised elections that:

> Results for the presidential and the national assembly elections *were transmitted using different routes from the ward collation centre.* While the destination for the national assembly election results was the constituency centre, the Presidential results were forwarded to the district centre for onward transmission to the national command centre in Harare.

The ZEC Report further confirms that:

> The results were taken to the *national command/collation centre* physically by the District Elections Officers *where they were captured and collated* on a results collation template at the National Collation Centre.

ZEC did not capture and collate the result for the 2018 presidential election in the manner outlined by Malaba. I have shown throughout this book that in fact ZEC did not follow the prescribed manner. The only reason why ZEC did not follow the prescribed process was to enable the rigging of the result at the behest of "the system" through Defence House. There can be no other rational explanation.

On the facts, there is no dispute that, from ward centres, ZEC invented a different route with a different destination for the transmission, capture and collation of the results for the 2018 presidential election. The route and destination were different from that used for the transmission, capture and collation of the results for the national assembly election.

Contrary to the noise made about V11s in the ConCourt, the fact is that the case had nothing to do with polling-station returns. Malaba was too fixated about V11s when they were irrelevant. Their number was not an issue and it was not necessary to produce them. The fact is that the 2018 presidential election was invalid, having been voided by the hijacking of results from ward collation centres to where they were illegally captured and collated at the national command centre in Harare. It is enough to establish this, and the official confirmation has been provided by ZEC itself in its Report on the 2018 harmonised elections. There is no need to get into any election residue in the sealed ballot boxes or the sealed election packets.

The route and destination used by ZEC to transmit, capture and collate the results for the presidential election was illegal. The illegality not only disharmonised the harmonised elections but, critically, it voided any outcome of the illegal process. The voiding of any outcome of the

---

[110] Judgment, No. CCZ 21/19, page 76.

route and destination used means that the election result declared and announced by Priscilla Chigumba on 3 August 2018 was invalid. In this connection, and if the definition of an election as a political process which is a legal event is applied, Emmerson Mnangagwa is in the Office of the President and Cabinet illegitimately, in terms of the political process, and illegally at law.

But why did ZEC do such a manifestly illegitimate and illegal act of commission in such a brazen manner?

ZEC acted in the manner it did at the behest of Defence House because Mnangagwa had lost the election. The loss was first captured by ZEC's main server by "the rigging system" well before the results for the harmonised elections reached "civilians, including ZEC civilians". By the time the results reached the 1,958 ward centres, a decision had already been made to disharmonise the presidential and national assembly elections and to divert the results for the presidential election by using a different route with a different destination. The purpose of the diversion was to reverse Chamisa's victory to stop the reversal of the coup, which would have been the consequence of Chamisa's victory. As far as "the system" was concerned, the presidential election was the second phase of the coup and thus had to be won by any and all means available.

It was in this context that "the system" pulled out all the stops, to ensure a Mnangagwa victory by hook or crook. While the mechanism for this is as outlined in Chapter Three of this book, the main actor in the operation was Mavis Matsanga, shown below.

Matsanga, ZEC's Chief Information Security Officer and Active CIO Divisional Intelligence Officer, was seconded to the Commission in 2008. She oversaw the rigging operations and logistics for the 2018 presidential election.

Matsanga's operation was supervised from Defence House and involved coordinated action with the CIO's Data Recovery Centre, the Army's Africom Zimbabwe, a subsidiary of the army-owned Fairhaven Investments and the CIO's Chiltern Trust.

The involvement of an active CIO officer seconded effectively to run the key operations and logistics for the 2018 elections through CIO structures (Data Recovery Centre) backed by the CIO's Chiltern Trust and the army's Africom most definitely produced a poisoned chalice, to the detriment of ZEC's constitutional duty and obligation enshrined in s235(1)(a) which provides that:

> **The independent Commissions are independent and are not subject to the direction or control of anyone.**

In the 2018 presidential election, ZEC was infested with securocrats from the ZDF and the CIO who, together with Priscilla Chigumba, reported to and were controlled from Defence House.

Given the foregoing, only a deceitful, incompetent and corrupt electoral body would, as a Chapter 12 constitutional institution, conduct a presidential election in such a manner, and only a compromised court would endorse that kind of conduct. Yet this is precisely what happened in the 2018 presidential election. A deceitful, incompetent and corrupt ZEC conspired with a compromised Chief Justice to deliver a rigged election to "the system". It should be recalled that on 31 July 2018, Priscilla Chigumba, as ZEC chairperson, revealed her commitment to the rigging conspiracy in a WhatsApp that message she shared with her close contacts in which she said:

> They [MDC] don't have to agree. We will announce based on our own V11. We don't need any party's V11. It's just courtesy for us to ask them to verify. Agree or not, we announce.

Chigumba adopted her rigging position before ZEC instituted its verification process for the determination of the result for the presidential election which commenced on 1 August 2018 at the electoral body's national command centre in Harare. Chigumba's position was complemented by Malaba's stance taken while he was at the Pretoria Sheraton hotel for his son's wedding in South Africa where, after reading through Chamisa's application that had just been lodged with the ConCourt on 10 August 2018, Malaba turned to the judicial officer who had given him the application and asked, "Is that all?", and when the officer replied, "Yes, sir" Malaba, shaking his head, said: "OK. *Akula lutho la*" [There is nothing here]", by which he meant that there was no case and that he was going to dismiss the application, even before the case was heard in the ConCourt.

On the one hand, Chigumba already had a method for ensuring that ZEC would use its V11s to secure a Mnangagwa win even before the verification and determination of the result for the presidential election had commenced. On the other hand, Malaba took the position that the ConCourt would dismiss Chamisa's application even before the arguments were made and the case was heard in court. This means that Chigumba and Malaba were critical parts of the rigging system, as pointed out in Chapter Three of this book.

The prejudicial positions taken by Chigumba and Malaba in favour of Mnangagwa and against Chamisa were, in reality, against the people of Zimbabwe.

In terms of s88 of the Constitution of Zimbabwe, "Executive authority derives from the people of Zimbabwe", and, in terms of s162, "Judicial authority derives from the people of Zimbabwe". As such, the people have a constitutional right and duty to assert their authority in accordance with the Constitution and to reclaim that authority where those vested with it become delinquent by abusing the trust bestowed on them by the people.

Over and above the fact that ZEC's hijacking of the results for the 2018 presidential election through the use of a different route with a different destination from the prescribed manner deprived Chamisa of his victory as captured by the results in ZEC's main server which was severed to facilitate rigging, the ultimate victims of the rigging were Zimbabwean citizens, as the electorate, whose political rights are enshrined in s67 of the Constitution of Zimbabwe:

(1) *Every Zimbabwean citizen has the right –*

(a) *to free, fair and regular elections for any elective public office established in terms of this Constitution or any other law; and*

(b) *to make political choices freely.*

(2) Subject to this Constitution, every Zimbabwean citizen has the right –

   (a) to form, to join and to participate in the activities of a political party or organisation of their choice;

   (b) *to campaign freely and peacefully for a political party or cause;*

   (c) to participate in peaceful political activity; and

   (d) *to participate, individually or collectively, in gatherings or groups or in any other manner, in peaceful activities to influence, challenge or support the policies of the Government or any political or whatever cause.*

(3) Subject to this Constitution, every Zimbabwean citizen who is of or over eighteen years of age has the right –

   (a) to vote in all elections and referendums to which this Constitution or any other law applies, and to do so in secret; and

   (b) *to stand for election for public office and, if elected, to hold such office.*

(4) **For the purpose of promoting multi-party democracy, an Act of Parliament must provide for the funding of political parties.** [emphasis added]

The premediated corruption in the capturing, collation and transmission of the results for the presidential election from ward centres to ZEC's national command centre violated the justiciable political right of Zimbabweans to free, fair and regular elections to choose the President of Zimbabwe. An election which is not free and not fair violates not only the rights of the affected candidates or political parties but also, and even more fundamentally, the rights of the electorate. This situation was made worse not only by the ConCourt's endorsement of an audaciously stolen election, but also by the fact that Malaba took more than a year to release his "fully dressed judgment" that also audaciously endorsed the electoral theft, with the consequence that justice delayed became justice denied. It is in this connection that the 2018 election was stolen from Zimbabweans.

In the circumstances, and given that executive authority and judicial authority are derived from the people, when officers and offices vested with such authority to exercise on behalf of the people fail to discharge their constitutional duty, the people have the right to reclaim their authority. In the case of the stolen 2018 presidential election, the people have the right to reclaim their stolen vote that was captured in the ZEC server before "the system" intervened to change it by hijacking V11s and V23As with that result at ward centres and illegally transmitting them to the national command centre where they were unlawfully captured and collated.

The inescapable situation before Zimbabweans is that Emmerson Mnangagwa illegally occupies the office of the president to exercise the executive authority that is derived from the people but that the people did not vest in him. Section 67(3)(b) provides that:

> **Every Zimbabwean citizen who is over eighteen years of age has the right to stand for election for public office and,** *if elected, to hold such office.*

In terms of the Constitution of Zimbabwe, a person who has not been lawfully elected by the people has no right to hold the public office to which they sought to be elected. By the same token, a person who has been elected by the people to a public office has the right to hold that office. Mnangagwa was not elected to the public office of the President of Zimbabwe,

Chamisa was; yet it is Mnangagwa who is holding the public office to which he was not elected. This is the source of the crisis of legitimacy in Zimbabwe: a person who was elected to a public office is prevented from holding that office, while a person who has been rejected by the electorate ends up holding the public office to which he was not elected. It is for this reason that Mnangagwa faces intractable questions of illegitimacy and illegality.

Given that the concept of an election as a political process is a legal event, the situation obtaining on the ground is that Mnangagwa's presidency is bedevilled by a twin challenge of illegitimacy and illegality. The result of the 2018 presidential election declared and announced by Priscilla Chigumba was invalid because it was based on an invalid route and destination used by ZEC to transmit, capture and collate the results from ward centres. The invalid result has engendered political illegitimacy.

Moving forward requires the restoration of legitimacy and legality. There is also an urgent need to demilitarise state politics in Zimbabwe. The current constitutional provisions have proved to be inadequate. The militarisation of ZEC is a total onslaught on democracy. ZEC has been so compromised that it cannot run any credible election without undergoing root-and-branch reforms. So bad is the situation at ZEC that it is structurally and functionally worse than the election machinery that used to be run by the discredited former Registrar-General, Tobaiwa Mudede. The role of independent constitutional commissions needs to be revisited.

The framers of the new 2013 Constitution created independent constitutional commissions as institutions of society to support democracy. As such, constitutional commissions are not state institutions or organs of the state. It is tragic that Priscilla Chigumba literally took directions and orders from Defence House. That should not be possible. A fresh start is required.

Malaba's conduct in the whole saga around the theft of the 2018 presidential election is perhaps the most treacherous. The rule of law is the cornerstone of a constitutional democracy. In this connection, an independent judiciary is a *sine qua non* for the rule of law. Malaba's conduct in the manner he handled Chamisa's ConCourt challenge has damaged the integrity and reputation of the Constitutional Court. If truth be told, the ConCourt has become a laughing stock.

It now remains for the people to reclaim their stolen vote by asserting their sovereignty, from which executive and judicial authority are derived. The provision in s162 of the Constitution that stipulates that "judicial authority derives from the people of Zimbabwe and is vested in the courts" is important to interrogate and unpack, so as to establish the options available to the people when the courts abuse that authority. The way in which Chief Justice Luke Malaba and the ConCourt judges who heard Chamisa's election challenge handled the case is an example of the abuse of judicial authority. Malaba dismissed the case even before he had received, let alone heard, the arguments. The result has been to create a crisis of confidence in the judiciary.

As I have highlighted, the hijacking of the results for the presidential election from wards to the national command centre, where they were captured and collated, did not only violate the law to the detriment of Nelson Chamisa but also prejudiced the political rights of the electorate. It is necessary that registered voters should seek the enforcement of the fundamental right enshrined in s67(1) of the Constitution which provides that:

> Every Zimbabwean citizen has the right –
>
> (a) to free, fair and regular elections for any elective public office established in terms of this Constitution or any other law; and
>
> (b) to make political choices freely.

The enforcement of s67(1) is necessary in the interest of curative justice under s85 of the Constitution.

The mishandling of Chamisa's election application by Chief Justice Malaba is a sobering reminder that judges are not gods but are human beings, and, as such, they are liable to the tension between virtues and vices that can cause them to make fundamental errors. While the decisions of the lower courts can be reviewed, appealed against or revised as the case may be, the Constitutional Court cannot make changes to its own judgment in a decided case. Yet this can lead to corruption and the denial of justice.

ZEC's admission that it hijacked the results for the 2018 presidential election means that Priscilla Chigumba's declaration and announcement of Emmerson Mnangagwa as winner on 3 August 2018, and the ConCourt's endorsement of that declaration and announcement on 24 August 2018, were a gross and intolerable miscarriage of justice which must be cured and prevented. Either the ConCourt can use its inherent powers to reconsider its own judgment or the people can use their sovereignty to reclaim their judicial authority. In India, the Supreme Court has, under the novel doctrine of curative petitions, exercised its inherent power to correct its own decisions in the interest of justice.[111]

There is no prospect that, having dirtied its hands in the matter, the ConCourt under Chief Justice Malaba will be moved by the interest of curative justice to review its own decision to uphold ZEC's illegal and thus invalid declaration and announcement of Emmerson Mnangagwa as the duly elected President of Zimbabwe on 3 August 2018.

It is for this reason that the only available option is for the people to reclaim their vote by asserting their judicial authority to redress the illegality and restore constitutional order and to bring those behind the unprecedented electoral theft to justice. There is a clear and present case of criminal abuse of office by ZEC and the ConCourt, among other individual and institutional players.

In this regard, the people should demand the setting up of an international commission of inquiry into ZEC's admission that it invented a different route with a different destination for the transmission, capture and collation of the results for the 2018 presidential election in brazen violation of the Electoral Act.

---

[111] See: Supreme Court of India in the matter of *Rupa Ashok Hurra* vs. *Ashok Hurra and Anr.* (2002)

APPENDIX: THE COUP MINUTES

SUMMARY OF THE MAIN ISSUES AND CONCERNS OF THE COMMAND ELEMENT COMMUNICATED TO HIS EXCELLENCY THE PRESIDENT OF ZIMBABWE, AND COMMANDER-IN-CHIEF OF THE ZIMBABWE DEFENCE FORCES, CDE R. G. MUGABE, THROUGH THE FATHER FEDELIS MUKONORI TEAM IN THE TWO DAYS FROM THE 15TH TO THE 16TH NOVEMBER, 2017.

INTRODUCTION

This Report summarizes main issues to emerge from communication, both mediated and direct, to the President of Zimbabwe and Commander-in-Chief of the Zimbabwe Defence Forces, Cde Robert Gabriel Mugabe, by the Command Element following an operation mounted by the Zimbabwe Defence Forces in the early hours of Wednesday, 15th November, 2017. The sequel to that operation, dubbed "Operation Restore Legacy", was a morning meeting called by the Commander of the Defence Forces (CDF), General C.G.D.N Chiwenga, at the Army Headquarters at Josiah Magama Tongogara Barracks (JMTB), formerly KGVI, comprising the Command Element (including Police, Prisons and the President's Department), the Chief Secretary to the President and Cabinet, Dr M.J.M. Sibanda, Chairman of the Civil Service Commission, Dr Mariyawanda Nzuwah, Secretary for Foreign Affairs, Ambassador Joey Bimha, Secretary for Information, Media and Broadcasting Services and Presidential Spokesperson, Cde George Charamba. Later, Father Fidelis Mukonori joined the same meeting.

1

AN FM

Broadly, the CDF explained the rationale behind the Operation stressing that this was not a military take-over of Government, but a time-bound Operation meant to extricate the President of Zimbabwe and Commander-in-Chief of the Zimbabwe Defence Forces from negative elements who encircled and had developed tentacles around him, thereby over threatening his legacy and interfering with the proper execution of his duties as Leader of the ruling Party, Zanu-PF, and as President of the Republic of Zimbabwe. Explaining that the Command Element had had several meetings with the President at which it had repeatedly expressed grave concern over this negative development, especially on the defence and the upholding of the ideals and vision of the National Liberation Struggle; on his Legacy and symbolism as the only surviving leader from that epochal Struggle; as the founding father of the Zimbabwe Nation; on the electability of the ruling ZANU-PF Party in the impending 2018 Harmonized Elections and, on the preservation and reproducibility of the whole ethos of the National Liberation Struggle as the dominant, enduring and governing idea in and for Zimbabwe, the CDF requested both the Chief Secretary and Chairman of the Civil Service Commission to help with a quick return to normalcy in respect of the functioning of the three pillars of the State, namely the Executive, the Legislature and the Judiciary. The Operation would not interfere with the normal functioning of society and was only targeting criminal elements who, over the years, had surrounded the President and Commander-in-Chief of the Defence Forces, thereby stifling the proper running of the Party and Country.

The CDF also requested Father Fidelis Mukonori to assist with restoring contact and communication with His Excellency the President, Cde R.G.

2

Mugabe, who remained free and secure at his private home. Further, the CDF requested the Secretary for Information, Media and Broadcasting Services and Presidential Spokesperson, Cde George Charamba, and the Acting Director-General (A/DG) of the Central Intelligence Organisation, Cde Aaron Nhepera, to accompany and assist Father Fidelis in the said contact and communication with the President and First Secretary of ZANU-PF. The Report which only covers the Father Fidelis Mediation Mission, consolidates issues and concerns raised by the Command Element, and put to His Excellency the President in the two days that have gone by since the Wednesday 15 November 2017 Operation.

All told, the following chronology represents meetings held in the two days of November 15 and 16:

Inaugural Meeting of Wednesday morning (from about 0930HRS) of 15th November, 2017, called by the CDF, at which tasks were given as outlined above;

First Meeting involving the President, Cde R.G. Mugabe, the First Lady, Amai Grace N. Mugabe, Father Fidelis Mukonori, Secretary Charamba and Acting Director General Nhepera, held at The Blue Roof, the private residence of the First Family, later in the morning of 15th November, 2017;

First Feedback Meeting from about midday of Wednesday, 15th November, 2017, involving the Command Element (minus a

3

representative of the Zimbabwe Republic Police) and the Father Mukonori Team, held at JMTB.

Second Meeting of the First Family and the Father Mukonori Team held late afternoon of 15th November, 2017, at The Blue Roof. The meeting went into the early hours of the evening.

Second Feedback Meeting involving the Command Element, Father Mukonori and Secretary Charamba from about 1000HRS on Thursday, 16th November, 2017, at JMTB. Commissioner-General of Prisons and Correctional Services, Cde Paradzayi Zimondi, who had been away on a foreign mission, also attended.

Third Feedback Meeting involving President Mugabe, Father Fidelis Mukonori, Secretary Charamba and A/DG Nhepera at State House, from about 1200HRS on Thursday, 16th November, 2017. A/DG Nhepera was later excused to prepare for a meeting between His Excellency the President and a visiting, fact-finding South African Delegation dispatched by His Excellency President Zuma in his capacity as the Chairman of the Southern African Development Community (SADC).

Meeting between President Mugabe and the South African Delegation led by the South African Minister of Defence, and comprising South African Minister of State Security, the CDI of SANDF, and South Africa's Ambassador to Zimbabwe, in the afternoon of Thursday, 16th

4

AN FM

November, 2017, at State House. The President's side comprised Defence Minister Sydney Sekeramayi, State Security Minister Kembo Mohadi and CDF Chiwenga, with Secretary Bimha, Air Vice Marshal (AVM) E. Moyo, Father Fidelis Mukonori, Secretary Charamba and A/DG Nhepera in attendance.

Inaugural face-to-face Meeting between His Excellency the President of Zimbabwe and Commander-in-Chief of the Zimbabwe Defence Forces, Cde R.G. Mugabe, and Commander of the Defence Forces, General C.G.D.N. Chiwenga, held at State House, late afternoon, Thursday, 16th November, 2017, and chaired by Father Fidelis Mukonori, with Secretary Charamba, A/DG Nhepera and AVM Moyo in attendance.

Third Feedback Meeting with Command Element at JMTB, early Thursday evening, 16th November, 2017, on the inaugural face-to-face meeting between the President and General Chiwenga. Father Fidelis Mukonori and Secretary Charamba represented the mediating side.

CONSOLIDATED REPORT ON ISSUES RAISED WITH HIS EXCELLENCY THE PRESIDENT AND COMMANDER-IN-CHIEF OF THE ZIMBABWE DEFENCE FORCES, CDE R.G. MUGABE, BY THE COMMAND ELEMENT.

Rationale for "Operation Restore Legacy".

The Father Fidelis Mukonori team reported to His Excellency the President that the Wednesday 15th November 2017 Operation by the Zimbabwe Defence Forces as explained by the Command Element was

5

not a military take-over of Government or a challenge to the Constitutional position and authority of the President as Head of State and Government, and Commander-in-Chief of the Zimbabwe Defence Force. Rather, the Operation was meant to prop the authority of the President and buttress his Constitutional roles in running the affairs of both the Party, ZANU-PF, and the Nation of Zimbabwe. Equally, it was reported to the President that the Command Element undertook to ensure the safety and welfare of the entire First Family both in the present and for all times. The Command Element pledged loyalty to the President and expressed reverence to him as the only surviving leader from the epochal National Liberation Struggle; as the founding President of the Nation of Zimbabwe and, above all, as a symbol and personification of the founding process, the Struggle for National Liberation and Independence. Operation Restore Legacy had been prompted by grave concerns on the part of the Command Element to threats to the integrity, role and legacy of the President posed by a cabal of negative, counter-revolutionary elements who for long had hung around him, and who appeared to take advantage of his advanced age to besmirch his impeccable legacy as a living icon of the Struggle, while systematically destabilizing and misdirecting the ruling Zimbabwe African National Union - Patriotic Front (ZANU-PF), itself the Party of Struggle and National Liberation, and who interfered with the smooth functioning of Government and related institutions critical to the sustenance and endurance of the ethos of Struggle. The goal of the Operation was thus to extricate and redeem the Principal from this cabal which encircled him and which threatened his image in the public eyes, through its acts of wanton corruption and ambitions. The drastic intervention had been prompted and necessitated by repeated

6

representations made to His Excellency the President by the Command Element, but which appeared checkmated by the said cabal whose strength and influence on the President, the Party, Government and the First Family seemed to grow by the day, at the expense of the ethos, the ideals, values and traditions of the National Liberation Struggle, and at the expense of the President's otherwise hallowed legacy as a symbol of the freedom struggle and a renowned Pan-Africanist. More worrisome were the divisive, manipulative and vindictive acts by the same cabal which threatened the electability of ZANU-PF in the impending 2018 Harmonized Elections, thus raising the spectre of an electoral defeat which harkened to the 2008 Electoral Crisis and more broadly, to a similar fate suffered by Zambia's founding UNIP in the early 1990s. The President was informed that it was the view of the Command Element that the activities of the group, if left unchecked, threatened broader social cohesion and thus National Security and Stability.

Destabilization and subversion of the Ruling ZANU-PF Party.

The President was informed of the grave concern of the Command Element over the methodical subversion by the same cabal of established Party hierarchy, processes, procedures and values, all in ways that divided and destabilized ZANU-PF from within. Specific mention was made of the wanton suspensions, and destabilization of Party structures across all but one Provinces by the same group in the hope of rigging intra-party electoral results in order to influence the forthcoming Extraordinary Party Congress whose outcomes would be rendered illegitimate in the eyes of members and supporters already

7

riled by the open and wanton arbitrariness which characterized the management of Party affairs. The ongoing purging of Party officials across the country, including senior officials holding leadership positions in Government, threatened overall stability in the Party and in Government. Against such a baneful background, the Party risked creating conditions for the rise of "Independent" candidates in the forthcoming National Elections drawn from its embittered members, thereby dividing its vote to its own detriment and against its own electoral prospects. Feedback from the over 2 000 Commissars comprising retired senior officers from the Army already embedded in communities across the country pointed to worrisome, widespread disaffection and malaise within the Party, against its leadership, its decisions and management style. Presidential Interface rallies had been manipulated and stage-managed to create a veneer of normalcy and Party popularity on the ground. In reality, these rallies deceptively involved same faces bused to different venues, or ordinary citizens force-marched to these meetings against their will. The Operation by the Military was thus meant to reinstate *bona fide* party processes for legitimate outcomes. It was the wish of the Commanders to ensure that the President presided over clean and just Party processes in the run-up to the Congress, all for legitimate outcomes. It was the view of the Command Element that all Party members needed to be allowed to participate in elective processes leading to the Congress, without being blocked through trumped-up charges and arbitrary suspensions. Further, the Command Element said while the President's view that the Party leadership would come from the people (through processes of Congress) was unimpeachable, in reality, Party processes had been so badly interfered with as to render Congress outcomes predetermined

8

AN FM

and thus lacking in legitimacy. This rendered the President's well-meant protestations against arbitrary appointments appear to sound hollow and even deceitful, to the extent that the said acts of interference were being carried out in his name and that of members of his Family.

Threats to National Cohesion and Unity

The President was informed of the Command Element's acute concern with strident and persistent messages by high-ranking Party officials that threatened National Cohesion and Unity. Recalling the baneful legacy of violent conflicts and divisions in Zimbabwe's recent past, the Command Element sought to draw His Excellency's attention to the fact that the National Liberation Project of Nation-Building stood imperiled by the said recklessly divisive talk by high-ranking Party officials which threatened the country with what the Command Element termed "hondo yemarudzi", the war of linguistic tribes and regions. Such a discourse which was traceable to the divisive cabal, threatened the country with a throwback to the era of conflicts which this time around, was bound to be more complex and more widespread as to rip the Nation apart. In any case, ZANU-PF needed to muster votes from all provinces for a resounding victory, and thus could not afford alienating entire communities and regions through divisive political rhetoric.

Economic Crisis and non-fulfillment and execution of Public Projects

His Excellency was advised of the Command Element's reading of the dire economic situation obtaining in the country, and which posed a real threat to National Security and the overall electability of ZANU-PF.

9

Noting the unfulfilled promises made in the 2013 Harmonized General Elections, the Command Element expressed fears that ZANU-PF faced another election without evidence of real economic recovery by way of completion of flagship projects, or pointers to the general amelioration of the socio-economic conditions of an expectant voting populace. The President was informed that it was the view of Command Element that most of the Projects which would have taken off had stalled because of divisions caused by the said cabal which, apart from causing general paralysis in the execution of projects and programmes, was also extorting and demanding kickbacks from such projects. Apart from the Kariba Power Project, the ZANU-PF Government had little else to show. Much worse, acts of corruption had alienated many in the country, and Zimbabwe's all-weather friends like China who found little or no acknowledgment from Zimbabwe's Foreign Policy thrust and concrete day-to-day economic decisions. A sore project, the President was told, was the Dualisation of the Beitbridge-Chirundu Project which had long stalled, much as the President had been led to commissioning it several months ago. Another sore project was the Solar Project sited in Gwanda which had been mired in, and stalled by, endless controversies.

Non-fulfillment of Commitments to, and sidelining of, War Veterans

His Excellency was informed that no benefits promised to the War Veterans following an indaba with them more than a year ago, had materialized. The integration of War Veterans into operations of both Party and Government was still outstanding. What seemed to be happening instead was a systematic removal and alienation of War

10

Veterans from all levels and programmes of the Party and Government, thereby deepening the isolation of the President from his wartime associates and ethos. Although legal instruments were being finalized on gratuities of serving War Veterans, the general attitude promoted by the counter-revolutionary cabal undermined a sense of belonging for the Veterans. Even Veteran Commissars seconded to the Party by the Military had been dropped or sidelined. This did not bode well for the future of the revolutionary culture in the Party which now seemed controlled by well-known corrupt counterrevolutionaries.

Abuse of Office and Hierarchy by the Cabal

The President was told of the Command's concerns over Party officials who overreached their official designations for selfish, arbitrary and ambitious ends. Examples included the Secretary for Science and Technology, Professor Jonathan Moyo, who had morphed into the driving ideologue of factional politics known as G-40, itself at the heart of the mayhem in the Party. Through his baneful influence over Party structures, and especially over the Secretary for Administration and the National Political Commissar, Professor Moyo, whom the Command Element described as a deserter from the struggle and party to negative forces behind the infamous 1978/79 Internal Settlement, and as an agent of a hostile State, had exerted a negative and disproportionate influence in the Party and in Government. He had also created the bogey of "Lacoste" faction as a counterpoise to his G-40 faction. His association with the First Family, both direct and indirect, constituted a grave threat to national security, apart from undermining the standing of the First Family in public eyes. The President was informed of the

11

Command Element's frustration following repeated and well-substantiated representations against the Professor revealing that he was in the employ of hostile States, and was a nucleus of espionage activities in the country (Wikileaks Reports being cases in point). Other cited examples of portfolio and hierarchical distortions pointed to the Women's and Youth Leagues, both of which had overrun the Main Wing of the Party. The President's attention was drawn to the Command Element's criticism of the way the National Political Commissar was executing Commissariat work. Instead of healing differences and benignly correcting erring cadres in the Party, his style of running the Commissariat Department was overridingly vindictive and judgmental, thereby worsening tensions in, and alienation from, the Party.

Perception of protection of offenders by the First Family

His Excellency the President was informed of the anger and frustration of the Command Element following confirmed reports that both the ruling Party's National Political Commissar, Cde Xavier Kasukuwere, and Secretary for Science and Technology, Professor Jonathan Moyo, and their families had been granted refuge at the First Family's Blue Roof Residence. The President was informed that the Command Element regarded the two and Cde Chombo as key members of the cabal it blamed for misleading the President and threatening his legacy, as well as for the mayhem in the Party. The Command Element also alleged that the three were part of criminals who, in spite of facing overwhelming charges of corruption, had defeated the course of justice by exploiting their proximity to the First Family. The President was told

12

that Professor Jonathan Moyo faced charges of abusing the Zimbabwe Manpower Development Fund (ZIMDEF), but had used various dilations and other subterfuges to delay or even forestall his day in court. Cde Chombo had aided and abetted the abuse of ZIMDEF funds by authoring a letter that allegedly sought to exonerate the Professor. All three faced charges related to the abuse of residential land and stands in many suburbs in Harare and in different parts of the country. The seriousness of the matter was underlined to the President when he was told the Command Element expected him to release the two, failure which it may even consider plucking them out of Blue Roof, with the attendant consequences. The President was also told of the fears on the part of the Command Element that the duo's continued stay at the Blue Roof represented its lingering hold and influence on the First Family at a time when delicate attempts were underway to reopen clogged channels of communication between the President and the Command Element. The Command Element, the President was advised, feared the duo would continue to negatively influence the ongoing communication between the two sides. Equally, the Command Element's assurances that all arrested officials would be delivered to the Police for due process, was communicated to the President.

Repeated Attacks on Seniors

Also drawn to the attention of the President was the Command Element's extreme concern and displeasure at the culture of open disrespect of seniors in the Party, including public humiliation, chastisement, innuendos and even direct denunciation of officials at Interface Rallies, contrary to the dictates of decency, respect and

13

comradeship in the Party. This insidious culture of disrespect and public confrontation demeaned the Party and its personages in the eyes of the people.

Undermining of official communication through the Press and social media

Concern of the Command Element regarding the integrity and management of information and decisions of the Party was drawn to the attention of the President. There was a generalized tendency of preempting or ventilating decisions of the Party, the thinking of the President, and discussions and decisions of Government through the social media. Much worse, serious pending decisions or intentions of the Party and Government would be leaked to the Press and social media as rumours, only to be validated by subsequent actions. All this created an atmosphere of uncertainty, insecurity and victimization in the Party and Government. It also suggested an unofficial inner ring which enjoyed a position of privileged knowledge, on the basis of which it terrorized the broad membership in the Party and Government. This undermined the dignity and sincerity of the President, including the credibility of his decisions.

Provocations against the Defence Establishment

The President and Commander-in-Chief was informed that his Command Element felt painfully irked and provoked by repeated attacks on the Military, including public charges of conspiracy of a violent overthrow of the Constitutional Order and physical threat to the

14

President and his Family. The Command Element had put up with such repeated abuses and charges, which themselves had created bitterness within an already disgruntled rank and file. Such irreverent comments coming at a time when the welfare threshold in the military had markedly declined, threatened discipline in this very sensitive Organ of the State. For Commanders coming from the Struggle, such charges were particularly painful given both their longstanding loyalty and commitment to the safety of His Excellency the President, both before and after Independence.

Insecurity of Tenure within the Zimbabwe Defence Force and the weeding out of the core corps of War Veterans

The President and Commander-in-Chief of the Zimbabwe Defence Forces was alerted to growing anxiety within the Command Element arising from well-publicized threats of dismissals or arbitrary retirement of wartime commanders from the Zimbabwe Defence Force. Particularly riling to the Command Element, the President was told, was the fact that such pronouncements came from individuals who fell outside the Defence Establishment and Defence Chain of Command, but who delightfully abused claimed proximity to the Commander-in-Chief and/or the First Lady. The Command Element made reference to a list circulated by a Party Official in the Harare Province, one Mashayamombe, pointing to a planned systematic elimination of veterans from the Command Structure. Such threats which could no longer be discounted or treated lightly in the context of the atmosphere of generalized purging in the Party, and a strident anti-war veterans rhetoric, suggested a systematic attack on the ethos, values

15

and culture of the Struggle which needed to be nurtured in the Security Establishment as a permanent legacy and philosophy guiding the Command Element for all times. The President and Commander-in-Chief was informed of the precipitously declining numbers of war veterans in the Command Structure as a result of natural attrition and previous retirements. This, coupled with the fact that officers with combat experience deriving from various post-independence operations, whilst numerically significant, were still in need of command exposure, argued for a gradual and well thought-out Command transition in the Military, if the country was to retain its defence and offensive capabilities, as well as retain its liberation struggle-time philosophy and ethos. The Commander-in-Chief was informed that only the positions of the Commander of the Zimbabwe Defence Forces, Commander of the Zimbabwe National Army, Commander of the Airforce of Zimbabwe, Commissioner-Generals of Police and Prisons and Correctional Services, and the Director-General of the Central Intelligence Organization, had term limits in terms of the reigning Constitution. However, the Command Element could not understand why there seemed to be an attempt to invoke the term-limit clause retrospectively, and in ways that selectively applied to the Security Establishment only. The Command Element is of the view that apart from focusing on only those posts with Constitutional term limits, regard had to be given to the fact that the new constitutional dispensation ushered in 2013 gave everyone occupying such constitutionally abridged posts a new countdown date.

Undermining of Inter-Agency Cohesion within the Security Establishment.

16

His Excellency the President and Commander-in-Chief was informed of a serious attack on Inter-Agency Cohesion within the National Security Establishment by the aforementioned cabal which appeared to have influenced key departments of National Security. The impact had been the virtual collapse of the National Joint Operations Command (JOC) through which issues relating to National Security were dealt with collectively, and jointly presented to the Head of State. This vital structure had given way to narrow departmental reports and de-briefings which not only misrepresented the overall National Security situation, but also provided a conduit for briefings to the Commander-in-Chief that were based on self-serving falsehoods and character assassinations calculated to settle vendettas. The obtaining selective access to the Commander-in-Chief had undermined the spirit of intelligence-sharing and collegiality which all along had underpinned the institution of the National Joint Operations Command. On this score, the Command Element blamed the Police Commissioner-General, Cde Augustine Chihuri, and the former Director-General of the Central Intelligence Organization (now Minister of Justice, Legal and Parliamentary Affairs), Rtd General Happyton Bonyongwe.

Concern over claims of Treason arising from both the Monday, 13th November, 2017 Press Briefing and the Wednesday 15th November, 2017 Operation Restore Legacy.

The President and Commander-in-Chief was informed of concerns of the Command Element over dangerous claims of treasonable conduct arising from a public expression of their disavowal of the state-of-affairs in the country and the Party expressed at the Press Briefing of 13th

17

November, 2017, and the subsequent Operation mounted two days later. The Command Element cited a Press Statement by the Minister of Information, Media and Broadcasting Services, Ambassador S. K. Moyo, which was issued in his capacity as the Spokesperson of the ruling Party, and an address by Youth League Secretary Chipanga, both of which alleged high treason. They also claimed that the new Minister of Justice, Legal and Parliamentary Affairs, was crafting a legal instrument meant to indict the Commanders for both actions. The noble intentions behind the actions had to be acknowledged to quash fears of indictments in the future.

Rumours of preparations for a counter-operation led by the Police and Rtd General Bonyongwe.

The President was informed about mounting tension and concern within the Command Element triggered by a mobile communication message attributed to the new Minister of Justice, Legal and Parliamentary Affairs, and former Director-General of the Central Intelligence Organisation, Rtd General Happyton Bonyongwe, to Air Marshal Parrence Shiri who is in Dubai on official business allegedly urging him to fly back to join in efforts towards a counter-operation whose backbone would be the Police Force commanded by Commissioner-General Augustine Chihuri. It was drawn to the President's attention that Commissioner Chihuri had not attended the inaugural Wednesday morning meetings, or any thereafter. His Deputy, Deputy Commissioner-General Godwin Matanga, had only attended the inaugural Wednesday morning meeting, after which he did not turn up for the rest. Instances of friction between the Military and the

18

Zimbabwe Republic Police were also drawn to the President's attention, culminating in what appeared to be a withdrawal of the Police Force from policing duties at least in the National Capital, Harare. The President was informed that the Command Element had made it clear that a counterforce against their operation would constitute an escalation which was bound to lead to a bloody outcome.

Disinformation and Falsehoods amidst the Operation.

The Mediating Team was able to provide the President with facts which dispelled rumours and falsehoods which continued to swirl around the whole operation. These included claims that three deaths had been reported when Finance Minister and ZANU-PF Secretary for Administration was arrested at his home during the Operation; claims that the Commanders had evacuated their families to safety ahead of the Operation; claims that CDF Chiwenga had made a diversion and stop-over in South Africa en-route to Zimbabwe from China, in order to meet with the dismissed former Vice-President Emmerson Mnangagwa and his team thought to include Cde Christopher Mutsvangwa and Zimbabwe's Ambassador to South Africa, Ambassador Moyo. More critically, the Mediating Team informed the President that the Operation by the Command Element was not calculated for a top leadership change in the Party and country, a process which had to be left to the Party and its Organs running in a fair, clean and just way, all of which had to be superintended by the President himself without undue influence. However, the President was told, hard decisions could not be stalled any longer, and had to be made in the interest of the survival of the Party and its revolutionary traditions.

19

Fear of the development of a vacuum in Government, and prolongation of the Operation

Amidst reports of ministers reportedly fleeing or attempting to flee the country, coupled with various suspensions of Party Officials who are also Government Ministers, the President was advised on the Command Element's fear of a vacuum developing in Government Ministries, thereby impairing the delivery of essential services, to the detriment of national security and stability. The President was told of Ministers who had attempted to skip the border through different points. He was also told of Ministers who were in a state of limbo as a consequence of suspensions or threats of dismissal from the Party. Both factors had created a situation of paralysis in Government which could trigger unrest or a generalized revolt in the country. Equally, the President was told of the Command Element's anxiety to call off the Operation so soldiers could go back to their barracks, in favour of a return to normalcy. However, the President was further advised, the Command Element would not scale down its operations until all the criminal elements had been accounted for, and the way cleared for the President to resume his functions and role without undue influence.

Clear Roadmap for the Party and Country

His Excellency the President was briefed on the Command Element's anxieties over mounting uncertainties surrounding the future of the Party and country should he decide to take a rest and retire. The Command Element's view was that the current programme of

20

victimization through manipulative suspensions and dismissals did not inspire confidence in a harmonious succession process. Hard decisions had to be made whilst there is still time, including weeding out negative elements from the Party, while planning for the survivability of ZANU-PF and its revolutionary ethos and legacy well into the future.

Attachments to this report are:

- Signed "Talking points for CDF's meeting".
- Statement by Youth League Chairman, Kudzanayi Chipanga, denouncing the CDF.
- Statement by Youth League Chairman, Kudzanayi Chipanga, retracting his denunciation of the CDF and linking the First Family to the original statement of denunciation.
- Transcript of edited statement by Kudzanayi Chipanga aired on ZTV on 15th November, 2017.

Father Fidelis Mukonori S. J.

Secretary George Charamba

A/DG Aaron Nhepera

Mediation Team, Harare

17/11/17

21

AN F. M

TALKING POINTS FOR CDF'S MEETING

Politicians to stop reckless utterances against the military wh
are causing alarm and despondency within the rank and file wh
may result in anarchy thereby threatening peace and security i
the country.

The Party to afford every Party member a fair and equal chan
of being heard or elected and the whole democratic process to
observed from the cell up and no imposition of candidates.

Cease all purging in the Party and Government and reunite the
Party by reinstating all previous victims.

Implement the recommendations of the War Veterans Indaba
and reintegrate all war veterans into the mainstream of the Par
and Government.

The known counterrevolutionary elements who have fomente
the current instability in the Party be weeded out both in the Pa
and Government .

Security of tenure of employment as it relates to the provisio
of the current Constitution of Zimbabwe.

A clear cut roadmap for succession in the Party including a fre
start and going for a new election in 2018.

Constantino Chiwenga
CDF
16th November 2017.

REFERENCES

Alexander, Jocelyn, "Militarisation and state institutions: 'Professionals' and 'soldiers' inside the Zimbabwe Prison Service", *Journal of Southern African Studies* 39, 4 (2013), pp. 807–28.

Alexander, Jocelyn and Tendi, Blessing-Miles, "A tale of two elections: Zimbabwe at the polls in 2008", *Concerned Africa Scholars Bulletin*, Winter 2008.

Bland, Gary, Green, Andrew and Moore, Toby, "Measuring the quality of election administration", *Democratization* 20 (2), 358–377, 2013.

Bleck, Jamie and van de Walle, Nicolas, *Electoral Politics in Africa Since 1990*, Cambridge University Press: Cambridge, 2018.

Bratton, Michael and Masunungure Eldred, "AD223: Zimbabwe's Presidential Race Tightens One Month Ahead of July 30 Voting", *Afrobarometer*, 20 July 2018, http://afrobarometer.org/publications/ad223-zimbabwes-presidential-race-tightens-one-month-ahead-july-30-voting

Dorman, Sara Rich, "Make sure they count nicely this time: the politics of elections and election observation in Zimbabwe", *Commonwealth and Comparative Politics* 43 (2), 155–177, 2005.

Flyvbjerg, Bent, "Five misunderstandings about case-study research", *Qualitative Inquiry* 12 (2), 219–245, 2006.

Gramsci, Antonio, "Between Past and Present" in *Prison Notebooks* (*Selections 272–76*), translated by Buttigieg, Joseph, Columbia University Press, New York, 1992.

Grofman, Bernard and Lijphart Arend, *Electoral Laws and their Consequences*, Algora Publishers: Ottawa, 1986.

Jacobs, Walter Darnell, "Rhodesian Independence After the Fearless", *World Affairs*, 131 (3) 1968, 162–176.

Koppell, Jonathan G.S. and Steen Jennifer A, "The effects of ballot position on election outcomes", *Journal of Politics* 66, 1 (1004), pp. 267–281.

Levitsky, Steven and Lucan Way. "The rise of competitive authoritarianism", *Journal of Democracy* 13, 2 (2002), pp. 51–65.

Marc, Meredith and Yuval Salant, "On the causes and consequences of ballot order effects", *Political Behaviour* 35, 1 (2013), pp. 175–197.

Mhanda, Wilfred *Dzino: Memories of a Freedom Fighter*, Weaver Press, Harare, 2011.

Moyo, Jonathan, *Voting for Democracy: A Study of Electoral Politics in Zimbabwe*, University of Zimbabwe Publications, Harare, 1992.

Ncube, Cornelias, "The 2013 elections in Zimbabwe: end of an era for human rights discourse", *Africa Spectrum* 48 (3), 99–110, 2013.

Nicole Beardsworth, Nic Cheeseman, Simukai Tinhu "Zimbabwe: The coup that never was, and the election that could have been", *African Affairs*, 118 (472), July 2019, 580–596.

Ninsin, Kwame A, "Introduction: the contradictions and ironies of elections in Africa", *Africa Development* 31 (3), 1–10, 2006.

Noris, Pippa, "The new research agenda studying electoral integrity", *Electoral Studies* 32 (4), 563–575, 2013.

Opitz, Christian, Fjelde, Hanne and Hoglund, Kristine, *Journal of East African Studies* 7 (4), 713–731, 2013.

Owen Gagare, "Tensions between Mnangagwa and army commanders grow", *The Zimbabwe Independent*, 16 February 2018, https://www.theindependent.co.zw/2018/02/16/tensions-mnangagwa-army-commanders-grow (12 January 2019).

Plato, *The Republic*, Simon & Schuster: New York, 2010.

Pocock, J.G.A., *The Machiavellian Moment: Florentine political thought and the Atlantic Republican Tradition*, Princeton University Press: Princeton, New Jersey, 2016.

Raftopoulos, Brian, "Reflections on opposition politics in Zimbabwe: The politics of the Movement for Democratic Change", in Karen Alexander and Brian Raftopolos (eds), *Reflections on democratic politics in Zimbabwe*, Institute for Justice and Reconciliation, Cape Town, 2006.

Raftopoulos, Brian, "Zimbabwe: The 2018 elections and their aftermath", *Solidarity Peace Trust*, 1 October 2018.

Research and Advocacy Unit, "Syncopated Numbers: Arithmetic discord and Zimbabwe's 2013 'harmonised' election", *Research and Advocacy Unit*, March 2014.

Tordoff, William and Young, Ralph, *Electoral Politics in Africa: The Experience of Zambia and Zimbabwe*, Cambridge University Press (Online): Cambridge, 2014.

We the People of Zimbabwe, "Violence around election day: reports from the We the People of Zimbabwe call centre, July 28–August 3, 2018", *We the People of Zimbabwe*, 3 August 2018.

Weber, Max, *On Law in Economy and Society* (Edited by Max Rheinstein), Harvard University Press: Cambridge, Massachusetts, 1954

Downloads

http://kubatana.net/2018/08/10/chamisas-constitutional-court-application-presidential-election-results-challenge/

https://www.scribd.com/document/386534407/Chigumba-Opposing-Papers-CCZ42-18

http://veritaszim.net/sites/veritas_d/files/mnangagwa-opposing-papers_Part1.pdf

https://www.newzimbabwe.com/full-text-chamisas-heads-of-argument-in-con-court-showdown/

http://kubatana.net/2018/08/20/zecs-heads-argument-nelson-chamisas-presidential-election-legal-challenge/

http://kubatana.net/2018/08/20/mnangagwas-heads-argument-nelson-chamisas-presidential-election-legal-challenge/

https://au.int/en/documents/20190514/Report-african-union-election-observation-mission-30-july-and-8-september-2018

https://eeas.europa.eu/election-observation-missions/eom-zimbabwe-2018_en

https://www.iri.org/sites/default/files/2018-10-29_final_zieom_report.pdf

http://www.hrforumzim.org/publications/reports-on-political-violence/2018-post-election-violence-monitoring-Report-01-09-august-2018/

http://www.postelectionviolencecommission.gov.zw/wp-content/uploads/2018/12/Final%20Report%20of%20the%20Commission%20of%20Inquiry%2018%20%20DEC%2018.pdf

http://thecommonwealth.org/media/news/zimbabwe-election-commonwealth-releases-observer-group-report

https://www.sadc.int/news-events/news/sadc-electoral-observation-mission-2018-harmonised-elections-zimbabwe-launched/

https://www.theindependent.co.zw/2017/01/20/chidyausiku-forced-retiring-early/

https://www.zesn.org.zw/wp-content/uploads/2018/12/Final-ZESN-2018-Harmonised-Election-Report.pdf

http://www.zhrc.org.zw/download-category/2018-harmonised-election-reports/

INDEX